*The publication of this book was made possible,
in part, by grants from:*

the Société des Auteurs et Compositeurs Dramatiques

the Cultural Services of the French Embassy, New York

the Quebec Government House, New York

UBU REPERTORY THEATER PUBLICATIONS

Individual plays:

Swimming Pools at War by Yves Navarre, 1982.

Night Just Before the Forest and *Struggle of the Dogs and the Black* by Bernard–Marie Koltès, 1982.

The Fetishist by Michel Tournier, 1983.

The Office by Jean–Paul Aron, 1983.

Far From Hagondange and *Vater Land, the Country of our Fathers* by Jean–Paul Wenzel, 1984.

Deck Chairs by Madeleine Laik, 1984.

The Passport and *The Door* by Pierre Bourgeade, 1984.

The Showman by Andrée Chedid, 1984.

Madame Knipper's Journey to Eastern Prussia by Jean–Luc Lagarce, 1984.

Passengers by Daniel Besnehard, 1985.

Cabale by Enzo Cormann, 1985.

Enough is Enough by Protais Asseng, 1986.

Monsieur Thôgô–gnigni by Bernard Dadié, 1985.

The Glorious Destiny of Marshal Nnikon Nniku by Tchicaya U Tam'si, 1986.

Intelligence Powder by Kateb Yacine, 1986.

The Sea Between Us by Denise Chalem, 1986.

Country Landscapes by Jacques–Pierre Amette, 1986.

Nowhere and *A Man with Women* by Reine Bartève, 1987.

The White Bear by Daniel Besnehard, 1992.

The Best of Schools by Jean–Marie Besset, 1992.

Jock by Jean–Louis Bourdon, 1992.

Family Portrait by Denise Bonal, new edition, 1992.

A Tempest by Aimé Césaire, 1993 (new edition), 1997.

The Free Zone and *The Workroom* by Jean–Claude Grumberg, preface by Michael R. Marrus, 1993.

A Modest Proposal by Tilly, preface by Tom Bishop, 1994.

The Case of Kaspar Mayer by Jean–Yves Picq, 1995.

Parentheses of Blood by Sony Labou Tansi, preface by Maryse Condé, 1996 (new edition).

Ubu Repertory Theater:1982–1992, A bilingual illustrated history with personal statements by various playwrights and theater personalities, 1992.

*Distributed by Ubu Repertory Theater, 15 West 28th Street, New York, NY 10001. All other titles distributed by Theatre Communications Group, 355 Lexington Avenue, New York, NY 10017.

Anthologies:

Afrique I: New plays from the Congo, Ivory Coast, Senegal and Zaire, including *The Daughter of the Gods* by Abdou Anta Kâ, *Equatorium* by Maxime N'Debeka, *Lost Voices* by Diur N'Tumb, *The Second Ark* by Sony Labou Tansi, and *The Eye* by Bernard Zadi Zaourou. Preface by George C. Wolfe. 1987.

The Paris Stage: Recent Plays: *A Birthday Present for Stalin* by Jean Bouchaud, *The Rest Have Got It Wrong* by Jean–Michel Ribes, *The Sleepless City* by Jean Tardieu, *Trumpets of Death* by Tilly, and *The Neighbors* by Michel Vinaver. Preface by Catherine Temerson and Françoise Kourilsky. 1988.

Plays by Women: An International Anthology: *A Picture Perfect Sky* by Denise Bonal, *Jocasta* by Michèle Fabien, *The Girls from the Five and Ten* by Abla Farhoud, *You Have Come Back* by Fatima Gallaire–Bourega, and *Your Handsome Captain* by Simone Schwarz–Bart. Preface by Catherine Temerson and Françoise Kourilsky. 1988, 1991. (Out of print).

Gay Plays: An International Anthology: *The Function* by Jean–Marie Besset, *A Tower Near Paris* and *Grand Finale* by Copi, *Return of the Young Hippolytus* by Hervé Dupuis, *Ancient Boys* by Jean–Claude van Itallie, and *The Lives and Deaths of Miss Shakespeare* by Liliane Wouters. Preface by Catherine Temerson and Françoise Kourilsky. 1989, 1991.

Theater and Politics: An International Anthology: *Black Wedding Candles for Blessed Antigone* by Sylvain Bemba, *A Season in the Congo* by Aimé Césaire, *Burn River Burn* by Jean–Pol Fargeau, *Olympe and the Executioner* by Wendy Kesselman and *Mephisto*, adapted from Klaus Mann by Ariane Mnouchkine. Preface by Erika Munk. 1990.

Afrique II: New Plays from Madagascar, Mauritania and Togo including *The Legend of Wagadu as Seen by Sia Yatabere* by Moussa Diagana, *The Crossroads* by Josué Kossi Efoui, *The Herd* by Charlotte–Arrisoa Rafenomanjato, *The Prophet and the President* by Jean–Luc Raharimanana and *The Singing Tortoise* and *Yevi's Adventures in Monsterland* by Sénouvo Agbota Zinsou. Preface by Henry Louis Gates, Jr. 1991.

New French–Language Plays: *The Orphan Muses* by Michel Marc Bouchard (Quebec), *Fire's Daughters* by Ina Césaire (Martinique), *The Ship* by Michèle Césaire (Martinique), *Talk About Love!* by Paul Emond (Belgium), *That Old Black Magic* by Koffi Kwahulé (Ivory Coast). Preface by Rosette C. Lamont. 1993.

Plays by Women: An International Anthology. Book 2: *The Orphanage* by Reine Bartève (France), *Game of Patience* by Abla Farhoud (Quebec/Liban), *The Widow Dylemma* by Werewere Liking (Cameroon), *The Tropical Breeze Hotel* by Maryse Condé (Guadeloupe), *Beware the Heart* by Denise Bonal (France). Preface by Ntozake Shange. 1994.

Monologues: Plays from Martinique, France, Algeria, Quebec: *Another Story* by Julius Amédée Laou (Martinique), *Night Just Before The Forest* by Bernard-Marie Koltès (France), *The Sifter* by Michel Azama (France), *All It Takes Is Something Small* by Martine Drai (France), *Madame Bertin's Testimony* by Fatima Gallaire (Algeria), *Anatomy Lesson* by Larry Tremblay (Quebec). 1995.

Plays by Women: An International Anthology. Book 3. *Always Together* by Anca Visdei (Romania), *Bonds of Affection* by Loleh Bellon (France), *Lapin Lapin* by Coline Serreau (France), *A Country Wedding* by Denise Bonal (France), *Your Handsome Captain* by Simone Schwarz-Bart (Guadeloupe), *You Have Come Back* by Fatima Gallaire (Algeria). Preface by Françoise Kourilsky, 1996.

Playwrights of Exile: *Lady Strass* by Eduardo Manet (Cuba/France), *My Mother's Eyes* by Leila Sebbar (Algeria/France), *Class Photo* by Anca Visdei (Romania/France), *Wedding Day at the Cro-Magnons* by Wajdi Mouawad (Lebanon/Quebec), *Such Great Hopes* by Noureddine Aba (Algeria/France). Preface by Andrei Codrescu, 1997.

FRANCE • ROMANIA • QUEBEC

ALGERIA • LEBANON • CUBA

Playwrights of

EXILE

An

International

Anthology

UBU REPERTORY THEATER PUBLICATIONS
NEW YORK

CAUTION

Ubu Repertory Theater Publications
General Editor: Françoise Kourilsky
Assistant Editor: Isabelle de Rezende
Distributed by Theatre Communications Group, 355 Lexington Avenue, New York, NY 10017

Printed in the United States of America, 1997
Library of Congress Catalog Card Number: 94-012045
ISBN 0-913745-48-0

Price: $19.95

CONTENTS

PREFACE

EXILES ALL

For my literary generation, exile had only one direction: France. When my mother and I made the momentous decision to leave our homeland forever, my interests and hers differed. I looked forward to being in the company of Tristan Tzara, E. M. Cioran, Paul Celan, and Eugène Ionesco, the great French-bound exiles of previous generations. My mother, on the other hand, looked to the bourgeois comfort of America. I despised her for this utilitarianism and vowed to conquer France as soon as I could get away from my mother's America, which she imposed on me by the sheer force of her seniority and economic clout.

The romantic myth of exile was possible in its full, unexamined glory only in the mind of an adolescent in the mid-sixties of our century. At that time, alienation was philosophically fashionable (necessary, like a tie in a fine restaurant), and exile had become the *crème* of alienation, the acme of youthful despair. We maintained the generation gap with all the assiduity of housemaids. Every removal from home, from my very real exile to a pre-college grand tour of Europe on a shoe-string, was gravely experienced by my contemporaries as an existential estrangement. (In different concentrations, of course; the metaphorical containing, usually, only 10% of the potency of the real thing.)

The reality of exile, visible in a realistic light several decades later, had in fact been very different for my predecessors. Far from a celebration of estrangement, it had been heartbreaking. For Cioran, the author of *Un Précis de décomposition*, his condition was a prompting to suicide. Paul Celan, whose parents were murdered by the nazis, saw his continued existence as a mistake and committed suicide, finally, in Paris. Ionesco, who had taken Europe by storm by pointing a mirror at its absurd manners, was situated at the intersections of two totalitarianisms, a position that was hardly playful. Tristan Tzara, who had founded the Dada provocation, became a communist, which was a form of artistic suicide very much like a real one. The list of literal and metaphorical suicides of Romanian exiles is long, and the same is true for exiles from every other country who had the misfortune of being born in one of the centuries' dark decades.

The playwrights of exile gathered here belong to different generations, and their attitudes toward their adopted language and country are quite different in each case.

Noureddine Aba, the senior playwright, is an Algerian born in 1921. His mythic-sized characters make their points gravely from within a betrayed revolution and a suffering homeland. They speak French to the French as if making their case before a grand global tribunal. The language they speak is that of advocacy, though the subject of their defense is an untranslatable crime against love, faith, and patriotism.

Eduardo Manet was born in Cuba in the 1930's and had a rich literary career in Spanish before choosing exile. His play *Lady Strass* evinces no particular anguish about his adopted language, he is at home in it. His meditations on language, borders, and history, are the pure credentials of an exile but they do not make an issue of either the difficulty or the ideology of writing in French. For Manet, as for the Romanians of his generation, France had long ago made herself hospitable to the seductive anguish of wanderers.

This is not the case for Leïla Sebbar, who was born in Algeria of mixed parentage. In her play, *My Mother's Eyes*, the young protagonist is wholly surrounded by the French language, which is both a trap and an escape. She can only tell her story in French, the language of a culture that has assigned her to second-class citizenship. She looks warmly to the language of her mother, but the culture of that language rejects everything she is. Suspended like a wounded bird between languages and cultures, the girl does the only thing she can: speak as violently and as freely as she can.

The characters of Wajdi Mouwad's *Wedding Day at the Cro-Magnons'* are, paradoxically the most culture-specific people in this book. Paradoxically, because the playwright is a Lebanese writing in French in Quebec, thus twice removed from the matrix. Although the members of the Lebanese family preparing for the wedding suffer from the displaced *maladies de rigueur,* they yet have a cultural model that nourishes them. Perhaps, the practice of exile in the provinces is a gentler form of alienation.

The French language, for the Romanians, was a sister Latin language which stood for true culture in this largely francophile region. In Anca Visdei's *Class Photo,* this is evident in the envy of her classmates when she returns to her high school class reunion. They envy her presumed affluence, but in truth they envy her escape into the *a priori* superior France where they have been taught to believe all culture comes from. The protagonist knows better, but she will not abandon her only ace-in-the-hole: the national superstition.

The French colonials, or those caught in mid-allegiance between France and her former colonies, have a painful attachment to the language of their literary successes, never quite at ease with its in-built assumptions. The Spanish, the Romanians, and, to some extent, the Lebanese, come to French with nearly unconditional love, free to express their anguish in a medium that is transparent to them.

This collection is a good sampler from the work of playwrights working in an area that is vast and fascinating. The umbrella-term "exile" gathers under its fold a tremendous diversity of viewpoints and attitudes. It is impossible to look at literature and art now without considering exiles: their articulation has become one of the main (if not *the* main) way we look at ourselves, no matter where we were born. The exiles' view has become the *native* view, which is good, as far as I'm concerned.

ANDREI CODRESCU
New Orleans, May 6, 1997

Eduardo Manet

Lady Strass

Translated from the French by
Phyllis Zatlin

UBU REPERTORY THEATER PUBLICATIONS
NEW YORK

Eduardo Manet was born in Santiago de Cuba in 1930 and began writing film reviews for a Havana newspaper at the age of fifteen. In 1952, Manet left Cuba for Paris and studied theatre with Jean-Louis Barrault and Jacques Lecoq, and became a member of Lecoq's famed mime troupe. Alerted that it would be unwise for him to return home during the repressive Batista regime, he next moved to Italy, where he received a degree in teaching Italian language and literature at the University of Perugia. In 1960, at the invitation of Fidel and Raul Castro, whom he knew from University days, Manet returned to Havana. He became director of the National Dramatic Ensemble at the National Theatre of Cuba, where he established cultural communication between Havana and the international stage and wrote the first novel of the Cuban Revolution, *Un Cri sur le rivage* ("A Cry from the Shore"). In 1968, when Castro sided with the Soviets against Czechoslovakia, Manet left for Paris once again. In 1979, he became a French citizen, and has been prominent among intellectuals opposing Castro's rule of Cuba. His first French production, *Les Nonnes (The Nuns)* was directed in 1969 by acclaimed avant-garde director Roger Blin, shortly after Manet's arrival in Paris. This play, which was published in *L'Avant-Scène,* has been translated into 21 languages and staged around the world. *Lady Strass* (1977) was also published in *L'Avant-Scène. Le Jour où Mary Shelley rencontra Charlotte Brontë (The Day Mary Shelley Met Charlotte Brontë, 1979), Mendoza en Argentine* ("Mendoza in Argentina," 1983), *Un Balcon sur les Andes* ("A Terrace Overlooking the Andes," 1979) have been published by Gallimard. His latest play, *Monsieur Lovestar et son voisin de palier (Mr. Lovestar and his Next Door Neighbor, 1995)* was published by Actes Sud and premiered in Paris in 1996. As of 1996, eighteen of Eduardo Manet's plays have premiered in prestigious French theatres, including the Comédie-Française and the Avignon Festival. In addition to his long and successful career as a playwright and man of theatre, Manet is also well-known in France as a novelist. He has published nine novels.

Three of these, a trilogy dealing with pre-revolutionary Cuba, have been nominees for the prestigious Prix Goncourt: *La Mauresque* ("The Moorish Woman," 1982), *L'Île du Lézard Vert* ("The Island of the Green Lizard," 1992) and *Habanera* (1994). His latest novel, *Rhapsodie Cubaine* ("Cuban Rhapsody"), published by Grasset in 1996, was awarded the Prix Interallié. Ubu Rep presented the American premiere of *Lady Strass* in October 1996.

Phyllis Zatlin holds a doctorate in Romance Languages from the University of Florida and is professor of Spanish at Rutgers, the State University of New Jersey, where she coordinates an M.A. program in translation. Her translations of plays by Spaniards José Luis Alonso de Santos, Paloma Pedrero and Jaime Salom have been produced or given staged readings in New York City, London, Washington, Kansas City and Miami. Her translation from French of Jean-Paul Daumas's The *Elephant's Graveyard* has been published by Modern International Drama. Author of numerous books and scholarly articles on contemporary Spanish, French, and Latin American theatre, she has recently completed a book-length study on the multi-cultural novels and plays of Eduardo Manet.

Lady Strass, in Phyllis Zatlin's translation, had its American premiere at Ubu Repertory Theater, 15 West 28th Street, New York, New York, 10001, on October 1, 1996.

Director...**André Ernotte**
Set Designer....**Watoku Ueno**
Lighting Designer....**Greg MacPherson**
Costume Designer....**Carol Ann Pelletier**
Sound Designer....**Robert Gould**

CAST

Mrs. Eliane Parkington-Simpson..........................**Susanne Wasson**
Bertrand LeBrun, alias Slick..**Paul Albe**
Manuel Sierra, alias Flash....................................**Robert Jimenez**

Produced by **Ubu Repertory Theater**
Françoise Kourilsky, *Artistic Director*

"Memory is all that an indomitable woman has salvaged from life, and it is an inescapable trap for her in Eduardo Manet's surreal play *Lady Strass* at the Ubu Repertory Theater. André Ernotte's direction of this 1977 work by the Cuban playwright, who lives in Paris, draws an audience so deeply into it that viewers, too, may feel trapped in its disorienting vision. [...]"
—D.J.R. Bruckner, *The New York Times,* October 14, 1996.

"[...] Manet, who has been exiled in France since the pre-Castro Batista dictatorship, uses a kind of post-Surrealist approach to the pathology of colonization. Set in Belize, Manet's claustrophobic drama unfolds when two fugitive ne'er-do-wells break into the home of an aging, seemingly wealthy widow of an English businessman. It's high tea in the tropics, and the two famished con men are willing to do the Charleston, pretend they're in Paris, engage in all manner of charades for the chance to steal Mrs. Parkington Simpson's jewels. [...]"
—Ed Morales, *The Village Voice,* October 23-29, 1996.

"[...] Self-deception in all its forms is the theme of *Lady Strass* by Eduardo Manet; "strass," in fact means paste or fake jewels. At the height of a tropical storm, two low-grade swindlers take refuge in what seems to be an abandoned house. Trapped inside, they are confronted by pistol-toting owner, Mrs. Eliane Parkington Simpson, the last grand dame of the British Empire. [...] Mr. Manet creates a seductive, personalized space for Mrs. Simpson's delightful world of delusion: tossing white petals about to Isolde's "Liebestod", her betrayal and desertion vanish. [...]"
—David Lipfert, *This Month on Stage,* Vol. VI, No. 11, December 1996.

AUTHOR'S NOTE

Structurally, this play has been inspired by the *pas de trois* of classical ballet. Three actors take turns at center stage. They dance as soloists, in *pas de deux* and in *pas de trois*. They are always attentive to one another, respecting each other's moments of emotion.

The idea for the play comes from a real situation. In Buenos Aires, someone told me about an aunt of Irish origin who lived in Rosario (near the border with Uruguay); she had locked herself up in a dilapidated old mansion and nailed the doors and windows shut. Friends and members of the family kept her supplied with food by passing the boxes through a basement window. They promised to take me along on delivery day. It seems there was a sort of ritual established between the people on the outside and the recluse. The old lady had been living like that for ten years, quite happy, lucid, and calm. I wasn't able to make the trip to Rosario but later, while traveling through British Honduras, I saw an empty house with boarded up windows and doors. It was said that a murder had been committed there and that the house had been vacant a long time.

But, who can say that for sure?

EDUARDO MANET

CHARACTERS

MRS. ELIANE PARKINGTON SIMPSON
BERTRAND LE BRUN, ALIAS SLICK
MANUEL SIERRA, ALIAS FLASH

SETTING

The livingroom of a dilapidated old house that had once known days of splendor. Stage right (against the theatre wall), a kind of raised balcony or pulpit; at the beginning of the action, it is closed off by a curtain. Several steps lead up to it. Stage left, an authentic little theatre; that is, a small stage where at one time Mrs. Parkington-Simpson and her friends put on plays. It is also concealed by a curtain. Upstage, center, a window, or rather, a kind of hole in the wall. Above this hole, a special mechanism: a simple but clever device, like a guillotine, that is held up by a pulley and chains but can quickly drop a panel that closes off the hole completely. The chains lead up to the balcony, where Mrs. Parkington-Simpson can manipulate them. In order to hide the back of the stage (except for the area with the hole and the mechanism), there are dusty, torn tapestries or drapes. The space between the little theatre and the area beneath the balcony is cluttered with pieces of furniture that have been turned upside down and covered up. There are spotlights visible everywhere, because Mrs. Parkington-Simpson lives her life theatrically.

ACT I

Throughout the beginning action, there is the sound of heavy rain from outside. Also the sound of Bertrand and Manuel banging on the window, trying to open it. For several moments, the stage is in total darkness. Then we hear the boards splintering and the voices of the two men.

BERTRAND'S VOICE: *(slight French accent)* There! I've broken through!

The beam from Bertrand's flashlight sweeps the center of the stage.

MANUEL'S VOICE: *(slight Spanish accent)* What do you see?

BERTRAND'S VOICE: Not a damn thing! A black hole! You could break your neck if you're not careful!

MANUEL'S VOICE: So, are you going in? That's not the way to do it. If you'd put your ass through first instead of your head...

BERTRAND'S VOICE: Goddammit. You do it then. You're the young, thin one.

MANUEL'S VOICE: Maybe so. But you're the one who wanted to go down first. You're there, so jump, cojones. It's raining buckets, and I'm going to catch my death of cold.

While Manuel is talking, Bertrand has followed his directions. Instead of going down head first, he has come in backwards and touched the floor with his foot.

BERTRAND: Well, that's that. Nothing's caved in, at least not yet. Your turn! Go ahead and jump.

*He leans over to help Manuel, who slips through easily. They
remain standing for a moment in front of the window.
Manuel, who is now holding the flashlight, sweeps the stage
with a beam of light. The audience thus sees the stage, with
the closed curtain, then the covered pieces of furniture.*

BERTRAND: Good God! What is it? Look what we've fallen into!

MANUEL: It looks like a church.

BERTRAND: No. A theater.

MANUEL: At any rate, it's shelter. And maybe there's something to eat.

BERTRAND: What? The rats? Maybe an old snake in the bathtub? No, haven't you seen the outside of this shack? It's literally falling apart. It's been abandoned for at least twenty years. And you talk about food! Ouch! *(He is walking in the dark, closely followed by Manuel, who is guiding him with the flashlight.)* Hey, Flash, let's have some light up here! I almost slipped in this goddamn mess!

MANUEL: So take the light and stop yelling. If you think that...

A loud noise: the "guillotine" has just fallen, closing the "window." The sound of the rain stops.

MANUEL: I don't know. Something must have fallen.

BERTRAND: Obviously, but what?

MANUEL: Look around. You've got the flashlight.

*Bertrand sweeps the set slowly. Starting from the far left and
aiming the beam up high, he makes a kind of semi-circle, then*

lowers the beam to the center where they, and the audience, see that the panel has fallen, hermetically sealing off the window.

BERTRAND: What the hell is that?

Bertrand tries to open the mechanism with his free hand.

MANUEL: Can't you open it?

BERTRAND: I've only got one hand, for chrissake! You could at least hold the light so I could see.

MANUEL: *(taking the flashlight)* Here. Don't get nervous. Above all you can't get nervous when this kind of thing happens. You end up doing something illogical and stupid. And then you look back with regret: oh, if I hadn't been so dumb, if I'd only done this or done that. Remember what happened in Nicaragua when...

In the beam of the flashlight we see Bertrand's desperate efforts at opening the panel.

BERTRAND: Cut the chatter and try to open this thing. You used to be a mechanic, right? So use your skills. Open it.

Bertrand takes the flashlight. Manuel goes immediately to work. He gives it a try, stops, looks at the joints.

MANUEL: So what is this already... Oh, so that's it! Well... I... No... I think... Madre mía!

BERTRAND: What? So you can't figure it out either? It's not so easy, huh.

MANUEL: It's fishy, that's what it is, fishy. Give me that!

He takes the flashlight back from Bertrand and looks carefully at the chains.

BERTRAND: So what is it?

MANUEL: It looks like a trap. We're shut up in here like rats.

BERTRAND: You must be nuts! This house is empty! All the doors and windows are closed from the outside, and boarded up.

Bertrand speaks loudly and quickly to give himself courage. Manuel has been running the flashlight beam along the chains and has discovered the balcony. He replies in the same tone.

MANUEL: I'm not saying that the house is empty or that it's inhabited. I'm only saying that, according to the most elementary laws of mechanics, that THAT *(He points the beam at the panel.)* looks just like a trap: for wolves or wildcats or dumb bastards, whatever, but a trap all the same!

The stagelights come on, with two strong spotlights in the area where Bertrand and Manuel are standing. The mechanism closing off the window does indeed look just like a trap.

ELIANE'S VOICE: *(slight British accent, heard over loudspeakers situated at several locations around the stage)* Don't move! No se muevan! You are under surveillance! Estais siendo vigilados!

Bertrand and Manuel look at each other in panic. They hide behind pieces of furniture, downstage center. The two men are barefoot and dressed like Central American peasants. They are wearing large straw hats. Their clothes are soaking wet.

MANUEL: What's going on?

BERTRAND: You were right, we've fallen into a trap.

MANUEL: We've got to do something.

BERTRAND: Do what? Do you have an idea?

MANUEL: We've got to negotiate.

BERTRAND: We've got to shut up. Let the others show themselves.

MANUEL: What others?

BERTRAND: You mean you didn't hear...

He makes a vague gesture, pointing at everything.

MANUEL: So far I've only heard one woman.

BERTRAND: Bravo! You're a real macho! He hears one woman and he's reassured. Well, listen, I think that bitch is surrounded by guys. We don't know how many or where they are. That's why we have to lay low and wait.

MANUEL: Well I say we should go out, with our hands up.

BERTRAND: Okay, go ahead. Go on out. You speak for both of us.

Bertrand does not budge.

MANUEL: I'm going. *(He gets up and walks around the stage. At times he takes backwards steps or turns from side to side.)* Madame, Señora, Lady... wherever you are, whoever you are, if you're alone or with somcone, don't be afraid. We're peaceful men who wish no harm to anyone. With all due respect, we'd just like to have a little friendly talk with you. Would you please show yourself and answer us?

> *There is a moment of suspense. Bertrand comes partway out of his hiding place. He and Manuel look at each other without knowing what to do. Suddenly we hear music from the original version of the opera "Tristan und Isolde." The volume is very high. Bertrand leaves his hiding place and crosses to Manuel, at center stage. He looks all around, not daring to say or do anything. Then the music stops as abruptly as it began. The balcony curtain opens, revealing Mrs. Parkington-Simpson, seated on a kind of throne and dressed in riding clothes; she is pointing a rifle at the two men.*

BERTRAND: Oh my God!

MANUEL: *(between his teeth)* I told you it was just a woman.

ELIANE: Mrs. Parkington-Simpson. You are in my home, and you are guilty of breaking and entering.

> *Manuel takes a step forward.*

MANUEL: It's pouring outside, Señora, and we...

> *Bertrand also steps forward and touches Manuel on the shoulder. He points to the hat Manuel is still wearing. Bertrand has taken his off and is holding it in front of him with the humble gesture that he has seen the Indians use to speak to their bosses.*

BERTRAND: Please excuse us, but we were convinced that the house was empty.

ELIANE: Can't you read?

Bertrand and Manuel look at each other.

BERTRAND: Yes, Madame. We know how to read.

ELIANE: Well, then you have no excuse. Just a mile up the road, before you reach the house, there is a rather impressive sign warning trespassers that this land is private property, under the protection of the British Empire.

The two men exchange another glance.

BERTRAND: Yes, Madame, we noticed it, but allow me to say that the sign is no longer very impressive. You can barely read it. And perhaps you have not been out of here for a long time and you don't have a radio or a television, but the British Empire is a bit like your house and the sign: in ruins.

Eliane aims the rifle and fires twice, handling the weapon with surprising skill. Bertrand and Manuel run, screaming, and hide behind the furniture.

MANUEL: Madre mía!

ELIANE: Wherever one finds an Englishman and an Englishwoman with a stout heart, there the British Empire lives and shall live in all its glory. And you should know that I can hit a fly at a hundred paces. One more insult, and it'll be curtains for you.

BERTRAND: But Madame, there has been a misunderstanding. I have nothing against the British Empire. Quite the opposite. Indeed, we deliberately came here to the English zone to seek asylum and protection. Do you understand? We need help! Protection! We love England. Yes, we do!

He begins to sing the British anthem. The two men have retreated stage left, trying to shield themselves next to the little theatre stage.

MANUEL: *(aside to Bertrand)* Shut up, godammit! Stop clowning around. This woman is crazy. We've got to escape.

ELIANE: *(calming down a bit after Bertrand's declaration of principles)* Hombres, who are you?

BERTRAND: *(to Manuel)* You see? I've got her! Let me handle this. *(He gets up and crosses to center stage.)* My friends call me Slick. And *(pointing to Manuel)* he's Flash.

Bertrand smiles brightly. Pause.

ELIANE: *(resuming her cold tone)* No pseudonyms. Please give your Christian names.

Bertrand is a bit taken aback.

BERTRAND: Excuse me, I've lost the habit of using them. My name is Le Brun, Bertrand Le Brun, and this is...

Manuel steps forward.

MANUEL: Manuel Sierra.

ELIANE: Very well, Mr. Le Brun or Mr. Sierra, what's going on in our noble Central America? Has there been a flood or an earthquake? Has a volcano erupted? What made you break into my home?

She has placed the rifle between her knees and, to the astonishment of the two men, has lit a long cigar.

MANUEL: Nothing like that, Señora. There's been a coup d'état in Tegucigalpa.

ELIANE: And you panicked over that? Since I've been living here, on the border between these two countries, I've heard of at least a hundred coups d'état by generals overthrowing other generals.

BERTRAND: *(responding before Manuel has a chance to)* Yes, indeed, it's a common thing, but the problem now is that each new one wants to outdo his predecessor. The one who took power today is shooting at anything that moves. "Only the dead never rebel," is what he said in his last speech. Now Flash—pardon me, Manuel—and I, we said to each other, that we're fed up. One of these days, they're going to use us for target practice. We have to beat it. We have to find a place where there still are honorable people, where we'll get a warm welcome, and voilà, here we are...

> *Bertrand smiles, very pleased with himself and his cleverness. Pause. Eliane looks at them pensively while smoking her cigar.*

ELIANE: Are you hungry?

BERTRAND: Oh, oui, Madame!

MANUEL: Sí, Señora, sí.

ELIANE: Very well. *(She gets up.)* You shall have something to eat. And I'll get you some clothes so you can change.

> *She slowly comes down from the balcony, with the cigar in her hand and the rifle under her arm.*

BERTRAND: Merci, Madame. *(To Manuel, loudly)* I told you:

we should go to the English zone. It's the only place where we will be treated well.

MANUEL: We should also say that if we'd known your house was occupied, we'd have knocked at the door.

Eliane crosses to her right, climbs the steps to the stage, and disappears behind the curtain. Manuel quickly goes over to Bertrand.

BERTRAND: Don't overdo your buttering up. Knock where? All the doors and windows are nailed shut from the outside, meathead. There it is again, it's got me again. I can't stand being closed in. I need air. As soon as we've chowed down, let's split.

MANUEL: How?

Pause. They look around.

BERTRAND: The way we got in.

MANUEL: Try it.

They look at each other, then Bertrand goes over to the window to open it. He makes a concerted effort. Nothing moves.

BERTRAND: Impossible. I knew it!

Pause. They are crushed.

MANUEL: Wait! I have an idea.

Manuel crosses to the panel that covers the window. He traces the chains that support the pulley, following them to the balcony. He climbs up and finds the lever that operates the pulley. He tries to move it.

MANUEL: Puta y reputa de la chingada de su madre! What the hell!

Bertrand goes over to Manuel.

BERTRAND: What's wrong?

MANUEL: This is where you operate the goddamn trap alright, but the lever has a lock on it. She must carry the key on her, the bitch.

Bertrand crosses to center stage. He tries to look innocent. We hear the voice of Eliane, coming closer. She is singing Isolde's aria in German. Manuel quickly comes down from the balcony and moves to center stage. Eliane emerges from behind the curtains. She has two hangers with clothing draped over her arms.

ELIANE: Here, take these.

The men go over to her to take the clothing.

BERTRAND: Thank you, Madame.

MANUEL: Gracias, Señora.

Eliane disappears again. The men go behind the overturned furniture to change their clothes. Only their heads are visible.

BERTRAND: It smells a bit like mothballs, but with a little fresh air...

MANUEL: You should talk about fresh air. If you'd listened to me, we'd be in Mexico by now.

BERTRAND: Or down some ravine, with vultures happily pecking away at our bullet-riddled bodies. We'll chow down, we'll rest up, and we'll nonchalantly cross the border. A week from now, we'll be in Veracruz.

MANUEL: No way. I'm going straight to Chihuahua. I already told you my cousins are waiting for me.

BERTRAND: Why the big hurry? We'll go later. Besides, if I were you, I'd be leery of those yokels who've invited you to go work on their farm. You realize what kind of job that is? Bending over from dawn to dusk in order to live just as badly as the Aztecs or the Toltecs.

MANUEL: If you've got a better idea...

BERTRAND: Veracruz, I tell you. Acapulco. That's where business is booming. *(Singing)* "From Sierra Morena, Cielito Lindo comes softly stealing. Laughing eyes, black and roguish, Cielito Lindo, beauty revealing, Ay, ay, ay, ay... "

MANUEL: Business, you say! Bad luck, is what you mean. Three months in jail in Maracaibo. Four months in Costa Rica. Getting kicked around by the cops in Nicaragua.

BERTRAND: Everybody has some bad breaks. Besides, that's life. One day you've got a chicken in the pot, and another your ass is hanging out. And may the best man win. Besides I can feel it that we're about to have a spell of good luck. I told you: let's go see what's in that house. And here we are, dressed like gentlemen.

> *They come out from behind the furniture, elegantly dressed in costumes from 1900-1910. Manuel's suit is a bit too large for him while Bertrand's is on the tight side. They look at each other.*

MANUEL: Well...

BERTRAND: Say, how's that for class!

He turns around like a model.

MANUEL: Don't you think they're a bit old-fashioned? We're sure to attract attention.

BERTRAND: *(disappointed)* Okay, they're a bit bizarre. But what a shame. Look at this material!

MANUEL: She must have some other suits, newer, more practical ones. Keep your eyes open, Slick. When we clear out of here, we want to grab at least enough to pay for the trip to Campeche.

BERTRAND: *(who has found a mirror behind a curtain)* Don't worry. I'll be on the lookout. There's no air in this shack; I've no desire to kick off here.

> *Bertrand looks all around. So does Manuel. They have turned serious and are concentrating. The atmosphere in the room has become oppressive.*

MANUEL: It's like a tomb, or a museum. How can that woman live here in...

> *A gong sounds, and the little theatre curtain opens.*

ELIANE: Gentlemen, tea is served!

> *On the little stage, there is a small table with three chairs, a grandfather clock, and a pedestal with a vase containing artificial flowers. We can faintly hear "Roses of Picardy," sung by a tenor. Eliane has also changed. She is wearing a summer dress, Creole style of 1900-1910. Her hair is also in the style of that period. She is pouring tea. On the small*

table, besides the tea service, there is a plate of cookies, a bottle of whisky, a small bucket of ice, and three glasses. Bertrand and Manuel, in astonishment, climb the steps to the little stage.

BERTRAND: Look at that...

MANUEL: Caramba!

The men are fascinated by the plate of cookies.

ELIANE: Sit down, please, gentlemen. *(Bertrand and Manuel sit. A moment of hesitation. Embarrassed smiles. They don't dare help themselves. Eliane makes an expansive gesture. The two men attack the food at the same time. They become engrossed in finishing off the cookies, stuffing their faces in silence and smiling from time to time at Eliane.)* Would you care for a drop of whisky with your tea? *(They nod affirmatively.)* With ice? *(Bertrand nods yes. Manuel shakes his head no.)* On the rocks, for Monsieur Le Brun; straight, for Señor Sierra! *(She serves each of them two shots and fills almost half a large glass for herself.)* Drinking whisky with tea is a custom I acquired from my first husband, the late Colonel Kenneth W. Parkington, officer of the British army. He spent almost all his youth in Southeast Asia: Burma, Benares, Madras, and never an illness. Good old Scotch kills the germs. He used to say to me, "Eliane, I lived thirty years of my life among the filthiest, most wretched people in the world. I've even drunk the polluted waters of the Ganges. And not a day's illness. Not dysentery, nor yellow fever, nor malaria. Wherever you are, Eliane, always have your tea with a drop of whisky to clean the intestines and purify the blood." *(She raises her half-empty glass.)* To you, Kenneth W. Parkington. Wherever you are, darling, cheers!

Bertrand and Manuel raise their glasses.

BERTRAND: Tchin-tchin, mon Colonel!

MANUEL: Salud!

They drink. Elaine refills her glass as generously as the first time. Then she takes out a cigar holder from a large, white cloth handbag that is hanging on the back of her chair. She lights her cigar, inhales a puff, and looks pensively at the lighted end.

ELIANE: Life! *(She makes a gesture as if to ward off a sad thought.)* Smoking cigars is a custom I acquired from my second husband, the late William F. Simpson. He used to say to me, "Eliane, the cigar was invented by God. It is a present he made to man to sustain him in moments of sadness, to help him to live, to chase from his lungs the putrid fumes of this world." Tobacco: the leaves of dreams. Simpson spent all his youth over here, in this hemisphere, working for the glory and prosperity of England. He was a financial genius. He had business in his blood. He's the one who built this house. "Eliane," he used to say to me, "on this narrow strip of earth between the Pacific Ocean and the Caribbean Sea, flies the flag of the British Empire, exalting the nobility of our people." *(She has been taking sips of the whisky. Suddenly she laughs.)* Parkington and Simpson were very different in most ways but they had two things in common: a deep distaste for anything native, mestizo, half-breed, and their love for me. What husbands! What men! Parkington married me when I was twenty and he was sixty. Ten years later I remarried, when Simpson had just turned sixty-five. They were both sturdy and strong, like elm trees or oaks or baobabs. You just don't find men like that anymore. The world has changed. For the worse. Traditions are dying. Men have lost their character. Today they are nothing but weaklings. *(Bertrand scowls.)* William was right when he said to me, "Here you are in your house, in English territory; even if you're surrounded by savages, you are protected from all attack by the British flag. If some day life becomes too disillusioning and the times too difficult, lock yourself in this protective tower and wait for the storm to pass. Here nothing can reach you, Eliane." *(A moment of silent reverie. Bertrand and Manuel have finished eating. The plate is empty and their hunger satisfied.)* To you, too, William F. Simpson, wherever you are. Cheers!

BERTRAND: Skoll.

> *Manuel lifts his glass without saying anything. He has not yet recovered from the story about the natives. He decides to have his revenge and therefore becomes insolent.*

MANUEL: Señora, may I try one of your cigars?

> *Moment of suspense. Bertrand motions Manuel to get hold of himself. Eliane stares at him coldly, searchingly. Her face has suddenly become strangely expressionless. Then she relaxes and smiles.*

ELIANE: Of course, dear. Pardon me. I didn't realize that men like cigars, too.

> *She holds out a box of cigars. Bertrand quickly takes one, but Manuel chooses carefully, finally taking one and putting it against his ear like a real connoisseur. He makes an opening with the little pair of scissors that Eliane has placed on the table, puts the cigar in his mouth and waits for Eliane to light it for him. Another moment of suspense, with Bertrand's glances, as he tries to get Manuel under control, and Eliane's coldness. Then she smiles and, with great feminine charm, lights Manuel's cigar. She serves another round of whisky. All three have a cigar in one hand and a glass in the other.*

ELIANE: You're from this area, Señor Sierra? Honduras? Nicaragua?

MANUEL: Guatemala. I was born in Quetzaltenango. A mestizo, Señora. The late Mr. Simpson would not have wanted to see me in this house, seated at this table.

They exchange glances.

ELIANE: *(very softly, articulating with care)* The late Mr. Simpson is dead, Señor Sierra. And besides, I shared a great many things with my husbands but never their phobia about the natives. I always used to say to one or the other of them: Kenneth... Bill... you're wrong, dark-skinned men can be soft, generous, warm-hearted. Besides, if one sets them a good example, they learn very quickly. And when one shows them the way of faith, they set aside their barbarian gods. It's a fact, absolutely. The Indian, the Black can become good, polite, God-fearing. And as for the problem of hygiene... we have tea, whisky, and cigars to protect us. Cheers!

She empties her glass and then refills it. Bertrand and Manuel look at each other.

BERTRAND: Pardon my indiscretion, Madame, but you have been locked up in here for... ?

She makes a vague gesture.

ELIANE: A long time. Yes, for a long time.

She smokes, staring at nothing. A new glance between the two men.

MANUEL: And this, where does this come from?

ELIANE: My grocers bring it to me. The Harlington-Dexters, honest English merchants who've been doing business in Belize for half a century. We have our faults, you know, but a real Englishman, I mean someone of old Anglo-Saxon stock, knows how to respect the individual and the particular traits of his peers. Old Angus Harlington-Dexter is dead. But his son Jimmy continues to bring me my provisions regularly. He brings up the boxes and sends them in the way you two entered the house. Sometimes we chat a bit. "Well, Jimmy, how's life? "Hard times, Mrs. Parkington, hard times." They know my tastes and my preferences, from father to son: Always the right whisky, the best cigars. *(She shows a cigar.)* Porridge, crackers... and all that.

Manuel takes a swallow of whisky before asking his question.

MANUEL: And... for money?

ELIANE: Oh, Simpson was an efficient man who planned ahead. I have a bank account to last the rest of my days. Not a cent here, except the jewels that my late husbands gave me. As for money, el dinero, l'argent, la plata, le fric, money... you never see any around here. I write a number on a slip of paper and I sign Mrs. Parkington-Simpson. My name, now that's money.

She has spoken these words with all the arrogance of her social class while looking first at one and then at the other of the two men. Pause. Bertrand crushes the end of his cigar in the ashtray.

BERTRAND: Mrs. Parkington-Simpson...

ELIANE: Eliane.

BERTRAND: Pardon?

ELIANE: You may call me Eliane. And I shall call you Gabriel, because I detest the name Bertrand. On the other hand, I like Manuel. *(She closes her eyes in order to appreci-*

ate the sound of it.) Manuel... So *(She points to them as if playing a children's game.)* Eliane... Gabriel... Manuel... Agreed?

Uncomfortable smiles from the two men.

BERTRAND: Agreed. So, Eliane, Manuel and I—Gabriel— are very touched by your welcome, very happy, too, to have met you but... we have some plans that require us elsewhere.

A brief pause.

ELIANE: And what does that mean?

BERTRAND: Well... some work. Manuel has a proposal from some cousins in Chihuahua. There's business waiting for us in Veracruz. I don't wish to be impolite, but... *(He smiles, very ill at ease because of Manuel's silence and Eliane's attitude.)...* we have to think about leaving.

A brief pause.

ELIANE: Manuel, are you in as much of a hurry as Gabriel?

A pause. The two men look at each other.

MANUEL: He'll have to speak for himself. As for me, I'm not in a hurry.

Manuel drinks. Eliane refills his glass. Bertrand explodes.

BERTRAND: What? But you were the one who's been wearing my feet out since we left Nicaragua with the bug up your ass. Let's go. Move it, move it. Chihuahua, Chihuahua, Chihuahua. Ándale, ándale, ándale...

Bertrand talks like a cartoon of Speedy Gonzales mimicking a horse race.

MANUEL: That was before, Gabriel. Now ze external circumstances zey have changed.

BERTRAND: Ze external circumstances... my ass. Who was it who was desperate because this... lady had locked us up in this shack.

In his anger, Bertrand has stood up.

MANUEL: Bertrand! *(He looks at Eliane and smiles.)* Excuse me. *(To Bertrand)* Gabriel, it's pouring outside. If we have whisky, music, and good tobacco, and the company of the charming lady who has made us welcome, then why hurry? Let us taste of the fruits and flowers before the winter comes.

Eliane and Manuel exchange smiles.

BERTRAND: Speaking of tasting, up to now all we've had to eat were cookies that are sitting in my stomach like a ton of bricks. And besides, I'm claustrophobic, dammit! I don't want to stay shut up here one second more! I'm getting the hell out of here. I'm taking off. I'm splitting. Rain or no rain. What difference does that make! *(He tries to get himself under control, to regain his dignity.)* Madame, the key.

Suspense. Exchange of looks.

ELIANE: I beg your pardon?

BERTRAND: You heard me well enough. The key. The key that opens your machine up there.

ELIANE: Excuse me?

BERTRAND: Did you hear?

MANUEL: This is her house. She's within her rights.

BERTRAND: Including shutting us up like rats in a mousetrap?

MANUEL: That, too. We are trespassers, guilty of breaking and entering. She has every right to lock us up until the police arrive.

Bertrand is angry once again.

BERTRAND: You're loco or the whisky's gone to your head. Okay, okay. You stay if you want. But I'm getting the hell out of here, and quick. I'll find a way to open that contraption. *(He quickly steps down from the little stage and crosses to the panel, which he tries unsuccessfully to open. Agitated, he finds a poker in a corner and tries to use it to pry open the joints. When that effort fails, he becomes more and more agitated. He kicks the panel and pounds on it with his fists.)* Jesus Christ... what in the hell... *(During this time, Elaine and Manuel drink and smoke and watch him as if they were in the balcony of a theatre. Then Eliane takes a revolver from her handbag and points it at the spot where Bertrand is standing. She has a cigar in her mouth. With her left hand, she cradles the right hand that holds the gun in perfect marksman stance. Manuel drinks and smokes unperturbed. Eliane shoots. Frightened, Bertrand screams and runs stage right to protect himself under the balcony. Eliane shoots a second time. Bertrand runs to the stairway that leads up to the balcony. A third shot. Bertrand, at top speed, takes refuge up above, in the balcony, hiding himself as best he can. We hear him cry out.)* Do something, Manuel, for godsake! Stop that nutcase. The bullets are getting closer and closer. *(Manuel puts his hand on Eliane's wrist and gives her his most charming smile.)*

MANUEL: Eliane, please.

*Eliane smiles back at him, blows on the revolver barrel, and
puts it away.*

ELIANE: All right, all right.

Manuel gets up.

MANUEL: Is there a pipi-room around here? *(He points at the
tea.)* That always gets to me.

ELIANE: Go down the hall and up the stairs. There's a hallway to the right. You'll find the loo at the end.

> *Pointing to the balcony, Manuel speaks to her in a confi-
> dential tone.*

MANUEL: Talk to him. To calm him down. He's a nice guy,
but he goes off the deep end when he's excited.

> *He smiles and exits. Eliane sits thinking, then takes a com-
> pact out of her bag, looks at herself in the mirror, touches up
> her lipstick and powders her nose. Then she gets up and goes
> down the steps. She has her bag in her hand. She stands at
> center stage, leaning on a piece of upended furniture.*

ELIANE: Gabriel, you can come out. I won't shoot anymore.

Slowly Bertrand pokes out his head.

BERTRAND: I suppose that's another custom acquired from
your husbands.

ELIANE: Parkington. A crack shot. Great tiger hunter in Bengal.

Bertrand gets up, looks at his suit, and dusts himself off.

BERTRAND: Look, because of your funny habits, I've gotten the suit dirty.

ELIANE: Don't worry. I have others. That one was used by the late Mr. Simpson to put on *The Importance of Being Ernest* by Oscar Wilde. At the time, we were crazy about theatre. Besides, you look a lot like Mr. Simpson. Where are you from, Gabriel?

BERTRAND: A little town in Brittany. Out in the sticks. Natives in the jungle. Tom-tom, tom-tom... ah... ah... ah..

Bertrand imitates drumbeats and Tarzan's yell.

ELIANE: Just what I was saying. Bravo, Gabriel. I can see you playing Wilde, or Giraudoux.

BERTRAND: Of course. Or piloting a plane or commanding a submarine. I could perfectly well do all of that.

He starts down the stairway.

ELIANE: Why not? A man or a woman can do anything, Gabriel. If he or she has a strong character and an iron will.

BERTRAND: My foot. That's baloney. A missionary line for making converts. To succeed, even if it's only that much *(He indicates a small amount by making a space between his thumb and index finger.)*, you have to have some dough to begin with. A baby born in a dungheap is handicapped for life, just like a mongoloid. Period.

Bertrand and Eliane are now at center stage, surrounded by the upended furniture. Two survivors of a world in ruins.

ELIANE: So how do you account for Abraham Lincoln,

Thomas Edison, and even Henry Ford? They all came from humble origins.

BERTRAND: That's something else. Yankees are born with dollars stamped on their behinds. *(He taps himself on the forehead.)* We French are born believing in the joy of living, in good food, in art.

Eliane steps over to Bertrand and puts her hand on his shoulder.

ELIANE: Gabriel, we were meant to understand one another. Surviving children of two fallen nations, two crumbling empires. Two old fogeys, past their prime, who've seen so much, who've won and lost and waited in vain. Why then are you in a hurry? To go out and take some more low blows? To be continually humiliated? These walls are real ramparts. You'll see how gradually your life will become sweeter. Gabriel, stay.

Bertrand looks at Eliane, fascinated. Her voice and eyes hypnotize him. He is about to answer when there is the sound of boots. Someone is approaching from behind the little theatre, and Bertrand looks in that direction.

BERTRAND: My God, who's that?

A man, dressed in an SS uniform, has just entered, walking backwards, and stands at the edge of the little stage, his back to Bertrand and Eliane. Eliane also turns around, looks, and lets out a cry.

ELIANE: Hans, oh, Hans!

We hear in the distance, almost inaudibly, "Lili Marleen," sung by a Wehrmacht chorus. The man turns slowly, clicking his heels, with one hand resting on his leather belt and the other arm raised in the Nazi salute. It is Manuel.

BERTRAND: Oh! That's clever. *(Pause. Frozen image.)*

MANUEL: I saw the uniform when I was walking past a wardrobe. I couldn't resist. *(He starts to come down the steps.)* Who is Hans?

ELIANE: He arrived one evening. During the rainy season. Like you. He was sick, bruised. A ghost from hell. He had wandered across Europe and South America. Poor. Pursued. Trailed. His life hanging by a thread. But, wherever he went, he never let go of that uniform even though it could mean prison or death for him. SS Leibstandarte Adolf Hitler. Look. *(She crosses to Manuel.)* There's a bullet hole! *(She caresses Manuel's left arm where the bullet left its mark.)*

MANUEL: Where's Hans?

ELIANE: Dead. In Germany. Shortly after his return. He had wandered the whole continent, from Buenos Aires to Caracas, from Rio to Bogota, searching for his leaders whom he believed were still alive. Sometimes he would have attacks of fever and would cry out: "They are not dead. Men like them cannot die." And he would call to them by name: "Seep Dietriech, Martin Bormann, Heinrich Himmler! Hans Schildcraft, present!" One day he said to me: "Deutschland über alles, Eliane." "No, Hans, no. Don't go away!" But he left me, giving me his only treasure: this uniform. "I shall no longer need it, Eliane. One Germany is dead. Another will rise from her ashes. And this time, victory will be ours. I shall have a new uniform. Keep this one in memory of our heroes. And of me. Heil!" And he left for Frankfurt. Three months later I received a little note: Our sympathy. No signature. No address. Perhaps one of his old comrades. I... Hans... oh, Hans... *(As she speaks, she has been touching the uniform, slowly caressing it. She ends up clinging to Manuel.)* When he died, I closed up all my doors and windows. I nailed them shut myself, with my own hands. Hans! Oh, Hans!

She remains clinging to Manuel for a moment, then looks at him as if he were Hans. She draws away and runs up the steps of the stage, exiting while hiding her face in her hands. Pause.

BERTRAND: Well?

MANUEL: Well what?

BERTRAND: Can you explain to me why you changed your mind? You wanted to beat it as fast as possible, right?

MANUEL: Didn't you hear her?

BERTRAND: Of course I heard her. Tap-tap. Hans is dead, the doors are sealed, boards are nailed across the windows, a genuine cemetery. And bang-bang if anyone disagrees with her. I'm sure not going to sleep here tonight.

He paces nervously back and forth.

MANUEL: And the loot? The jewels she's hiding somewhere. Her signature on a piece of paper. The number? A name. And Mrs. Parkington-Simpson makes you a gift of... how much? Twenty dollars? Two hundred? Two thousand? We could live like kings in Veracruz on that. And you want to toss it all out the window with your asinine claustrophobia and your impatience?

He has walked around Bertrand. His new image in the SS uniform has made an impression on Bertrand. Eliane's voice is heard from a distance as she approaches.

ELIANE: Muchachos! Manuel! Gabriel! I know what we'll do this evening. A party! *(She enters. She has put overalls on over her dress and is wearing a scarf to protect her hair. Under her arm she has a broom and housecleaning paraphernalia.)* We're going to relive the beautiful soirées that I used to give when Simpson was still alive. The gaiety! The music! The laughter! Una fiesta! Come on, don't stand there with your hands folded. Show some life, some enthusiasm. One, two... Do you know what the advantage is of living walled up, cut off from the world? Time. One cheats time. One plays tricks on it. Here Gabriel, take that... and that... and that... *(She quickly removes dust covers from the furniture and passes them to Bertrand. Manuel, who is sweeping the floor, discreetly exits by the little stage. Bertrand also disappears, with the covers.)* What is the weather like today, Mrs. Parkington-Simpson? I have no idea, my friend. And I don't care. I know that sometimes there's a cyclone out there somewhere, that it's raining cats and dogs, like tonight. I know it in a vague sort of way. Nothing very precise. The doors are sealed. My windows are firmly closed. My roof is sturdy. Let the wind growl! Let the rain pour! So what? Eliane Parkington-Simpson has duped the weather! *(She has been bustling about happily, sometimes interrupting her speech to sing snatches of a song.)* The weather outside, the passage of time. When was yesterday? When will tomorrow be? Eliane knows not. But today Eliane is spending the summer with her parents at Brighton. Today Eliane arrives in Bombay with Kenneth Parkington. Today she discovers beauty, love, and above all... *(With a mocking little laugh because Eliane never loses her sense of humor)* her soul. Belize. Simpson. Hans. Everything is today. I have stopped the clock, the seasons, and history. Eliane has conquered time! *(She has finished taking off the covers and putting the furniture in place. A feather duster in hand, she looks around.)* Such a victory deserves a party. The British Empire may be crumbling, but Eliane Parkington-Simpson is still here. Do you hear? *(She listens as if she is waiting for a response. She presses a button or moves a spotlight. In either case, there is a moment of darkness. We hear the beginning of "Ramona." Manuel and Bertrand take their places. Lights come up.)* Good God! My dress! *(She exits running.)*

ACT II

For a long moment we hear the theme song from Dolores del Rio's film "Ramona"—sung in English by a tenor with a Spanish accent. The curtain opens and the stage lights come up. All the dust covers have been removed. Stage right, under the balcony, there is a little table with an old RCA Victor phonograph, of "His Master's Voice" vintage. To right and center, a small sofa, two chairs with high, straight backs, and a long narrow table. In the far left corner, against the little stage, we see the end of a buffet table. The characters can go over to serve themselves, but the audience can only see the end of the table or guess that it is there. Manuel and Bertrand are seated on the chairs as stiff as boards. Bertrand is wearing a summer tuxedo, with a white jacket. Manuel has on a long tail coat; he has his hair plastered down. The two characters are posed like mannequins in a shop window. The initial contact with the audience should last a good minute. Then:

MANUEL: We sure look like damn fools.

BERTRAND: I don't think so. You, I'd say you look like a newly-wed waiting for his bride. Or that American actor we saw in the movies in Tegucigalpa. What was his name? Fred something or other?

> *Manuel gets up, crosses behind Bertrand, and leans both hands on Bertrand's chair back.*

MANUEL: As for you, you look like what you are: a big ham. We're not here to clown around but to find out where she hides her jewels and how many zeros she's going to put on the check. Agreed?

BERTRAND: That's all I think about, old buddy. I keep saying to myself: Bertrand Le Brun, alias Slick, alias Gabriel, like the archangel, opportunity is finally knocking at your door. Fortune awaits you: dough, loot, your wildest dreams, are all there, within arm's reach. But I don't see why I shouldn't savor the moment, the late Simpson's tuxedo, the Turkish cigarettes, the Manhattans, the buffet that awaits us. I can already imagine myself there, in Acapulco, in a luxury hotel on the ocean front. Gorgeous babes coming toward me, with naked breasts. "Señor, what would you like... ? What would you like?"

The record has ended. Manuel crosses to stop it.

MANUEL: In order for your dreams to become reality, sometimes you have to get your hands dirty. I know you all too well. You're unbeatable when it comes to projects, to talk. But as for action... *(He has taken the record off the machine and, holding it in his hand, turns to look at Bertrand.)* When you get down to it, Bertrand-Gabriel-Archangel, you've only got one flaw: you're a nice guy. *(Manuel states this as fact, without any aggressiveness. Bertrand responds in the same tone.)*

BERTRAND: And you, Manolo, you're a hoodlum, but charming.

They end up smiling at each other. Manuel goes over to put on the other side of the record, but the closed curtain now opens. Eliane appears, wearing an evening dress from the 1940s. Pause, as she freezes. Manuel puts the record down on the table and applauds. Bertrand follows his lead. A radiant Eliane steps down from the little stage. Bertrand gets up and goes over to kiss her hand. Manuel, who has also gone over to her, does so as well.

MANUEL: You look so... so...

He cannot find the words.

BERTRAND: Belle, très, très belle.

Eliane motions them to sit down. She sits on the sofa. The others return to their chairs.

ELIANE: Merci, Monsieur, merci. *(She motions around the room with an expansive gesture.)* You can imagine what this house was like in the good old days. William and I gave the most lavish parties in all the Caribbean here. People came from everywhere: Mexico, Florida, Jamaica, Havana. William and Eliane? Eliane and William... That was the password for mad, intoxicating, exhilarating nights. *(Pause as she takes a cigarette from the box on the table and puts it in a cigarette holder.)* It was during the war. One day, at dawn, after an insane night, I was terribly depressed and I said to my husband, "Bill, we have to tone down our lifestyle, or at least be more discreet in our pleasures. There's the war back home, Bill, the war. They're bombing London." And do you know what he answered? *(Bertrand leans forward to light her cigarette. He shakes his head. Eliane assumes a serious tone.)* Just this, my dear: The more blows we receive, the more we must prove our courage and endurance. Our house here, on the other side of the world, is a bastion of proud old England. Our way of fighting, yours and mine, is to show that we firmly believe in victory, that we have never doubted it and that we are already celebrating it. Let us show the natives, the enemies who are watching us, and our friends everywhere, that we are already behaving like victors. Hip, hip, hurray, for old England! *(She bursts out laughing, then continues, without a transition.)* It was the darkest moment of the war, the winter of 41-42. And Bill was talking of victory! Bill! A man of vision.

During the last part of her monologue, Bertrand has taken a shaker from the table and filled three glasses. Bertrand raises his glass.

BERTRAND: Cheers!

They drink.

MANUEL: Salud.

ELIANE: When England won, then we truly celebrated. During weeks, months, I think. I didn't know what else to dream up: charity raffles, masked balls, carnivals around the estate, theatre. Then, gradually, things resumed their normal pace. Business affairs became more and more important in Simpson's life. The Middle East, Africa, Asia.

MANUEL: And Hans came.

Pause.

ELAINE: Hans came. *(Pause. Then she jumps up.)* Enough of memories. We're here to celebrate our meeting one another. Let bygones be bygones. *(She goes over to the phonograph.)* Gabriel, how about getting us a little snack and some champagne?

> *She is searching among the records. Bertrand recovers his spirits as soon as someone mentions food. He goes over to the buffet. Throughout Eliane's monologue, Manuel has been concentrating on his smoking.*

BERTRAND: I'm just the man to prepare and serve all sorts of meals. I'm going to tell you a secret, Eliane: I used to be a waiter in a cafe. In Marseilles. On the Canebière.

> *Eliane has put on a record of "Smoke Gets in Your Eyes," in a sugary version like Mantovani's. Lots of violins. She listens a moment and then goes to center stage.*

ELIANE: *(to Manuel)* May I have this dance, Señor?

Manuel gets up.

MANUEL: You'll have to excuse me, but I don't know how to dance to that.

Pause. They look at each other.

ELIANE: And what do you know how to dance?

MANUEL: The Veracruz zapoteado, the Venezuelan merengue, the Cuban bolero, everything the natives in this part of the world dance.

He speaks very softly. He knows that Eliane likes his half-ironic, half-insolent behavior.

ELIANE: Yankee go home, in other words. That's your style. Well, that's too bad; this evening you'll make an exception. *(She takes him by the hand.)* And you are going to dance with me to "Smoke Gets in Your Eyes."

Bertrand returns with a tray.

BERTRAND: I was still just a kid back then. Twenty years old. What a phony war. *(Bertrand crosses to sit down. He pours himself a drink.)* When I think that you and your pals were stuffing yourself like pigs on this side of the globe while I was stealing from the kitchen to send food to my family in the occupied zone. And that's not all. I sent packages without worrying what they had inside. Just like that. To help out some pals. A bit of contraband, I told myself. It was Marseilles. And sometimes I hid some okay kind of guys in my digs. Then one day one of those guys I was passing stuff along for came to see me on the run and said, "You'd better beat it, Slick, and fast. The Gestapo is looking for you."

ELIANE: Hans adored this music.

BERTRAND: That's when I found out that I had been in a Resistance network. They pretty much forced me onto a boat that was leaving for Maracaibo.

MANUEL: Don't you ever wear your jewels?

ELIANE: Yes, sometimes, for special occasions.

MANUEL: Rubies, pearls, diamonds?

ELIANE: Yes, but mostly emeralds. Hans loved them, too.

BERTRAND: So, when I saw Manuel in that uniform, I panicked for a moment. That's it, there they are again! Twenty years later and they've come to get me. I had to see Manuel's mug! And then, hell, the war's over, the Krauts are our buddies! Cabin boy on the boat to pay my passage. House painter in Maracaibo. Errand boy in Caracas. What didn't I do in those days to keep from starving?

MANUEL: I sometimes used to have a dream. Always the same. I kept having it, over and over. Very strange.

BERTRAND: Diver. Dog trainer, and even a peon on rubber plantations: in the jungle, the humidity. Scared stiff by the spiders, the poisonous snakes. And to top it all off, a drunken foreman who thought I was a Negro.

ELIANE: What was your dream?

MANUEL: A woman. Or rather a virgin. Blonde, like you. Elegant dress. Clouds all around. She floated on air. Her long blue and gold cape covered her feet. Covered with jewels, with stars. She lit up everything around her. Queen, virgin, mirage, that's what I dreamed.

BERTRAND: I almost died. So, when I got out of there, I said to myself: "Old man, work can destroy you and all it does is make the rich richer."

ELIANE: Who was the woman?

MANUEL: I don't know.

BERTRAND: "You've only got one life to live, my good fellow. So, stop and look around you. There has to be some way to make a living without breaking your back!" Fate takes care of things. Just then I met a certain Manuel Sierra, alias Flash. Right away we set up our first con job.

A nod of complicity between Bertrand and Manuel.

MANUEL: The Immaculate Conception. Saint Anne, Mary or Martha. "Quien quiera que seas," I said in my dream, "Whoever you are, watch over me, bless me."

BERTRAND: I had to teach him French so we could pass for two hair stylists. We went to the finest house in Bogota and there...

MANUEL: "Protect me. Protéjame." And who knows? Perhaps it was you.

Eliane turns joyously toward the living room. She sees Bertrand in the process of stuffing himself.

ELIANE: What? What may I ask is this? Take a look at this horse. *(She steps down from the little stage.)* He's stuffing his face! Oh, no, my dear, it's not going to be like that! *(She has crossed quickly to the phonograph.)* Eliane wants to have a good time, to dance, to laugh. And you, gentlemen, are my escorts for the evening. So, let's have a bit of self-control.

(She puts on a record. It's a charleston à la "Gold Diggers of 1933." She goes over to Bertrand.) You are too fat, Gabriel. There's only one cure for that: dancing. Come on, let's go!

> *Manuel in turn has come down from the stage. He goes over to the little table, takes the bucket with the bottles of champagne, and crosses to the buffet. There, half-hidden, he will open the bottles and put them in the bucket. Bertrand has gotten up but he passively resists Eliane. He stands there, clasping his hands.*

BERTRAND: I'm not fat. I'm bloated. All those good soups and tasty chickens and delicious meats I never ate have made me put on weight.

> *Eliane pulls Bertrand toward the little stage.*

ELIANE: Shameful! Glutton! And a liar like all gluttons! Let's dance, mon ami! The night's made for dancing!

> *They go up the steps to the stage.*

BERTRAND: I could never dance to that!

ELIANE: Rubbish! Anyone can do anything. It's never too late to learn.

BERTRAND: Teach me something else, please. I don't know. The tango, say. Or the waltz. I've always wanted to know how to waltz.

> *Eliane has already started to do the charleston by herself.*

ELIANE: Absolutely not. Silence. Look at me, now. You put your legs like this. Bend your knees, you clumsy oaf! Your hands like that. And you move like that, and that, and that...

(She has put him in position. He lets her adjust him as if he were a puppet.) Go on! Follow the rhythm. Let yourself go! The charleston, such a marvel. Ideal for rheumatism, arthritis, flatulence and constipation. Let's dance! Dance! Dance!

> *She dances. He tries to imitate her. At first he is very awkward but gradually, in his own style, he develops self-assurance. Eliane is having a wonderful time. Manuel has opened the champagne bottles—in that he is half-hidden, the stage manager can cheat—then he crosses to the balcony. He has the bucket with the bottles in one hand, a glass in the other, and a Turkish cigarette in his mouth. He looks more like Valentino than ever. He settles down in the balcony and watches the show on the little stage while smoking and drinking.*

BERTRAND: Well, say there, it's true what you said. Nothing like it for the digestion. Everything I've eaten is down in my heels.

ELIANE: Faster! Keep going! That's it. You're starting to loosen up.

BERTRAND: Really? You think so? I'm feeling more comfortable, that's true. But I just can't get this step.

> *He shows Eliane a step she has just done where she touches her thighs with her heels.*

ELIANE: Look, it's easy. Relax. Let your legs go. Listen to the music. Feel it. Dance. The body becomes something else. An instrument. A sudden breeze. A leaf in the wind. *(She is dancing to show him how and suddenly realizes that Bertrand is beginning to like dancing.)* Well, I'll be! But you're dancing, Gabriel Le Brun, you're dancing!!! Look, Manuel, look!

> *Eliane stops to look at Manuel who has not stopped smoking and drinking in the shadows. He is handsome, mysterious, inscrutable. Eliane looks at him a second time, rather*

dazzled. Then she slowly backs up until she disappears. Bertrand is immersed in his enthusiasm.

BERTRAND: Yes, Manuel, look, look at me dance! And it's the charleston! Something for the young! Not the waltz. And just like that: look at me! Gabriel-Angelfoot, that's what I'll call myself from now on. You, you're already resigned to being a senior citizen. I've been reborn to the rhythm of the charleston. I'm dancing! My feet carry me away. I forget the past. Oh, damn it, not to have known before! I should have danced like this all my life! A man who dances rises up... above the garbage that surrounds him. Gabriel... Archangel. You're taking off... it's getting farther away. Gabriel- Bertrand is climbing... in the clouds. You can take everything away from me... except my dancing. I'm dancing! I'm dancing! I'm dancing!

He has reached a kind of anguished joy when, suddenly, the record catches in a groove. The same musical phrase repeats and repeats. Bertrand tries to follow it without realizing that the record is cracked. Then, out of breath, panicked, Bertrand falls down. For a moment we hear his breathing and the record caught in the groove. Manuel has continued calmly smoking and drinking. Pause.

MANUEL: Don't be an ass, Bertrand. You're too old for this. You can die from that kind of exertion, you know.

BERTRAND: What a rotten dance! My motor's racing like crazy. Kaput! Fini le charleston!

He raps the machine to stop the music.

MANUEL: I bet William Simpson had a heart attack while dancing the charleston. Here, have a drink.

BERTRAND: But even so... It was good. I felt hope again. I'm gonna do it everyday, I swear. For exercise, to keep in shape. I'll dance, damn it, I'll dance even if I kick off because of it.

MANUEL: Drink.

Bertrand drinks. Manuel watches him. Pause.

BERTRAND: *(in a soft voice)* Manuel. Have I aged a lot lately?

MANUEL: No. Yes. Besides, what the hell does it matter? Everyone gets old. A little bit every day. People die and are reborn. Or maybe they're not reborn. They go to hell, or to paradise. They don't go anywhere. And God exists, and he doesn't exist. You shouldn't think too much about it. You'll end up loco, or depressed. In any case, it doesn't settle anything. You have to live, that's all. Just live. Right now, here, this evening, you, the unlucky wanderer, and I, the son of a Spanish prostitute and a stupid Indian. You, Bertrand, rebaptized Archangel and I, Manolo, called Señor for once, here, this evening: we're drinking champagne. While waiting for the jewels and the checks. We have no age, amigo. Because only the rich can buy everything: health, a nose job, the right to step on other people's toes, freedom. Let them come tell us, let them come tell us that we're free. When you don't have a cent in your pocket and you have to rent yourself, sell yourself in order to survive, let them come tell us, and you know what we'll do to them, Bertrand?

The handsome, mysterious side of Manuel has given way to a sort of wild joy. Bertrand drinks in his words like a child. He is exultant.

BERTRAND: No. What?

MANUEL: Let them come talk to us about the freedom to be poor and we'll piss right in their faces like this... like this...

He squirts the liquid from the bottle. They laugh like children. Suddenly, total darkness.

BERTRAND: Good God! What is it?

MANUEL: That sicko has struck again!

Filtered light on the balcony. Darkness at center stage. A traveling light on the little stage. We hear Eliane's voice from a distance, reciting John Keats' poem "La Belle Dame sans merci." Manuel and Bertrand lean forward, concentrating on the stage.

ELIANE'S VOICE:
>O what can ail thee, knight-at-arms
>So haggard and so woe-begone?
>The squirrel's granary is full
>And the harvest's done.

Louder music to prepare for Eliane's entrance. she appears wearing a long evening gown made of netting and fine material. It is elegant, but aged by time. She is literally covered with jewels, creating an image like a Catholic Madonna or Tantric goddess. The fabric might have come from Madras, a gift of the late Colonel Simpson. She delivers the poem with tact and sensitivity, but in a somewhat old-fashioned style. The total impression should be of a touching beauty, never ridiculous. The intention is not to create a caricature but rather to transmit the emotions of someone who lives in another world.

>I met a lady in the meads
>Full beautiful, a fairy's child,
>Her hair was long, her foot was light,
>And her eyes were wild.

I set her on my pacing steed,
And nothing else saw all day long,
For sidelong would she bend, and sing
A fairy's song.

MANUEL: The jewels!

BERTRAND: A fortune!

MANUEL: How they shine!

Eliane comes forward, her arms filled with flowers, performing in a world of marvels. Some items could fall from the flies, perhaps maneuvered by Eliane as she is performing. She is her own actress, machinist, director, electrician.

ELIANE: I made a garland for her head,
And bracelets too, and fragrant zone.
She looked at me as she did love,
And made sweet moan.

She took me to her elfin grot,
And there she wept, and sighed full sore,
And there I shut her wild wild eyes
With kisses four.

And there she lulled me asleep,
And there I dreamed—Ah! woe betide!
The latest dream I ever dreamed
And the cold hillside.

I saw pale kings and princes too,
Pale warriors, death-pale were they all;
They cried, "La Belle Dame sans merci
Hath thee in thrall!"

And this is why I sojourn here,
Alone and palely loitering
Though the sedge is withered from the lake,
And no birds sing.
And no birds sing...

The lights on the little stage begin to dim. Eliane withdraws. The curtain for the little stage closes slowly. We hear one more time:

And no birds sing...

The stage lights go on. Manuel quickly comes down from the balcony.

BERTRAND: Where are you going?

MANUEL: The jewels!

He steps up onto the stage and exits. Bertrand comes down from the balcony.

BERTRAND: Wait! That's not the way to do it. We have time, Manuel! *(We hear noises and cries from the wings. Bertrand climbs the steps to the stage, then stops on seeing what is happening back there.)* No! Stop! It's...

Gunshot. Bertrand exits.

BERTRAND'S VOICE: Manuel! *(The stage remains empty for a moment, then we hear Bertrand's voice coming closer.)* I told you, you imbecile. But you, you always have to have everything right away.

They enter. Manuel is wearing a white shirt, his left arm is hanging limply. There's a bloodstain on his forearm. Bertrand is holding him up. They step down and go over to the sofa.

MANUEL: The bitch! She aimed to get me!

BERTRAND: Don't complain, idiot! She warned us. So there. *(He takes Manuel's arm and rolls the sleeve up.)* Let me see! *(He looks.)* You lucked out. The bullet only grazed you.

> *Bertrand makes a bandage for Manuel with his handkerchief. Eliane appears, her hair disarranged and a revolver in her hand.*

ELIANE: Rotter! Ruffian! Petty hoodlum! *(She throws down the revolver and gathers up in her hands the jewelry that she's been wearing.)* Is this what you wanted? Is this the only thing that interests you? This, this and this? Very well, go ahead and take them. They're yours. This one, and that one, too, and this, all of them!

> *Eliane pulls off her jewelry and tosses it to the center at Bertrand and Manuel's feet. She is having a crisis and falls to her knees on the little stage.*

MANUEL: Madre mía, I don't believe it! The jewels! Would you look at the jewels!

> *Eliane, kneeling on the little stage, watches as the two men crawl around on all fours hunting for the jewels.*

ELIANE: The jewels! Take them all! Rings... bracelets... necklaces... Do you know why I'm giving them to you, little worm, two-bit thief? Because they're fakes, those jewels. Paste, shiny rubbish—strass. *(Manuel stops and looks at her.)* The others, the real ones, the lavish gifts of Simpson and Parkington are long since gone. I gave them to Hans. Because he asked for nothing, wanted nothing for himself. He gave everything to others. A prince, a real gentleman, that was Hans. *(Manuel does not take his eyes off her. Bertrand looks at the jewels under a lamp, throws them down, disillusioned. She leans back, her hands on the edge of the stage. Manuel is crouching, his hands filled with jewelry.)*

He deserved the jewels. He was a god. An empire for Hans. Not for you, you miserable, groveling, Indian beggar. For you, there's nothing left but paste. You dared touch me. You...

Bertrand goes over to Manuel. From the symptoms, he realizes that Manuel is about to have a crisis.

BERTRAND: Manolo, calm down. Take a deep breath, chico. Manuel.

Manuel rejects this sympathy with a violent gesture. He begins to throw the jewelry against the little stage, against the furniture.

MANUEL: Fakes... strass... worthless pebbles... like you... yes... you from head to toe. Mrs. Parkington-Simpson... pure fake. Take you? Caress you? Put my hands on your body? Vieja momia! The real jewels belong only to me, to my people, not to you or to your Hans, seigneurs and señoras from a race of thieves. For all the gold, the blood, the lives you took from us, the jewels belong to me, in the name of the father and of the son. For all the blows we received, for the stolen land, for five centuries of humiliation and injustice, I have the right to strip you of everything, to shove down your throat your fake jewels, your false words, your lies... I'll make you eat them, eat them!

Eliane has been fascinated by Manuel's fit of rage. Now he lunges toward her, grabs her throat by one hand, and crushes the jewelry against her face with the other. This time, Bertrand will make a real effort to stop him.

BERTRAND: Let her alone! Good God, Manuel. Basta! Enough already!

Bertrand succeeds in separating Manuel and Eliane. He then helps the woman to get up.

ELIANE: Oh Lord... good Lord!

BERTRAND: Come on, it's done, it's over. Go rest a bit. Wash your face. Your mascara is running. Then we'll have a drink and eat a bit. The buffet is still waiting for us. Why let such good things spoil? He hurt you.

ELIANE: No. I was overwrought. He was, too. Now we're even.

Bertrand has stepped up on the little stage to help Eliane get up. Manuel has picked up the revolver that Eliane threw down on the floor next to him. Now he is at the center of the little stage, pointing the revolver at the woman.

MANUEL: Don't move.

Eliane and Bertrand, who had started to exit, freeze.

BERTRAND: Oh my God!

MANUEL: Maybe the jewels are fakes, but not your signature on a piece of paper.

Overwhelmed by events, Bertrand sits down on the edge of the little stage and puts his head in his hands. Eliane, very dignified, takes a step forward.

ELIANE: What do you want, Indian?

MANUEL: Ten thousand dollars. He *(pointing to Bertrand)* will go get it. I'll stay here. When he comes back with the money, we'll leave.

ELIANE: And if I don't sign?

Pause.

MANUEL: I shoot.

Bertrand looks from one of them to the other.

ELIANE: All right, if you're a man, go ahead and shoot. *(She points to the living room.)* For quite some time I've been living in this tomb. I already belong to the world of the dead. Shoot then, if you like.

> *She slowly opens her arms. Bertrand is ready to jump Manuel, but Manuel gently lowers his arms, tosses the revolver on a piece of furniture, goes to the little table, and serves himself a drink. Bertrand steps down from the little stage and goes over to the table.*

BERTRAND: I'm thirsty too. And hungry. Emotions really take it out of you.

ELIANE: *(in a soft voice)* I have a proposition to make to you. To both of you. *(The two men turn and look at her.)* Two thousand dollars. For each of you. And the key.

> *From her bodice, Eliane pulls out a little chain with the key to the lever device. Pause. Bertrand and Manuel look at each other. They have recovered their complicity.*

BERTRAND: In exchange for what?

ELIANE: Some work.

BERTRAND: What work?

ELIANE: Two thousand dollars for each of you.

BERTRAND: What work?

ELIANE: A game! I'll explain it to you. Come!

> *Manuel nods. Eliane turns and exits. Bertrand fills both hands with little sandwiches and quickly follows her. Manuel makes a move toward the little stage. He stops. He looks at the revolver. He leans over and picks it up. He puts it in his pocket and likewise exits rapidly.*

ACT III

Punjabi flute music.

ELIANE: *(on tape)* Benares, June 17, 1936. The heat has been intense all day. I think that I shall never become accustomed to this hot breath that seeps from the sun, smothers the sky, bakes the trees and the stones. All the windows are open, but it is useless to dream of the wind. It will not come. Colonel Kenneth W. Parkington is waiting for me. He has summoned me, as one is summoned to appear before a court, in order to talk about Kouala.

> *The curtain to the little stage is closed, as is the curtain to the balcony. The lights are focused to right and center. Downstage right, almost under the balcony, there is an armchair with a uniform of the British forces in India. The audience should see only the hat and the elbows that are leaning on the arms of the chair. Eliane is sitting on the sofa, placed diagonally to the armchair. She has her legs stretched out on the sofa. At the moment, on the little low table there are a deck of Tarot cards, a tray with a glass, an ice bucket, an open bottle of champagne, a box of cigars, an ashtray, and a large cigarette lighter. Eliane is wearing a long summer dress, of a style from the late 1920s or early 1930s. She is playing with a long string of pearls in one hand and a long handkerchief in the other. Soft Indian music is heard in the background.*

ELIANE: To understand. To want to understand. To try to understand. Is that too much to ask of you, Kenneth? *(She waits as if listening to an answer, her gaze on the chair.)* No. It's not a passing fancy or a flirtation. I'm talking about friendship. *(Pause.)* Friendship between a man and a woman does exist, yes it does. And a spiritual bond between two beings who have not had, have not wanted to have, and will never have sexual relations. Friendship, Kenneth, friendship. *(She changes position, leaning slightly toward the little table to reach a cigarette.)* I know, Kouala is a native, if you insist on calling him that. But above all, he's a poet. *(She lights the cigarette, and looks at the armchair.)* And besides, I don't see why one always has to classify, to compartmentalize, to label. He doesn't do that. Ever. *(She puts the handkerchief to her mouth for a moment, to chase away a bad memory, then she pours herself a glass of champagne while continuing to talk.)* Yes, he writes in English. Yes, he explained why to me. *(She takes a quick swallow and closes her eyes to remember Kouala's words.)* "One often speaks," he said, "of economic and political colonization..."

> *The music grows louder for a few moments. Slight change in lighting. The theatre curtain opens. Manuel appears in a Hindu costume. He comes down the steps and stands a bit behind Eliane. The music fades to the background.*

MANUEL: One often speaks of economic and political colonization. But one speaks very little, in my opinion, of another form just as harmful: cultural colonization. The kind that stealthily infiltrates schoolchildren and enters the heart of the young student in the colonized land who has had the good fortune to attend the university. The kind that whispers in our ears: if you want to make your voice understood, speak the voice of your masters. One will not look at the color of your skin or your origins. Since you express yourself like us, you are one of us. No, it's not a question of betrayal, but of adoption. You will be able to speak about your people, about yourself, about an environment that is strange to us but which fascinates us, like your rather bizarre beliefs, your music that is so different from ours, and your sweet-tasting fruits. Speak to us about all that, for we do so love a change of scenery. To be perfectly frank, we adore all kinds of folklore. Speak. Speak. But in our language. *(The music becomes louder again. Manuel moves forward and sits on the cushion placed at the foot of the sofa. Eliane looks at him and gently touches him as if she were afraid that the "ghost" will disappear.)* I have succumbed to the temptation, Mrs. Parkington.

ELIANE: Eliane... Kouala and Eliane...

MANUEL: It took me time to understand, but one day I saw myself in the mirror and I said to myself: You are a traitor. You're nothing but an expensive talking parrot, singing and dancing to a music that is not your own. At least call things by their name: it's not a question of adoption but of betrayal. You are a traitor. *(He slowly gets up, resuming his ghostly manner, climbs the steps and disappears again behind the little theatre curtain.)* I'm a traitor. I'm a traitor...

> *The Indian music ends. Eliane watches Manuel leave, then, with her head still turned toward the little stage, she answers a question asked her by the character seated in the armchair.*

ELIANE: His poems? *(She turns her eyes back to the armchair.)* But you must be familiar with them, Kenneth. Your police must have put them on your desk at one time or another. *(She gets up and crosses to the left.)* Yes, yes, I've read his poems. You have nothing to fear for public safety. There's nothing subversive about them. They are subtle, tender. He talks about the seasons, about memories of childhood, of meetings... Sometimes he talks about love. The poems written in Hindi? *(She listens.)* They're not poems, but tracts, political articles? Maybe they talk about hunger, poverty, the suffering of his people! Those things exist. You know it as well as I. If poets are dangerous, is it because their voices convey the truth? By silencing those voices do you think you solve everything? Fair play? Is what you're doing fair play? You had him put in prison, not because he's my lover but because of his revolutionary articles. Your henchmen followed me, my letters were opened, you knew about every one of our rendez-vous, I was used as your bait, and you talk about fair play? *(She is next to the armchair. She leans over, gripping it.)* You had him bound, beaten, tortured, locked up and there... there... No! A man like him does not commit suicide. He was killed. You had him put to death, Kenneth W. Parkington. You! You! You! *(She falls on her knees and, in her rage, spins the chair around.)* You monster! William! Bill! Bill!

> *The audience now sees that the figure in the armchair is a mannequin, dressed in uniform, and with a death's head instead of a face. It ought to give the impression of being a real skeleton, as if Mrs. Parkington-Simpson had kept the remains of her first husband. The Indian music, which had grown louder at the end of the monologue, now stops. Eliane crouches on her knees, hiding her face in her hands. At the cry of "William," Bertrand rapidly enters from upstage left, next to the little stage. He is dressed in knickerbockers, a tweed jacket, and tennis shoes. He is wearing a fake British moustache. He has a bag of golf clubs slung over his shoulder. He sets the bag on the sofa, goes over to the armchair, and turns it against the right wall. The image of the skeleton disappears. Then he crosses to Eliane, helps her up, and leads her over to the sofa.*

BERTRAND: Now there, now there. It's nothing. Come along and calm down. Come, sit here.

> *The actor can adopt a slight English accent.*

ELIANE: He killed him. In cold blood. He had him put to death.

BERTRAND: Don't think about it anymore. You have to stop remembering. It never does any good to stir up things from the past. Do you know how to stay beautiful your whole life? *(She shakes her head.)* I know the secret: good health and a bad memory. Drink. *(He hands her the glass he has just filled.)* Smoke! *(He offers her the box of cigars so she can choose.)* And above all, my love, never think about the dead. Never talk about death. The natives of this region are a good example: do you believe they are happy with their ceremonies to the dead? No. By cultivating the past they have fallen asleep. They've missed the train of progress. Right here in the twentieth century, they are still in a savage state. It's life that matters, Eliane. The movement that brings life. The look to the future. Optimism! Dynamism! Learn from our dear cousins, the Americans: a force propelled like a rocket toward the future. You are here. I am here. You are no longer Mrs. Parkington, but Mrs. Simpson. And this evening, we shall have guests, that is what counts. This party. This evening dedicated to friendship, to happiness, to a full life. Cheers, Eliane, darling.

ELIANE: Cheers, Bill, my dear Bill.

They drink. They feign looks of happiness.

BERTRAND: Darling!

We hear, in the distant background, a Wehrmacht chorus singing "Deutschland über alles." The curtain to the little stage opens. Manuel is dressed in the SS uniform, but he now has on a blond, almost platinum, wig and eyeglasses with small blue-tinted lenses. The stage is empty except for mirrors that multiply Manuel's image. Manuel turns around the stage slowly, looking at himself first from one side, then from another. He moves almost in slow motion, raising his arm to make the Nazi salute, and trying out various poses.

BERTRAND: *(to Eliane, motioning toward Manuel with a discreet gesture)* So there: he's started again!

Eliane looks over to the stage and smiles as if in response to a childish whim. She gets up, a glass in her hand, and crosses

to the far left, where she finds a kind of colorful Indian cover.
She throws it over the armchair, completely concealing the
mannequin—and the late Parkington. Then she crosses to
the phonograph and begins to choose records. She talks
throughout this action.

ELIANE: Whom have you invited this evening?

Bertrand takes out a notebook and begins to read names.

BERTRAND: Larry Gordon, my associate, and his wife.

ELIANE: Lord!

BERTRAND: I couldn't avoid it, darling. The Smiths, the
Parkers... the Lopezes, a Puerto Rican couple. I couldn't
avoid that one either. They're mulatto, but actually almost
white. And very rich. The Milton Brooks...

ELIANE: What high society! It's a promising evening.

All the while he is reading, Bertrand casts rapid glances
toward the little stage. He is more and more nervous.

BERTRAND: The Perez-Serranos; they're Colombian million-
aires. The Hamiltons. Miss Lorna Sosa. In the name of God,
Eliane! Does he have to spend his day listening to those records,
getting all rigged out in that uniform, and making those gestures like... that other one... used to make to the masses in Berlin?

He has stood up, in indignation. Eliane has some records in
her hand but does not put any on. Bertrand crosses and
presses his abdomen up against the stage. He takes out some
binoculars from his jacket pocket and looks at Manuel as if
he were a great distance away.

ELIANE: That's his way of healing old wounds. Besides, locked up in his room in the northeast wing, facing the sea, who can see him? Who can hear him?

BERTRAND: I can see him, that's who. I can hear him. I know that he disguises himself and struts around.

> *Eliane decides not to put a record on. She picks the glass back up that she had put on the phonograph table and crosses to the balcony stairs.*

ELIANE: He does not disguise himself. He simply puts on the uniform he wore during the best days of his youth. He does not strut around. He practices certain gestures, trying to find once again a certain truth, to give a new sense to old customs.

> *She climbs the stairs and disappears from audience view behnd the balcony curtain. Bertrand puts his binoculars in his pocket and turns to the right, continuing to speak as if Eliane were still next to the phonograph.*

BERTRAND: I've placed a single condition on our under-standing, Eliane: discretion. The war ended just five years ago. Other people's wounds have not yet healed. I represent the commercial and financial interests of England in this part of the world. Most of my business transactions are with Americans and they, you know as well as I do, are mostly Jews. Do you know what would happen if it were discovered that we are harboring a former Nazi in our house? Jesus Christ! And not just any Nazi: an SS officer!

ELIANE: He's told me the whole story. He was eighteen years old. The war had just begun. His father had been a hero in 1914. His grandfather fought against the French in 1871. A long line of soldiers. At eighteen one has the right to believe in that tradition. One has the right to be mistaken, to be innocent.

Bertrand returns with a tray loaded with plates of cookies and little sandwiches. He sits down, puts the tray on the low table, and eats as he talks.

BERTRAND: I'd like to remind you of just one thing, dear: at the Nuremberg trials, the SS officers were condemned as a group and found to be dangerous criminals. And he *(Bertrand points toward the stage, a sandwich in his hand.)* was part of Adolf Hitler's personal guard. You see what I mean? As a group! Despicable, all of them!

He eats hungrily.

ELIANE'S VOICE: Who can ascertain a human being's degree of blame? God himself has been mistaken many times. Reread the Bible. Since the beginning of time, it is not wisdom but injustice that rules the hearts of men. I am in a good position to know. I've seen an innocent man killed.

BERTRAND: All right: Kenneth Parkington is dead. Your poet was assassinated. But let your personal cemetery be for a moment. Please. I'm talking about the present. You are Mrs. Simpson and this Danish guest who does not speak Danish and doesn't even know Copenhagen is becoming more and more embarrassing. People are starting to talk in the international business circles of Belize, Kingston and Tegucigalpa. That's why I'm asking you, politely but firmly, to have our guest clear out, tonight, after dinner. I'm prepared to pay his plane fare to wherever he wants to go, but the farther away, the better. I'll even give him a bit of pocket money, just so he'll get the hell out of here, goddammit! *(He smiles.)* Excuse me. Good Lord, Eliane.

The music stops. Manuel slowly comes down from the little stage. The curtain to the balcony opens in perfect synchronization. Manuel clicks his heels in the German military salute.

MANUEL: Herr Simpson, may I speak to you a moment?

Eliane has an ice bucket, a bottle, and some cigarettes next to her chair. She will watch the scene as if it were a play. She could even use opera glasses. A vexed Bertrand bites off the end of his cigar. He motions Manuel to sit down.

BERTRAND: Sit down. Excellent timing. I have some things to say to you, too. *(Manuel sits down. Bertrand offers him the box of cigars.)* Cigar?

MANUEL: No thank you.

BERTRAND: That's right. You don't smoke. No point in offering you a glass. You don't drink either. A prototypical romantic hero. *(Pause.)* Romantic heroes jealously guarded their virginity. At least they didn't cuckold their hosts and protectors.

Manuel remains unruffled. Bertrand, the cigar in his mouth, becomes a bit sullen. Eliane serves herself a drink.

MANUEL: Herr Simpson, I've reestablished contact with my old comrades in South America and with those in West Germany.

There is a moment of tension.

BERTRAND: So, are you going to put us through that again? The shock troops? The nights of terror? The prison camps? Is that what you want to tell me?

Manuel smiles disarmingly.

MANUEL: We have no interest in reliving old battles. What's done is done. Let's leave the desire for revenge to fools. I want to talk to you about solid, sensible things. In a word: I've been chosen to make you a business proposition, Herr Simpson.

Bertrand carries out a series of actions as Manuel speaks. He refills his drink, looks for his eyeglasses, reads his notebook, makes notations.

BERTRAND: What kind of business could I and my people do with you and your contacts?

MANUEL: *(separating each word)* Lead. Tin. Zinc from Bolivia. Fine wood from Paraguay. Argentine wheat. Brazilian coffee. Venezuelan oil. Our race has defects, to be sure, but can you deny that wherever they've gone they've created prosperity, thanks to their sense of discipline, their organization, their passion for work. Your people and mine. *(Short laugh.)* Herr Simpson, we are spiritual cousins. Anglo-Saxons also know how to draw the deepest sap from the roots of the territories where they've settled. There's no need for me to pay tribute to your colonial history. Didn't you show the world, centuries ago, how to make flourish the countless riches of vast continents neglected through the laziness of the natives or the mismanagement of the Spanish conquistadores? *(Bertrand is now listening attentively.)* Well then, five years, Herr Simpson, just five years have sufficed for a handful of German exiles, scattered here and there, to establish a major financial network. *(Pause.)* My friends would like to do business with you, Herr Simpson.

Pause. They look at each other.

BERTRAND: Mr. Hans Schildcraft. Sir, I am obliged to think in terms of my business partners. Their credit rating is important but even more so their... reputation. Your friends, who've set themselves up these past five years in Latin America under false names... we know them all too well. If I start to deal with them, by the next day my desk will be covered with notes from the ministry, official dispatches, threatening letters, and who knows what else. Even if I wanted to, you understand? Even if... I cannot deal with them, Mr. Hans Schildcraft, sir.

The tone has changed. The atmosphere is that of a discreet London club. Manuel leans forward and takes a cigar.

MANUEL: And who says that you should deal directly with them, Herr Simpson?

He selects a cigar. Bertrand quickly lights it for him.

BERTRAND: What do you mean?

MANUEL: The connection can be made through other businessmen in Germany with whom you've already had transactions.

BERTRAND: And the home office is where?

MANUEL: Frankfurt. Sound transactions. Impeccable reputation. Representatives and offices in all the major cities of the world.

BERTRAND: And what can I do for you?

MANUEL: Serve as a relay between South American farms, stockyards, and mines and the European market. No risk. Just profits.

BERTRAND: Commission?

MANUEL: That's negotiable. But it won't be less than 20% on transactions that will count in the millions of dollars and deutschmarks.

Eliane is looking at them, delighted. She raises her glass and murmurs, "Cheers."

BERTRAND: And why me, in particular?

MANUEL: My friends have done their homework: you're well respected here. No one would suspect you of being sympathetic to... us. Nevertheless, you have taken me into your home and protected me. They know that.

BERTRAND: Herr Schildcraft. Sir, life has taught me that we can sometimes be mistaken about our friends and our enemies. Only healthy, well-balanced people are incapable of resentment. And then, who knows? You, I, my people, your people? The next time, might we not find ourselves on the same battlefield, shoulder to shoulder?

MANUEL: May I count on your saying yes?

BERTRAND: I'll raise a toast to our friendship, to our future projects, to our collaboration. May it prove exciting and fruitful. Here's to Deutschland!

He rises. Manuel follows suit.

MANUEL: To England—cheers!

They drink. Then Eliane gets up.

ELIANE: Bravo! Parfait! Fantástico! That's exactly how it really was.

She applauds. Bertrand turns toward the balcony and takes a bow, like an actor. Manuel rapidly climbs onto the little stage and disappears.

BERTRAND: So, you're pleased!

ELIANE: More than that. Delighted. You've surpassed all my hopes. Come, let me give you a hug.

She comes down from the balcony. Bertrand happily turns toward Manuel and notices that he's gone. Worried, he quickly tries to go after him but does not have time because Eliane approaches him with open arms and kisses him soundly on both cheeks.

BERTRAND: Thank you. I'm very happy to have succeeded. *(Pause.)* So, that's how Hans and Simpson came to an agreement?

Eliane looks all around. She, too, is searching for Manuel. As she talks, she heads over to the phonograph.

ELIANE: I can see them as if they were right there. Hans, impeccable, imposing. Simpson blushing with joy. They had become great friends. Just as I had wished.

She beams happily. Bertrand takes off his moustache.

BERTRAND: And afterwards? Pardon my curiosity, but I don't want to leave without knowing why everything took a bad turn.

Eliane walks slowly, looking around and touching the pieces of furniture.

ELIANE: William died of a heart attack. Hans wanted to join his people in Germany, to continue their secret struggle. William only thought about money. He was a... boor. Nice enough, but boorish. Now Hans, he only dreamed of glory. He wanted to go off without anything. A poet, like Kouala. I couldn't let him leave, empty-handed. So I asked him to... I insisted that... Hans, take these jewels. Hans, to remember me by. Here, Hans... *(She is caught up in a kind of hallucination. Manuel reappears, with a portfolio in his hand.)*

MANUEL: You're lying!

Eliane comes back to reality. For a moment they look at each other. Eliane goes over to the low table to get a cigarette.

ELIANE: It's possible I've forgotten a few details. Twenty years have gone by. I...

Manuel comes down the steps, the portfolio in plain view in his hands.

MANUEL: No. You're lying about everything. I found this hidden in the back of a drawer.

He shows the portfolio.

ELIANE: Those are just some worthless old papers. You can't wrap life up like that in a bag. Nor can you define truth. Not ever. I find you quite pretentious, Señor Sierra.

Bertrand has stepped between them and motions for them to calm down. Eliane turns her back to Manuel and goes over to the phonograph. Bertrand takes Manuel by the arm and tries to lead him over to the little stage.

BERTRAND: Don't make a scene. We fulfilled our part of the bargain. She had what she wanted. It doesn't matter whether it was true or not. We take the dough and we split.

Manuel forcibly pulls away and goes back to center stage, near the little table.

MANUEL: That's a lie too, the dough.

BERTRAND: What? What do you mean? It's all a lie?

He, too, goes back to center. Manuel pulls a sheaf of papers from the portfolio.

MANUEL: It's all right there, in black and white. A paper signed by the late Simpson to a bank in London. In English. Copy in Spanish. *(He points to Eliane.)* She has a lifetime pension. Period. Her signature isn't worth a cent. What she signs isn't a check; it's a receipt. London pays the shops directly through their branch in Belize. *(He points to Eliane again.)* She can also have a return ticket to England. And that's the extent of the wealth of Mrs. Parkington-Simpson. And besides, there are the newspaper clippings. Hans...

As Manuel talks, he tosses papers on the floor and on the furniture.

BERTRAND: It's not true. It's not possible. Eliane is a lady. She promised us. There must be some dough some place. Eliane, say it isn't true. You couldn't lie. It's not... *(In his surprise he is searching for the right word and thinks of Simpson.)...* fair play! Nom de Dieu, Eliane, say something!

He crosses to her. Throughout Manuel's speech, Eliane has been looking, almost compulsively, for a record in the stack. At last she finds it. She puts it on: "Tristan und Isolde," sung by Kirsten Flagstad. There is a shifting of positions: as Bertrand reaches the area next to the phonograph, Eliane crosses in the opposite direction, gesturing with her arms as if she were singing. Manuel steps in front of Eliane. Both have their profiles turned to the audience. He shows her the clippings.

MANUEL: This photo: Hans Schildcraft between two policemen, in handcuffs. And this letter from the Interior Minister of Honduras thanking Señora Simpson for her collaboration: "Gracias a usted, señora, hemos atrapado al ladrón." "Thank you, Madam, for your help in catching the thief."

The music—Isolde's aria—is in the background. Eliane recites the German words as she earlier said the verses of Keats.

BERTRAND: The moola! We did what you wanted. We did the right thing by you. The money!

MANUEL: Hans!

BERTRAND: If you can't pay what you promised, we can work something out: three thousand for the two of us!

MANUEL: Hans Schildcraft!

BERTRAND: No? Two thousand then!

MANUEL: Hans!

BERTRAND: Five hundred dollars total!

MANUEL: The truth about Hans!

BERTRAND: Twenty dollars! For our busfare to Campeche!

MANUEL: Hans, goddammit, Hans!

BERTRAND: Ten dollars... five... you must have a bill you can give us, Eliane. A subway ticket! *(He is pleading.)*

MANUEL: Hans!!!

> *Eliane gets away from Bertrand and leads Manuel rapidly away. Eliane clasps Manuel, her arms around the young man's neck. She says something in his ear. Manuel transmits her words.*

MANUEL: Hans had made up the whole story of the business deals between Simpson and the ex-Nazis in Latin America.

BERTRAND: Your stories, Eliane, are a real paso-doble: a step forward, then a step backward... and a step forward, then a step backward... oh, shit!

He pours himself a drink.

MANUEL: Hans wanted to stall for time, but he knew one day or another Simpson would find out the truth. Time was against Hans. Then... yes? Hans? What?

> *Manuel and Eliane turn in place as if they were dancing. The Indian listens to what the woman tells him in his ear. Bertrand, who has finished off his drink to regain his strength, straightens up, like an angry whippersnapper.*

BERTRAND: Time was against Hans! Well, just you think that time is against us too! I've had it up to here! I'm cutting out! And this time for real! Even if I have to blow up this garbage dump of a trap!

> *He crosses quickly and exits. Manuel stops the dance movement and takes Eliane by the shoulders to look her straight in the face. With his SS uniform and his exasperation at the situation, he has fallen into the role and is transformed into a Nazi.*

MANUEL: What was it that Hans said? To go away? Did he suggest that you go away with him? And you? How did you answer him?

ELIANE: We're going away, Hans. Going away... going away... going away...

> *She takes Manuel's face in her hands and covers him with kisses, all the while convulsively repeating, "going away." Manuel breaks the embrace by taking Eliane by the wrists.*

MANUEL: Fine... we're going away... *(He straightens Hans's uniform.)* We're going away to where, Eliane, where?

ELIANE: To Ushuaia.

> *She cries the word the way Flagstad cries "Tristan." She clings to him to kiss him on the mouth. He spins her around and grips her tightly, a bit like a straight jacket, his arms on her arms and her wrists firmly clasped.*

MANUEL: Ushuaia? In Tierra del Fuego? Why so far?

> *His tone is harsh and dry, like a cop handling an interrogation. Eliane tries to free herself. His tone panics her, breaking her out of her state of self-hypnosis.*

ELIANE: Because I want to take you to the ends of the earth, Hans. There, where no one knows anything about Simpson, Parkington, or the war itself. There, where an SS officer from Leibstandarte Adolf Hitler can bury his past and his memories forever.

> *Her tone is tender and strong. Manuel has slightly relaxed his grip. Eliane forcibly frees herself and comes down from the little stage. She stops at center stage, rubbing her arms as if to recapture the warmth of the young man. Manuel does not move.*

MANUEL: But, are we going to be able to go away, Eliane?

ELIANE: Yes, Hans, as you said: we'll go away on foot.

MANUEL: We'll go away on foot.

ELIANE: Naked, if necessary.

MANUEL: Naked, if necessary. Penniless.

ELIANE: Penniless.

He takes the dossier back from her and puts it on the table.

MANUEL: We'll start over again from nothing.

ELIANE: We'll buy false passports. We'll dye our hair. We'll change our names.

She leads him over to the mirror.

MANUEL: What will we call ourselves?

ELIANE: Juan. You'll be Juan Almanza. And I'll be Rosa Barrios.

Bertrand enters.

MANUEL: Even in Ushuaia, there are guards, customs officers, cops. Do you understand? The beautiful story of Juan and Rosa will come to an abrupt end. A penniless couple doesn't interest anybody.

ELIANE: I've taken William's money. I have my own money. And the jewels. Enough to live on a long time. We'll have everything in Ushuaia, Hans. A safe haven. Love. A river. Mountains. A church. All of that's at Ushuaia. And the sunsets are the most beautiful in the world. What else could we ask for? Let's go, Hans. And they'll say about us: They found the secret for a love that life could not shatter. They fought against everything that makes life sordid—hatred, selfishness, fear—and they won. A new humanity has begun thanks to them. A miracle has taken place. Thank you, Juan-Hans. Thank you, Eliane-Rosa.

MANUEL: Eliane never became Rosa and Hans Schildcraft ended up in Honduras, in handcuffs. I made a promise to you in exchange for two thousand dollars. I kept my promise. For nothing. To find out... So, what happened? You finally convinced me. I've agreed to take the jewels. We've got everything ready for our departure. And, one day...

He speaks softly, as if telling a bedtime story to a little child.

ELIANE: Or rather one night. William was in Costa Rica...

She cannot go on. She gets up and goes quickly over to the next piece of furniture where she finds a bottle and a glass. She pours herself a drink.

MANUEL: You had the jewels, the letters of credit, the checks, all in your handbag...

Eliane has downed the glass in one swallow. She sets it down and resumes the gestures of a drowning person that she had at the beginning of the third act in the scene with Parkington.

ELIANE: Yes, I'd arranged everything, taken everything into account. I didn't want history to repeat itself. *(She goes over to the armchair and leans on the back.)* Kouala... beaten... murdered... I... I'd learned...

Manuel stiffens; he braces himself, with his arms resting on the armrests of the chair and his hands gripping the edge.

MANUEL: Yes?

ELIANE: That one has to defend love, that one has to protect the loved one... I wanted...

MANUEL: Yes?

ELIANE: I wanted to save Hans! To save you! To go away with you. Quickly. So nothing could happen.

She leans over to kiss Manuel.

MANUEL: Why am I in danger?

Bertrand, who has filled a bag with food, crosses to center in search of things to sell that he will put in a suitcase and in the big pockets of his raincoat.

ELIANE: Because I know why William went to Costa Rica. He suspects you of lying. He's going to meet your old comrades. I, I know that you lied...

She presses her mouth to Manuel's ear.

MANUEL: Yes, I lied. I didn't go from one end of the Americas to the other searching for my people but to hide from them. At the end of the war I panicked. I betrayed them. I sold some of them to the Americans, others to the Russians. I only wanted one thing: to forget the war... to go far away... far away...

Eliane has slowly separated herself from Manuel. Now she comes down from the balcony and crosses to center. Bertrand is at the opposite end of the room.

ELIANE: Everything was ready... we were going to go...

Manuel gets up, leans on the balcony, and says:

MANUEL: Come, Eliane... follow me!

She turns to look at him and cries out:

ELIANE: It's too late! He's here! William! We have to talk, to explain. Bill, I must tell you. No, Hans. Stop. *(She relives the scene in all her anguish. Bertrand does not dare move. Manuel braces himself to call out. Eliane collapses on the sofa. Manuel quickly comes down and goes over to her. Bertrand does not move. He just stares.)* Hans hit him. Bill fell to the ground. He tried to get up... but something strange had happened to him. I... I felt something break in my body. He... put his hands on his chest... as if he wanted to dig them in. He wanted to cry but no sound came from his wide-open mouth. Then, he looked at me. Help! I could read infinite terror in his eyes. Help! He struggled for a long time. Help! You can't abandon someone who clings to life like that. I'm here. *(She makes gestures as if holding someone up.)* Take a breath. Let me lift you up. You're so heavy? Hans, help me. Hans. I looked, I looked all around, and I, too, felt my heart break... sink... but I could cry out... I... with all my strength...

> *She opens her mouth to cry, but no sound comes out. She turns and hides her face in the sofa cushions and sobs. Pause.*

MANUEL: Hans didn't answer you. He'd already left, Hans had, taking your purse with all the money and the jewels. Hans wasn't a hero, but a hired hand, scum, an SS flunkey. And he died because you turned him in. Poor Eliane! Love stories don't repeat themselves. Hans was not Kouala. Period.

> *Manuel has taken off the blond wig and the military jacket. He exits. Bertrand, who had remained immobile on the little stage, goes over to Eliane.*

BERTRAND: You mustn't hold it against him. He's been like that as long as I've known him. Wherever he goes, Manuel tries to find out the truth. For all the good it does him! It's an illness like any other, truth! Go on, calm down. You're stubborn too, in your own way. *(He gently imitates her.)* Help me. I want to know everything about Hans... Simpson... Parkington... Let's relive the past. Go ahead, blow your nose.

Bertrand puts a handkerchief in her hand, and then goes rummaging in his grocery bag to find a bottle.

ELIANE: Yes, Nanny. Anything you say, Nanny.

BERTRAND: Wait! I'm going to salvage a bottle. We'll have a drink. And we'll say "cheers" a thousand times to chase away bad luck.

ELIANE: Little Liane will be good.

BERTRAND: What? What's got into you now?

ELIANE: *(while hugging him)* Anything you say, Nanny, but please, don't shout.

BERTRAND: *(leaving her in order to sink down on the edge of the little stage)* Oh my God! Oh no!

Eliane follows him, on hands and knees.

ELIANE: Liane wants to play in the garden. Liane loves the roses, the daisies and the lilies. Liane wants to be a daisy. A flower blooming in the moon. It shines up in the sky, the moon. It's like... music... very soft music...

Eliane strolls around the stage. Bertrand opens a bottle and drinks straight out of it without taking his eyes off Eliane. Manuel enters, wearing high boots, a raincoat, and a "Bolívar" hat; the total effect is elegant. He is carrying a backpack that appears quite heavy. His motions are quick and efficient.

MANUEL: *(to Bertrand)* Bravo! You really stripped all the closets. I've picked up a few trinkets that were scattered here and there.

> *He puts the backpack down next to the suitcase. For a minute, he looks at Eliane, who is now next to the phonograph. He takes a chain with a key out of his pocket, showing it to Bertrand.*

MANUEL: I lifted this from her a while back. This time, we're leaving.

> *Manuel quickly climbs the steps to the balcony. What he does will not be seen clearly because he will be half hidden by the curtain, but there will be the sound of chains, etc.*

ELIANE: Day is coming. Someone is coming from the sea. Listen. Do you hear? That voice. A poet's voice. So tender. Is it a voice? Or an angel singing the news? Do you hear, Nanny? The Lord is coming! The angel tells us! He's singing for us! Oh, Lord, I knew you were there! We're not alone, Nanny! An angel can't be untruthful! The Lord is coming! We're not alone!

> *The contraption slowly begins to rise during Eliane's speech. Finally one can see the window-hole. There is the vague sound of rain. Bertrand has not stopped drinking while looking first at Eliane then at the contraption going up. Manuel leans over the balcony and looks at the hole.*

MANUEL: We're cutting out. Come on, let's go.

> *Manuel gets ready to go down the steps.*

BERTRAND: No. We're not going.

> *Manuel stops short and leans over the balcony.*

MANUEL: Estás loco? What's got into you?

BERTRAND *(pointing to Eliane)* Look at her. We can't leave her like that. We're not Nazis like Hans. We're not going.

Eliane is downstage right, near the phonograph. She is talking to someone—Nanny—but the sound of her voice is not heard.

MANUEL: Jesus Christ! Whether we stay or go, that doesn't change anything. She was already crazy when we got here!

BERTRAND: Not like that! Not like now! You're the one who got her into this condition with your bullshit, your need to know the truth! There it is! There's your truth for you!

Bertrand takes a swallow.

MANUEL: All right. We're nice people. We're not from the SS. In the village we'll ask someone to come get her. They'll put her on the plane for England. They'll put her in a clinic. She has a lifetime pension. *(He tries to speak calmly but gets carried away by his words.)* Everything will turn out OK for her. Not for you. Not for me. For us, we have to get out of one mess after another just to survive. That's why we have to go.

BERTRAND: Maybe you're right. But it's still raining out. And it's not so bad here. There's good wine. And when we run out of something, the Dexter-what's-their-names will come to bail us out.

Bertrand drinks.

MANUEL: We planned this trip together. They're waiting for both of us in Chihuahua. You can't drop me, Slick. Besides, in your own way, you're a bit like her. Chihuahua's only a dream. We're going to get slapped around again. I don't want anyone to beat me anymore, to spit on me.

Manuel takes out Eliane's revolver.

MANUEL: I'm not going to let anyone humiliate us anymore. Bertrand... Gabriel... Archangel. We're armed. This time we'll give 'em back blow for blow. We'll shoot. We'll shoot.

> *Manuel continues talking but what he says cannot be heard because Eliane has put on the love duet from "Tristan und Isolde" at full volume. Bertrand, seated with a bottle in his hand and Manuel, standing, leaning over the balcony railing, are having a shouting match. Their mouths can be seen moving as if they were screaming. Eliane crosses the stage, making long motions as if she were dancing. She climbs the steps to the little stage and disappears for just a moment. She returns with her arms filled with flowers which she throws down around her. The volume of the music continues to increase, if possible.*

∼

Anca Visdei

Class Photo

Translated from the French by
Stephen J. Vogel

UBU REPERTORY THEATER PUBLICATIONS
NEW YORK

Anca Visdei was born in Bucharest, Romania, in 1954. She began writing at the age of 14 and later, at the University of Bucharest, studied to be a stage director. At 18, her first play, *La Revedere, Florentina*, was performed and published in her native city. The following year she emigrated to Switzerland. There, she studied law and criminology at the University of Lausanne, obtaining a doctorate before finding employment in the Swiss court system. But having decided to resume her original vocation, she began writing again, and soon newspaper articles, stories and plays followed in rapid succession. People she interviewed include Gabriel García-Márquez, Jean Anouilh and Milan Kundera. As of 1979, all her creative writing has been done in her adopted language, French. She is the author of a novel, *L'éternelle amoureuse* ("Woman Forever in Love"), two collections of short stories, and over a dozen plays, including *L'atroce fin d'un séducteur* ("A Seducer's Ghastly Fate"), *Doña Juana, René et Juliette, Toujours ensemble (Always Together), Photo de classe (Class Photo)*, and most recently, *La Médée de Saint-Médard*. Her plays have been translated into more than ten languages, and performed throughout Europe and in the United States. For productions in Romania, she herself adapts them into her native language. *Toujours ensemble (Always Together)* had its American premiere at Ubu Repertory Theater in February 1996. Anca Visdei currently resides in France and holds both the French and Swiss citizenships. She was awarded a Beaumarchais Foundation grant for *Photo de classe*.

Stephen J. Vogel has previously translated Anca Visdei's *Always Together,* Daniel Besnehard's *Passengers* and *The White Bear,* all published by Ubu, as well as two other plays by Daniel Besnehard, *A Simple Death (Arromanches)* and *The Child in Obock*. *The White Bear* was produced by Ubu Rep in 1992. *Always Together* was published by Ubu in *Plays by Women III* in 1996 and produced by Ubu twice to critical acclaim in 1996. It will go to Romania in June 1997. Other translations for Ubu Repertory Theater include *All It Takes Is Something Small* by Martine Drai (France), published in Ubu's Anthology *Monologues; The Prophet and the President* by Jean-Luc Raharimanana (Madagascar), published in *Afrique II; Intelligence Powder* by Kateb Yacine (Algeria); and *The Daughter of the Gods* by Abdou Anta Kâ (Senegal), which was included in the first *Afrique* anthology now out of print. He is co-translator of Raymond Queneau's *En Passant* presented at the French Institute/Alliance Française as part of Théâtre de la Cabriole's *Be-Bop at Saint Germain-des-Prés*. He recently translated *My Mother's Eyes* by Leïla Sebbar, which is also part of the Ubu anthology *Playwrights of Exile*. The translation of *Class Photo* was made possible by a grant from the Beaumarchais Foundation.

AUTHOR'S NOTE

UNGUIDED TOUR: VISITORS MAY SELECT THEIR OWN ITINERARY

Let the director regard this play as a kind of patchwork. To paraphrase that other woman exiled from love and letters, "Forgive me, I had too much to say to keep it short." And as there is still so much to say, each director may cut what is his or hers (the scenes), and I, as author, will try to recognize what is mine (the characters) in the resulting play. Consequently, the staging of scenes 2, 3 and 4 should be considered "optional." Including them here, however, seemed to me a necessity for the reader, the actors and the director. This play is like a grandmother's attic: each object there is real, having rendered service during a lifetime of its own. It has a memory, and a knowledge of exile. As in an attic, though, only a few pieces of the past can be brought to light. Selecting those pieces is a sign we have already sided with the future, with what it holds for us.

This play is a palimpsest deciphered by the light of a twenty-year absence. But what is it meets the eye if not layer upon layer of lives, times and rhythms, of intersecting destinies wherein each actor/copyist starts living an adventure, to be continued by someone else? What catches the eye of the woman, after her long absence, are the small segments of life, and beneath her gaze the forgotten codes are sometimes broken, sometimes not...

Time and again, someone will scratch out the text of another's life, of another's words, to make room for himself. A love affair is blotted out so that a combat in the professional arena can be recorded. A triumph is scraped away so as to spell out a private defeat. And, between the lines of the manuscript, in the spaces whose virginal whiteness owes its purity solely to her absence, Bianca, "returned from the Great Beyond," reads fragments of her own destiny and, all amazed, finds room there to record her future.

Such reading matter is deeply moving, for no matter the copyist, whether ardent or spiteful, finicky or fastidious, invariably we find therein a blend of extreme violence and infinite tenderness. We find emotions elsewhere, too, but never so extreme as here. Homesickness for this country is homesickness for that passion able to lay waste, and to affirm life...

ANCA VISDEI
1995

CHARACTERS

THE SOMMELIER
BIANCA
VIOLETA
KATIA
MARINA
ROBESCU
RADU
VINCENT
VLAD
SILE *(pronounced "see-lay")*

SILHOUETTES

These roles are to be played by the same actors cast in the parts above:
  A beggar in the métro
  A clerk at the "classifieds" section of a newspaper
  The customers at the same "classified" section
  The guests at a funeral
  Luca and Monica, Vlad's parents

SCENE 1: EVERYDAY LIFE, PARIS, DAYTIME

The prologue to follow, like the epilogue, will be performed on the bare apron of the stage, in front of the still-lowered curtain. The setting will merely be suggested, using sound effects. The sounds evoke the Paris métro. The sound of trains, the well-known signal as the doors are about to close, crowd noises. Bianca, wearing a gorgeous fur coat, hangs onto an imaginary strap in a métro train which is full to bursting. Swaying from side to side like someone trying to keep his balance, a man is holding a bundle of cloth in his arms, one that contains, in all likelihood, a baby.

THE MAN: Madame, Monsieur... I'm a refugee from Romania. I haven't got enough food for my child... If you can spare a coin or even a restaurant coupon... *(He goes over to Bianca.)* Take pity on a Romanian refugee. *(Bianca looks away and doesn't react. The man persists, sticking out his hand right in front of her.)* Have pity. I walked all the way from Romania. *(He makes a point of noticing her fur coat.)* Can't you spare anything for the Romanian refugees?

BIANCA: *(no longer able to contain herself, in a fit of temper)* Vorbiti româneste? *(The man stares at her, dumbfounded. Bianca's anger flares up.)* Biet refugiat, hein? Speak up, fratele meu alb, de ce taci, why don't you answer me, my white brother? *(The man steps back, very troubled. He looks left and right, as if seeking help from the other imaginary passengers around him.)* A Romanian refugee, huh? How's it going for you, Monsieur Romanian refugee? You know, I was born that way... *(She holds out her hand, like a beggar, right in front of the man's face, using the same gestures he used a moment before.)* Help a poor Romanian refugee... *(She moves threateningly toward the man. He backs up, holding the baby before him in a pitiful gesture.)*

THE MAN: I'm a gypsy myself, Madame, but the baby is Romanian. I swear it on the head of my... *(Searching for something)* of my children. The baby is Romanian. Honest...

> *The sound of the métro doors about to close. The man steps back and disappears, as if swallowed up by the curtain. The sound of the train leaving the station. Bianca holds her hands out toward the place where the baby was last seen. With the train now moving, she stumbles, and hangs on to the folds of the curtain, repeating to herself, as if hypnotized:*

BIANCA: The baby is Romanian. The baby is Romanian. *(Suddenly she begins to cry. She stops for a moment, between hiccups.)* Then time for baby to go back home.

SCENE 2: HERMES WITH WINGED FEET, BUCHAREST, MORNING

An official in a gray jacket over a shiny black shirt struggles to push back the curtain, which opens with the grinding sound of a piece of machinery badly in need of oiling. Once the curtain is up, we see a long line of people waiting on stage. Bianca is among them. She is the only one whose clothes stand out, because of her white coat. All the other cast members, wearing the same sort of khaki-colored raincoat, are waiting in this line. Bianca is among the last. Numerous small, silent disruptions, like confusion over someone's place in line, or pickpockets at work, occur every now and then. They are all settled in an equally silent fashion. A sort of ticket-window, behind a guillotine-like sliding panel, is set up downstage left. The official in the gray jacket and shiny black shirt walks to the head of the line, headed for the window. She counts the number of people waiting to see her and her mood grows progressively more sour. She communicates this through snarls, clicking of the tongue and various other noises, all indicating that her level of displeasure is dangerously high.

An air of absurdity, half everyday life-half melodrama, hangs over the group on stage. For example, to trick a person into losing his place in line, someone will point to a spot on the floor and when the first person bends over to see what it is, the second will quickly move to take his place. The first person takes this ruse in stride but then turns around and plays the same trick on someone else. And finally, after a veritable orgy of deception and double-crossing on the part of all those in the line, which by now has undergone multiple contortions, they wind up in exactly the same order that they were in at the beginning. In place of a shade covering the "ticket-window" of what, in fact, is the classifieds section of a newspaper, the dingy, guillotine-like beveled panel displays, in block letters, the name of the paper, "The Voice of the People."

Once this panel is raised, the first customer holds out a piece of paper to the clerk at the counter.

THE GROUCHY MAN: There's no sense of order.

THE SENSIBLE MAN: Anything goes around here.

THE FATALISTIC MAN: That's the way it's always been. It's because we're in the Balkans.

THE PUSHY WOMAN: Before there was a least a sense of discipline. Before!

THE ELDERLY MAN: That's just foolish talk. You weren't even born yet.

THE GROUCHY MAN: No, you fool. We weren't born yet; otherwise we wouldn't have let imbeciles your age set up a communist state.

THE ELDERLY MAN: *(furious, eager to protest)* Snotty-nosed kid.

THE SENSIBLE MAN: *(friend of the young man, very upset, to the elderly man)* Aren't you ashamed of yourself? Have you no shame, a gray-haired man like you, insulting a young man?

THE ELDERLY MAN: *(fuming with indignation)* But... but... it's supposed to be the other way around. He's the one who's not supposed to insult my gray hair... only...

THE GROUCHY MAN: These old fogies don't know what shame is. The grim reaper's knocking at their door, and they're out dragging their varicose veins all over town.

The elderly man is so put out that he almost has a heart attack, but suddenly a collective "shhh!" is heard. The line compresses, and everyone grows calm again. The window opens. The next customer hands over his ad, written on a piece of paper.

THE CLERK: *(reading)* "Will sell apartment Fatherland Square. Décor: traditional Romanian Arts and Crafts. Payment in dollars only." Three hundred and forty lei. *(Wistfully)* Everybody gets paid in dollars these days. Including the doctor. Including the butcher. I'm the only one that has to accept this toilet paper money.

THE SINISTER WOMAN: Three hundred and forty lei? I thought real estate was cheaper.

THE CLERK: *(eyes to heaven)* And to top it off, she's complaining.

THE GROUCHY MAN: She'll be getting thousands of dollars and she gripes about three hundred lei.

THE SENSIBLE MAN: What's three hundred lei? Not even a dollar.

THE SINISTER WOMAN: Okay, that's enough. What's it to you, anyway?

> *She counts the money out and hands it over with an elaborate little gesture, common to all the characters, a sort of secretive movement, reminiscent of the way a student will cover his notebook in class when he doesn't want his neighbor to copy from it.*

THE SENSIBLE MAN: I'll tell you what it is to me. You're holding up the line with all your bellyaching.

THE SINISTER WOMAN: *(exiting)* I suppose your case is an emergency, right?

THE SENSIBLE MAN: Right. Someone who can't wait.

THE CLERK: Stop your arguing or I'm closing up for the day.

> *All at once, complete order reigns. The next customer, "The Emergency," moves forward and hands over his slip of paper. The clerk reads it aloud:*

"It is with grief-stricken hearts that Mama, grandmother, Cousins Nae #1 and Nae #2, Godmother Tarda, little Nicolas, and the Fetesti cousins, announce the unforeseen and devastating loss of the dearest person in the world, their beloved Nae #3, affectionately known as Dirty Dog. Do not send flowers but sign up to make your contribution for the purchase of a marble headstone. Donations in dollars welcome. Nae, we miss you terribly. "

THE SENSIBLE MAN: Seventy-one words! A thousand three hundred lei. Here you are.

THE OPTIMISTIC WOMAN: Such dignity! He's lost the dearest person in the world and he just hands over a thousand lei without batting an eye.

THE PUSHY WOMAN: *(bitterly)* Maybe he got an inheritance from the dearest person in the world.

THE SENSIBLE MAN: *(exiting)* Neurotic bitch! What you need is a good lay!

THE CLERK: *(reading the next customer's ad)* "Bioelectrotechnochimica Enterprises, offering secure employment..."

THE FUNNY MAN: *(turning around)* Shhhh! I can't hear a thing!

THE CLERK: "...for experienced chauffeur to work in..." *(Half*

the line moves forward, hanging on every word.) "...Moldavia."
(General let-down, disappointed sighs.)

THE GROUCHY MAN: You'll never find one.

THE ELDERLY MAN: Unless you get a retiree.

THE PEACEFUL MAN: *(looking at the girl, worried)* You really think so?

THE FATALISTIC MAN: Trust me. The whole province wants to get working papers to come to Bucharest, and you think that someone's going to leave the capital to go out to the boondocks, in Moldavia?

THE PEACEFUL MAN: In Moldavia they have plenty to eat.

THE GROUCHY MAN: Yeah, but that's all they have. Not much to tempt a young man with.

THE FUNNY MAN: Make it clear that you're looking for retirees. They only think about food, anyway.

THE ELDERLY MAN: I beg your pardon!

THE PEACEFUL MAN: *(to the clerk)* Say, what about a retiree, think that's a good idea?

THE CLERK: Who else is there? So I'll just put in, "suitable work for retiree. "

THE PEACEFUL MAN: Better put in the address of the head office, "Red Army Square. "

THE OPTIMISTIC WOMAN: It's not called Red Army Square, any more. It's called People's Square these days!

THE PEACEFUL MAN: What was I thinking? Thank you, ma'am. So put in "People's Square, the Lenin District. "

THE FATALISTIC MAN: It's not the Lenin District any more, it's gone back to the old name, Sector 5, same as before.

THE PEACEFUL MAN: Are you sure about that?

THE FATALISTIC MAN: Absolutely. It was in this morning's edition of "The People's Cause. "

Half the line turns and stares at him.

THE PEOPLE IN LINE: You read "The People's Cause?"

THE FATALISTIC MAN: *(slightly abashed, but facing up to them)* Of course I do. When you want the official word, they're the first to have it, right from the source.

THE PUSHY WOMAN: That's the truth!

THE FATALISTIC MAN: *(emboldened)* You just have to make sure you buy it outside your own neighborhood.

THE PEOPLE IN LINE: Well, of course. Everybody knows that.

THE CLERK: Next! *(reading)* "Am moving abroad. Must sell..."

THE PEOPLE IN LINE: Lucky lady!

THE PUSHY WOMAN: Cowardly traitor!

THE CLERK: *(continuing to read)* "... Gründig TV..."

A WOMAN: Color?

A MAN: What size?

THE CLERK: "... a Renault..."

A MAN: How old?

ANOTHER MAN: What color?

THE CLERK: "... family tomb..."

THE WHOLE LINE: Which cemetery?

THE CLERK: "... and sundry items..."

> *The whole line swivels around, surrounding the person placing the ad, the Optimistic Woman, and draws her aside.*

THE PEOPLE: What do you mean exactly, "sundry items"? Have you got a fax, by any chance? Any blue jeans? How many rooms in the apartment? Where exactly do you work? What's your job? Do you want cash?

THE OPTIMISTIC WOMAN: Of course I want cash. I'm leaving in a week.

THE SENSIBLE MAN: Do yourself a favor. Don't use the classifieds. You'd be just throwing away your money. If we all go over to your place, you'll get everything sold in half an hour. Where do you live?

THE OPTIMISTIC WOMAN: Berceni.

A MAN: You got a car?

THE OPTIMISTIC WOMAN: No.

THE FATALISTIC MAN: Well, let's go. I'll drive you all over there. I'm a bus driver. The Number 94. I'm parked right outside. Just wanted to drop off my ad. I wanted to buy a TV set, but if you save me the Gründig, I'll drive everybody over for free!

THE OPTIMISTIC WOMAN: You're on!

EVERYBODY: You're on! *(They look ready to leave.)*

THE CLERK: *(still holding the ad)* Hey there! That woman wanted to place an ad.

EVERYBODY: Who needs the ad?

THE FATALISTIC MAN: This is the Market Economy in action!

> *They exit, exclaiming delightedly. Only a few die-hards remain in the line, including Bianca.*

THE CLERK: Good-for-nothing bastards! *(Wistfully)* I sure would have liked to get hold of that Gründig, though.

THE FUNNY MAN: *(reading his ad aloud)* "Seek copy of next fall's entrance exam, Bucharest Med School. Will pay cash."

THE CLERK: That's it?

THE FUNNY MAN: That's it.

THE CLERK: "Seek copy of... exam." I don't get it.

THE FUNNY MAN: Don't worry about it, comrade.

THE CLERK: We don't use "comrade," anymore.

THE FUNNY MAN: Oh, sorry. Force of habit. Don't worry about it, the ones who're supposed to get it, they'll get it. The judges on the entrance committee, they're all guys, right? They all piss standing up. And they need cash, like everybody else. And they're just waiting for a chance to get some. Here, here's your money.

He exits.

THE CLERK: *(to herself)* Not a bad idea, really. What section, though? Education... Job Opportunities... or Help Wanted?

She is startled out of her meditation by the voice of the next person in line.

THE FATALISTIC MAN: "Seeking commercial space ground level for pretzel shop. Have machinery and permits. Will buy sugar wholesale..."

THE CLERK: *(having processed the order)* And you? *(Bianca hands over her ad.)* "Bianca Sara organizing reunion for all classmates who took State Exams, class of 1973, at Camil Petresco High School, Bucharest. Meet Friday December 15th, The Jolly Mug Restaurant and Tavern... Gody... Gody-amos?"

BIANCA: "Gaudeamus!" That means, "Let's be merry!" in Latin.

THE CLERK: In Latin, huh? One thousand lei!

BIANCA: *(handing over the sum)* Here you are!

THE CLERK: *(looking at Bianca intently)* Are you sure that you counted this correctly? *(Slyly)* One thousand lei?

BIANCA: Why yes, that's what you said.

THE CLERK: *(long, uncomprehending sigh)* It'll take at least 10 days for me to run your ad.

BIANCA: But this is the window for this Friday's ads. If it's going to take 10 days, I'm not interested.

THE CLERK: *(stone-faced)* Well, I'm not interested in running this ad on Friday.

BIANCA: Am I imagining all this? A hundred people just gave you their ads to run and you never once mentioned a deadline to them.

THE CLERK: I didn't have to, but in your case, there's not a thing I can do in less than 10 days.

BIANCA: But in 10 days I'll be out of the country, don't you get it? What did I do wrong? Why all the others and not me. Have I got something on my forehead, or what? *(She is very upset.)* Is my fly unzipped?

THE GROUCHY MAN: *(to the clerk)* She must have been out of the country a long time. Can I talk to her a second?

THE CLERK: Sure. I'm only interested in one thing. That business is conducted... appropriately.

> *The man takes Bianca aside; the rest of the line grumbles because of the delay this causes.*

THE GROUCHY MAN: Have you been away for long?

BIANCA: Twenty years!

THE GROUCHY MAN: In my case, only two years.

BIANCA: Did you see how she treated me?

THE GROUCHY MAN: You've been gone so long... You've forgotten a few things.

BIANCA: I've forgotten about the injustice.

THE GROUCHY MAN: There you go with your lofty phrases. This isn't an injustice, you're just in the Balkans.

BIANCA: Sure, chalk it up to the Balkans, as usual. Balkans or no Balkans, everybody else placed their ads right away... but not me!

THE GROUCHY MAN: Maybe you've forgotten our customs, a certain way we have of doing things, our ritual gestures. We're very attached to our customs here... in the Balkans. Watch carefully...

> *Bianca watches the next man, in the process of paying for his ad. He does indeed execute a little gesture, beyond what is strictly necessary. The clerk takes the money from him, separating it into two piles. One pile goes into her pocket, the other into the cash drawer, all in a highly discrete, briskly executed motion suggesting a well-oiled machine: Bianca shows a sudden understanding.*

BIANCA: I'd completely forgotten.

THE GROUCHY MAN: Now you see. Even after twenty years, it all comes back. It's in our genes... in the Balkans.

BIANCA: Thanks! I didn't even consider the possibility... I thought that since the revolution...

THE GROUCHY MAN: What revolution? Please, lady, give me

a break. I helped you out because you strike me a nice sort of person. So don't go talking to me like some bozo from the West. The revolution? You know it wasn't like we swapped all our people for the people in some other country.

BIANCA: *(in amazement)* You're right. It's so crazy how quickly we forget.

THE GROUCHY MAN: You and I, we'll never forget. Because we were born here. We might overlook it but when it comes to forgetting: no way. I just had to tell you to take a look at what's going on, and you caught on right away. I doubt if somebody from the West would have caught on. That's how they look at everything here in these Balkans of ours, including our revolutions. Just the way you were looking at the line a while ago, eyes wide open but not seeing a thing.

THE CLERK: *(calling to Bianca)* Hey, Miss Thing, made up your mind yet?

BIANCA: *(whispering)* The little extra, in lei or... ?

THE GROUCHY MAN: Dollars. You can speak in a normal voice now. It's allowed. That's what's changed. We still do the same things but out in the open now.

BIANCA: *(to the clerk)* Here you go!

THE CLERK: *(suspiciously)* A thousand lei. *(Bianca hands over the money for the ad and, concealed in the rolled up paper containing her ad, the greenbacks.)* Okay, that's good. See, everything works out fine if you go about it with the right attitude. That'll be in the Friday edition. Next!

> *Bianca leaves the line, waving to the guy who helped her out.*

BIANCA: Thanks again!

THE GROUCHY MAN: Don't mention it. One citizen to another. How long have you been back in the country?

BIANCA: Since this morning.

THE GROUCHY MAN: You'll see. It'll all come back to you. It's like riding a bike!

BIANCA: Good luck!

THE GROUCHY MAN: *(skeptically)* If you can call this luck...

> *Bianca exits. The Grouchy Man hands a paper to the clerk who reads it aloud.*

THE CLERK: "Romanian engineer residing abroad for 2 years, applying for foreign citizenship, serious, practical, jealous, intending to marry, seeks beautiful, young university graduate, in perfect health, preferably a doctor or pharmacist." Five hundred and eighty lei!

SCENE THREE: THE SUPPLY ROOM, BUCHAREST, NOON

The stage goes dark. Depending on the size and shape of the theater, Bianca and the sommelier will appear in what seems an intimate and sheltered spot: a stage-box, a stairway, the apron of the stage. Stage right, a public phone. The sommelier wears his uniform with white jacket and bow tie. He is seated, or rather sprawled, on a chair. Bianca enters, in a great hurry. She carries a large envelope under her arm.

BIANCA: I'm the one who phoned you this morning. To make a reservation for a buffet dinner for thirty.

THE SOMMELIER: *(apathetically)* If you say so.

BIANCA: You're the sommelier, I suppose.

THE SOMMELIER: Given the etymology of the word "sommelier," meaning one who leads beasts of burden, I'm afraid... I am.

BIANCA: I gave you my name. Bianca Sara.

THE SOMMELIER: *(softly singing the José Feliciano song)* "Sarà, sarà... ché serà, serà... " That's the main thing, knowing who you are.

BIANCA: Do you remember me?

THE SOMMELIER: It would be hard for me to remember since I've never seen you before.

BIANCA: *(trying to control her irritation, to herself)* Stay calm. Let's not forget, we're in the Balkans now, the powderkeg of Europe, and to make things worse, we're in that part of the

Balkans where "the ox is slumbering idly... "

THE SOMMELIER: *(continuing the quotation)* "...as if upon the sere, scorched fields beyond the walls of Rome... "

BIANCA: You can quote Balcescu's work from memory. Bravo!

THE SOMMELIER: It comes with the territory. In my glory days, I used to lead a seminar in semantic topology at the university.

BIANCA: You were... let go?

THE SOMMELIER: No, I was kicked out on my ass.

BIANCA: By the new people?

THE SOMMELIER: By the old ones. *(Placing a knife between his teeth)* The real villains of the piece!

BIANCA: Well then, you'll be accepted back... after the revolution...

THE SOMMELIER: *(pointing the knife at Bianca)* You've been living abroad.

BIANCA: How do you know?

THE SOMMELIER: Because you think there's been a revolution.

BIANCA: Well then, what was it?

THE SOMMELIER: Just another noisy, tumultuous baïram... the usual thing. Perhaps you know the etymology of the word "baïram"? Perhaps not. Too bad. It's a festival, the word is Turkish... *(With a helpless shrug)* These are the Balkans, so what do you expect? Shall I show you, as I show all our visitors from the West who express an interest, the bullet holes on the front of our building? There are precisely seventeen. Highly visible... and authentic. I can testify to that. We put them there ourselves, my co-workers and I, using a rifle belonging to one of our friends, a retired gamekeeper. There was simply no way to go on, all the other restaurants on the square had bestowed upon themselves their own historic indentations. We were the only ones whose front wall was still untouched. And just think, The Jolly Mug, of all places. The capital's oldest tavern. The rendez-vous spot for the intellectual—and therefore, the revolutionary—elite since a century ago. We were starting to look positively reactionary. So we faced up to our responsibilities, took our hunting rifle in hand and went out into the street to give our century-old establishment its revolutionary credentials. Pow! Pow! One of us served as lookout, but it really wasn't necessary. Out in front of the dressmaker's, right across the way, the salesgirls were going through the same routine. We even gave them a helping hand with their bullet holes for fear of their hurting themselves. *(Sadly)* The little seamstresses. That evening we all went out dancing and dining and... *(With a gleam in his eye at the recollection)* we got very friendly...

BIANCA: But there *was* fighting, and victims...

THE SOMMELIER: Some people claim to have been tortured in basements by Babylonian terrorists, others say they sold sausages and brandy to gawkers on the so-called battlefield. Those are just the extreme cases...

BIANCA: *(to herself)* I should have been here. I belonged here.

THE SOMMELIER: You would doubtless have been the only one to run smack into a real Babylonian terrorist. You were smart to stay where you were. Where do you live?

BIANCA: In Paris.

THE SOMMELIER: So lovely. So expensive. The City of Light. Under the Mirabeau Bridge flows the Seine...

BIANCA: And our loves...

THE SOMMELIER: But where are the snows of yesteryear? You ought to meet two of my co-workers. One has a doctorate in French and one is a poet, the best translator of Villon in Romanian.

BIANCA: Are they sommeliers, too?

THE SOMMELIER: No, they just wait on tables. I'm the only "success story." *(He laughs, raises his fist, singing the song of University Square.)*
> Better a pauper than an activist...
> Better a corpse than an opportunist!

Bianca sings along with him.

BIANCA AND THE SOMMELIER:
> Better a pauper than an activist...
> Better a corpse than an opportunist!

The sommelier brings out a bottle of champagne and two glasses.

BIANCA: That's too much.

THE SOMMELIER: It's on the house. To celebrate the return of the prodigal daughter.

BIANCA: *(flattered, curtsying swiftly)* Master.

THE SOMMELIER: Margarita!

They toast each other.

BIANCA: This is so good!

THE SOMMELIER: *(whispering)* I know, I know, but don't tell anyone else. If they find out in the West we make good champagne, they'll think we don't need bread any more.

BIANCA: *(jumping right in)* And if they also found out that we have caviar...

THE SOMMELIER: Shhh!

They drink, each lost in thought.

BIANCA: Haven't your friends gotten their jobs back?

THE SOMMELIER: Why should they?

BIANCA: Because of the new government.

THE SOMMELIER: Oh, it's called the "new government" now? Thanks for telling me. Since I seem to recognize so many of the same faces as before, I hadn't noticed the change. New! *(He laughs.)* Intellectuals are always so divorced from reality. I noticed that you were in the class for math majors, correct?

BIANCA: Advanced level math... class of 1973.

THE SOMMELIER: *(taking out his reservation book but without really checking it)* I've written down your reservation. It's the only reservation for the evening.

BIANCA: Before it was always packed. We had our big dance here, to celebrate our last year at school. It was a real struggle just to get in.

THE SOMMELIER: *(wistfully)* Before. *(Returning to reality)* There will be thirty of you?

BIANCA: At a maximum. At a minimum, two. Myself and Vlad, my best friend. I called him a few days ago. From Paris. The first time after all these years! I've lost track of the others. Over twenty years. But I put an ad in the paper to try to locate them again.

THE SOMMELIER: In which newspaper.

BIANCA: "The Voice of the People."

THE SOMMELIER: You can count on three people, maximum.

BIANCA: In the old days, "The Voice of the People" was the only paper that could publish freely.

THE SOMMELIER: It still is.

BIANCA: Then why does it have so few readers?

THE SOMMELIER: Because the others want to continue to publish freely.

BIANCA: You talk like the Sphinx. Does that make me Oedipus?

THE SOMMELIER: I don't know whether you've murdered your father, but you've certainly come home again. Looking for survivors.

BIANCA: *(giving him the large envelope she was carrying)* Here they are. It's our class photo. Taken at the end of May, 1973. There are thirty of us.

THE SOMMELIER: *(studying the photo)* Wonder how many are still alive.

BIANCA: *(astounded)* You think some are dead? *(Taken aback)* But we're only thirty-eight years old.

THE SOMMELIER: *(studying the photo, smiling, bitter)*
　　　　Among the many masts
　　　　Setting sail from these shores,
　　　　How many will be wrecked
　　　　By the tempests, by the waves?

BIANCA: How many of us do you think there'll be?

THE SOMMELIER: You're one-of-a-kind, perhaps a bit eccentric. A madcap zany with a crackling wit. One of the things our country's famous for, like the Pan-pipes. You know the type, "Those Romanians are out of their minds." Elvira Popesco, the cousin from Bucharest... part of our folklore, right? I like that. You remind me of my first fiancée. My only fiancée for that matter. Just before the war. She used to wear a little gray hat with a violet on it, and she would read Hegel in the original. She was an excellent pianist... They broke the mold. Today all you've got are these frumpy old hags, worn out from standing in line all day, stressed out to the point of obesity, and shrewish from envy for all the consumer goods that others have and they don't. I'll buy you some flowers for your banquet table... in memoriam.

BIANCA: *(kissing him on both cheeks)* I'm dying to introduce you to my friend, Vlad. A poet at heart, like you. I'm off to his house, right away. After twenty years. Maybe he won't recognize me.

THE SOMMELIER: Was he your special boyfriend?

BIANCA: *(laughing)* Oh, no. Not at all, I didn't have a special boyfriend.

THE SOMMELIER: Are you married?

BIANCA: Till tonight.

She exits, rushing out.

THE SOMMELIER: *(waving nostalgically, then, sadly, to himself)* Till tonight, then. *(Worried)* A poet at heart? Me?

SCENE 4: THE CEMETERY, BUCHAREST, DUSK

*A burial in a little cemetery. Smooth, hard light of dusk in win-
tertime. All the cast members are dressed in mourning. The men
are in black coats, the women wear kerchiefs tied under the chin.
Each person lights a yellow candle characteristic of the Orthodox
faith. Downstage, small groups of people are gossiping in low
voices. Downstage right, a man and a woman kneel at a grave,
in deep contemplation. The woman is crying. People shake her
hand automatically and exit. Stage murmurs.*

A WOMAN: Just thirty-eight years old.

ANOTHER WOMAN: An only child.

A MAN: His parents will never get over this.

A WOMAN: He'd just been named chief architect on the project for the new Civic Center.

A MAN: I read that too... in "The Voice of the People."

A WOMAN: His mother always said he was a great architect,
but nobody knew he was... that great.

A MAN: "The Voice of the People" article said that for an architect of today, being in charge of a work site as important as
the Civic Center is the equivalent of building a pyramid.

A WOMAN: He was so nice.

A MAN: Are you sure it was really a heart attack?

A WOMAN: Shhh! His mother might hear you. *(She crosses herself. Stage murmurs.)*

ANOTHER WOMAN: His wife didn't even come to the cemetery.

ANOTHER WOMAN: She doesn't believe in God.

ANOTHER WOMAN: He was too nice.

A MAN: Blood is thicker than water. When you're the daughter of a colonel in the Secret Police, other people's lives, or their deaths...

A WOMAN: Even so, that's no reason.

A MAN: For what?

A WOMAN: For not coming to your husband's burial just because you don't believe in God.

ANOTHER WOMAN: *(crossing herself)* May God rest his soul.

> *Bianca makes her entrance from stage left. She is wearing a white coat and carrying some flowers in her hand. The man and woman kneeling still appear crushed. We see them from the back. A passerby, seeing Bianca looking lost, calls out to her in a friendly voice.*

A PASSERBY: Are you looking for the Ceausescu gravesite? It's over there, where you see the fresh flowers. *(Tenderly)* He's on the right, she's on the left.

BIANCA: *(bending down to get a better look)* There's no name on the cross.

THE PASSERBY: So as not to encourage trouble makers.

BIANCA: Just look at all the flowers on their grave!

THE PASSERBY: *(a quiver in his voice)* Not everyone is ungrateful.

He exits with a wink.

BIANCA: The alarm clock is going to ring in five minutes... and everything will be back to normal! I'm a naturalized French citizen, and I live on the rue Saint-Sauveur in the first arrondissement of Paris.

She goes over to the group gossiping in the middle of the stage.

I'm looking for a burial that's taking place... *(Starting over)* A young man... his name is Vlad... I mean, his name was...

A WOMAN: There they are... his parents. Crushed. If the father's on his feet at all, it's only because of tranquilizers. Be careful what you say... are you a relative?

BIANCA: Yes.

ANOTHER WOMAN: *(suspiciously)* On the wife's side?

BIANCA: No.

A MAN: One of Vlad's family, then...

BIANCA: No... I'm a... a friend. A very close friend.

The people look at her with suspicion.

A WOMAN: I've never seen you before. And I've lived in their building for 17 years.

BIANCA: I left the country... 20 years ago.

A MAN: 20 years ago... that was another century.

A WOMAN: And you think that they'll remember you?

BIANCA: I remember them so well... *(She stands uncertainly in the middle of the stage. Silent pressure from the other people propels her toward the couple. Bianca touches the kneeling woman on the shoulder.)* Hello... It's me!

The woman looks at her without recognizing her.

THE MOTHER: I don't know, dear. I don't recognize you. I don't recognize anyone. Sorry. I've been crying too much. I can't see anything any more.

BIANCA: I'm Bianca... Bianca Sara.

THE MOTHER: *(after a long moment of silence)* Bianca, my darling, you've come... *(She gets to her feet.)* You've come back... *(Bianca opens her arms and the woman rushes to her, in tears. Bianca embraces and consoles her, caressing her as if she were a child.)* Vlad was so glad you were coming back. He said he was going to show you... after 20 years... all the changes... and you've found us more dead than alive. *(She turns toward the man.)* Luca, it's Bianca... She's come back.

> *The man gets up. He goes to Bianca. He looks at her silently, only bowing his head, gently. Discretely, all the guests invited to the burial move as one toward the trio downstage, so as not to miss a word.*

THE FATHER: What a loss...

BIANCA: Sorry about my coat. *(She looks down, embarrassed by her white coat.)* I didn't know a thing. I went to ring your doorbell, to surprise Vlad... *(The mother bursts into tears.)* and the neighbors told me where you were.

THE FATHER: What a loss...

BIANCA: But only a week ago I called him on the phone... from Paris.

THE MOTHER: He was so happy after your phone call. He went around laughing and singing for the rest of the day... like when he was a child. For years he hadn't sung a note.

BIANCA: He seemed so well.

THE MOTHER: He was well... a heart attack... *(She weeps.)*

THE FATHER: Too much heart, too much passion... for one life.

THE MOTHER: *(noticing the people drawing closer, to the others)* Forgive us, forgive us. This girl is Vlad's friend. Leave us alone... Please. *(The others exit.)* If he had only lived three days longer, he would have seen you... and maybe everything would have been different.

THE FATHER: *(to his wife)* You're just torturing yourself, mother. *(To Bianca)* He was so happy at the idea of dancing with you.

THE MOTHER: Like at the banquet twenty years ago... *(She bursts into tears.)*

THE FATHER: Let's sit down... and try to be with him.

THE MOTHER: Luca is crushed.

They sit down on the edge of the grave.

LUCA: I'm not crushed. I just wonder how this kind of injustice is possible. To strike my child down in his sleep, without giving him a chance to cry out for help, to be rescued. Even a hunted animal gets one last chance.

THE MOTHER: Luca is Catholic.

THE FATHER: *(with a distant gaze)* I don't believe any more... I don't believe any more.

THE MOTHER: *(to Bianca)* Here, my darling. Have some of the cake for the dead. You haven't forgotten the old ways, have you?

BIANCA: I never really knew them. I was an orphan... But I'd be glad to learn... for Vlad's sake.

THE MOTHER: *(handing her a plate and a glass of wine)* Vlad loved the cake for the dead. He used to laugh when he was a child, with his little schoolboy cap on all crooked. He'd say, "Mama, how 'bout if we move near a cemetery so we can eat cake for the dead more often. " *(She takes her glass and lets a few drops of wine fall onto the ground.)* May God rest his soul.

BIANCA: *(doing the same)* ...rest his soul. I loved you all so much. You were so happy, the three of you. The parents I would've liked to have...

THE FATHER: We loved you, too, so very much.

THE MOTHER: Darling, don't ever have just one child... so you don't have to go through what we're facing.

THE FATHER: *(indignant)* It's against the laws of nature, it's a cowardly act, it's mean, lowdown...

THE MOTHER: *(not believing her own words)* There's no need for blasphemy, Luca.

THE FATHER: ...to let a son die before his father. How can He allow that?

THE MOTHER: *(in a low voice, to Bianca)* He loved you. When you invited him to come to Paris, he was so happy. After opening your letter, he took me in his arms and waltzed me around the apartment. I was wearing my apron and holding my duster. He was laughing *(She weeps.)* He was laughing... he loved you.

BIANCA: I never understood why he didn't join me over there.

THE MOTHER: They never issued him a passport.

THE FATHER: Tonight... at the reunion... don't be disappointed. There won't be many there. I said the same thing to Vlad. Don't get your hopes up! The political situation, the poverty has pulled people apart.

THE MOTHER: To think that he managed to stay out of the fighting, even though he ran into the streets every time, even when the miners descended on University Square.

BIANCA: Always the bravest.

THE FATHER: He used to say the same thing about you. But what's the use? What's the use? And who's going to show me how to go on with my life?

THE MOTHER: If you like, come stay with us. We'll let you have his room. It's just the way he left it. You can see his pictures, his letters, everything... He loved you so much. If you'd come back, who knows? Maybe everything would have turned out differently.

THE FATHER: And you Bianca, how are you doing? Do you have any children?

BIANCA: No. *(Barely audible)* I think I can't have any.

THE MOTHER: You're still young, my darling. Have a lot of them because otherwise it's just too hard. *(Dissolving into tears)* It's too hard.

THE FATHER: Are you still writing?

BIANCA: Yes.

THE FATHER: In French?

BIANCA: Yes.

THE FATHER: *(to his wife)* You see, mother. Vlad always said that Bianca would make it. *(To Bianca)* And what are you writing at the moment?

BIANCA: An essay. A meditation on a Romanian fairy tale: Youth-without-age and life without death. *(She dissolves into tears.)*

THE FATHER: *(standing up)* Let's go, mother. We're making Bianca cry. And she has to be pretty for tonight, for the party. The living with the living.

THE MOTHER: We'll come here every day. We'll wash the gravesite. We'll take care of the flowers. What else can we do? It's a shame he never had any children. Come on.

THE FATHER: I think she wants to be alone a while with Vlad.

BIANCA: Just a moment... and I'll join you.

THE FATHER: I remember so well that New Year's Day you spent with us. You were seventeen. For two years Vlad had been singing the praises of this smart, this brave, this pretty girl who never let anyone boss her around. And finally we got to see her, so petite in her pretty pink dress, and so nice. I told myself that Vlad was right, that she was different. She didn't say anything, all she did was look. But that look in her eyes... was hers alone. It's been twenty years, and I still haven't forgotten that look in your eyes, Bianca.

THE MOTHER: He only said, "Mama, Bianca is an orphan. I know you always wanted to have a daughter. So, you see, I've made up for what you lacked."

> *They both exit, bent over, inconsolable, each imprisoned in his sorrow. Bianca meditates for a moment, puts her flowers on the grave then speaks as if in prayer.*

BIANCA: My dear Vlad, my only real friend, what would our life together have been like if you had joined me over there? I was so afraid of people... I was only an orphan. And you held me so high. Like the others, so high, that I didn't dare even draw breath for fear of being unworthy of your admiration. You were so talented, so sensitive, so generous. When you found out I was leaving, I hear you said, "She'll be back when we've finished cleaning house." You see, I have come back. I was so frightened, of illegal abortions, of degrading myself, of making concessions to save my own skin, afraid of being too weak, of giving in. *(Angrily)* How can anyone die who's been loved so much? And you were always surrounded by lovesick admirers, they gravitated toward you... and me, in my role as Holy Virgin. I always thought that you only admired me for my intelligence. We behaved ourselves too well. Just take that banquet. We were so tired out from organizing it that we were the only two who didn't dance.

> *Vlad, stark white makeup on his face and dressed in a burial suit, appears on stage. Bianca at first views him with*

fright, then when she recognizes him, she bursts out laughing. He notices the cake for the dead, tastes it with one finger, then closes his eyes, savoring the taste. Bianca rushes into his arms. Vlad enfolds her in them and they begin to dance wildly about the stage, doing a waltz.

BIANCA: Why didn't you ever tell me that you loved me? Why did you die? Just now? Do you still love me?

He places a finger on her lips to signal silence. They continue waltzing around the full length of the stage. As they waltz they laugh uproariously. When the blackout comes, all that can be seen are the burial candles turning to the rhythm of the waltz.

SCENE 5: THE BANQUET, BUCHAREST, EVENING

Tacked to the wall is a blow-up of the class photograph. It shows a group of uniformed students smiling for the photographer with a large park as a backdrop. Noise of plates and tableware being set out.

THE SOMMELIER: *(off stage)* We need another set of tableware for the reunion banquet. We were told there'd be thirty people but there are only twenty-nine plates on the banquet table.

The sound of footsteps and of dishes. Robescu enters, wearing a large dark-colored overcoat. He carries a large package under his arm. He leans on a cane, despite which he limps badly. Each of his steps is accompanied by a horrible metallic sound coming from his leg brace. He wears black leather gloves which, like his coat, will only be removed much later. The sommelier appears, pushing a cart loaded with plates.

ROBESCU: Is this for the Petresco High School banquet?

THE SOMMELIER: They aren't here yet. Who are you?

ROBESCU: The thirtieth person. I'm going to sit down.

THE SOMMELIER: Well, you know... I'm not finished with the preparations. You're in the way. Oh, sorry. I didn't see...

ROBESCU: It's nothing. Polio... a childhood illness. Don't look so distraught. Even I can laugh about it.

THE SOMMELIER: *(very sympathetic)* Sit right down. Put your crutch down there.

ROBESCU: It's not a crutch. It's my leg brace!

THE SOMMELIER: Excuse me. I didn't get a good look. I only heard the noise. It's like Sarah Bernhardt. After they amputated her leg. You know how they signal the start of a play in France, by thumping loudly on the floor off-stage with a pole? Well, after the last three thumps, someone called out from the audience, "That must be Sarah, making her entrance." *(He laughs.)* That's a good one, don't you think?

ROBESCU: That depends. For whom?

THE SOMMELIER: Excuse me. I thought you could laugh about it. Well, you like to have it both ways, don't you?

ROBESCU: You're quite brilliant for a waiter.

THE SOMMELIER: *(embarrassed, calling off stage)* Where's that thirtieth tableware set?

He exits. Robescu approaches the class photo and stares at it.

ROBESCU: "Among the many masts..."

When the sommelier re-enters carrying a bouquet of flowers, he recognizes the poem and continues with the next line.

THE SOMMELIER: "Setting sail from these shores..."

He places the bouquet in the center of the banquet table. After he has finished, Robescu grabs him by the arm, very firmly.

ROBESCU: Which girl is the most beautiful? Tell me, since you're a connoisseur.

THE SOMMELIER: Why me?

ROBESCU: You're in the service sector. Wine stewards and taxi drivers know more about life than anyone else. *(Eyeing him, ambiguously)* They're the best informants... in the whole world.

The sommelier looks closely at Robescu, then, quickly, at the photo.

THE SOMMELIER: You're a believer in determinism, I see.

ROBESCU: A firm believer!

THE SOMMELIER: Therefore the son of an informant must be an informant... in your view.

ROBESCU: Now you've got it.

THE SOMMELIER: I hope your father was a worthy example.

ROBESCU: *(firmly, pointing to the photo with his cane)* The most beautiful?

THE SOMMELIER: *(servile, out of mockery)* If you really insist, sir. There are two: the vulgar one... and the other.

ROBESCU: *(egging him on)* The other?

THE SOMMELIER: The one in the middle. She reminds me... a delicate and refined little creature, the kind you don't find any more... I'm not an objective viewer!

ROBESCU: *(wistfully studying the photo)* You're being completely objective.

Hearing the sound of footsteps and laughter, Robescu hides behind a screen. Bianca enters, surrounded by Violeta, Vincent, Katia and Radu. They all wear overcoats which they will keep on throughout the scene. They are laughing.

Violeta is a young woman, rather self-effacing but extremely good-natured. Katia, cinched into a severe-looking suit, holds herself stiffly, with pursed lips. Radu is a paragon of good manners in his three piece suit and tie. Vincent displays a young "with it" look: jeans, leather jacket and white sneakers. The sommelier enters, looks around trying to find Robescu but, failing to do so, he gives up. He greets Bianca with a nod or a wave, then exits.

RADU: *(gazing at the photo)* May 30, 1973... *(Counting)* For once, everybody showed up. Nobody skipped class, that day. Twenty-eight... nine... thirty? *(To himself)* That's impossible! I remember perfectly, we were all there. *(Recounting)* Twenty-eight, twenty-nine! But who's the missing one?

KATIA: It was a perfect day. On the eve of our entrance into life... into adulthood.

Radu and Vincent exchange knowing glances at this untimely, rhapsodic outburst.

VIOLETA: What I was thinking was, "This is the last day we have to wear a uniform."

RADU: After twelve years of it, we were all a bit... weary.

VIOLETA: The park with the fountain in it, behind the school. That's where we had our picture taken... We were all there.

RADU: That's just it.

VIOLETA: *(cutting him off)* We took some boats out on the lake. The boys rowed.

RADU: I remember. Katia fell in the water.

KATIA: I was pushed.

VINCENT: And nobody wanted to pull you out.

KATIA: You still haven't grown up?

BIANCA: *(to Vincent)* Were you the one rowing?

VIOLETA: *(wistfully)* No, it was Silé.

VINCENT: *(allusively)* Ah, Silé. Silly Silé. See silly Silé row. Row, row Romeo. No, I wasn't rowing. I was the one who pushed Katia in the drink.

KATIA: That was very risky. I can't swim.

> *The sommelier enters and brings around glasses of champagne on a tray. Each of the guests takes one. Bianca clinks glasses with the others, then facing the photo, with her glass raised, begins singing:*

> Gaudeamus igitur,
> Juvenes dum suumus!

> *She motions for the others to join in, and little by little their voices blend in with hers.*

EVERYONE:
> Post molestum senectutem
> Post jucundam juventutem
> Nos abebit suumus!

> *They all raise their glasses, clink them together and drink.*

VIOLETA: That was so lovely. We should have gone on!

VINCENT: In Latin? Who remembers?

RADU: We were math majors.

KATIA: We barely know what the part we just sang meant.

BIANCA: It was about youth... taking advantage of it while you still can... while it lasts.

An embarrassed silence.

RADU: *(to Bianca)* It took you coming back from Paris to bring us together again.

BIANCA: I thought you got together every year, the way we promised we would.

VIOLETA: For the first few years we did... two or three times.

KATIA: Then we stopped. We each had our own problems.

RADU: We live in the same city, but I haven't seen Vincent in three years or Violeta and Katia in eighteen... eighteen years.

> *Marina enters, bustling and making noise, enveloped in a great, swirling eddy of ruffles and flounces and furbelows. She is of enormous size and wears garish make-up. With a dramatic gesture, she tosses her coat on a chair... and stands shivering under what is revealed to be a lightweight, red dress, of elastic material.*

MARINA : *(spotting Radu)* Lord! Even the Brahmans are here. Apparently, they lived to see forty. Indestructible. There's champagne, there are women... and *(Eyeing Katia)* beasts. Am I too awfully late?

Marina kisses everyone enthusiastically, but conspicuously avoids Katia. The sommelier enters with a new tray of champagne.

BIANCA: *(to the most recent arrival)* Not everyone is here yet. I called Marina, too. She'll be here.

A long, heavy silence.

MARINA: *I'm* Marina.

Bianca is silent for a moment then tries to make amends for her blunder.

BIANCA: Of course, of course you are. I knew it all along.

She kisses Marina again but this time with noticeably more affection.

MARINA: It's quite all right. Nobody recognizes me. I've put on almost ninety pounds. I've lost my hair, my teeth. *(To Katia)* Darling... I knew that "certain people" would be here, but it was so important that I see you again. So I silenced my heart and took a whip to it: "You're going... and you'll be quiet!" For twenty years that's all I've ever asked of my heart, just to keep quiet! *(They kiss.)* So you didn't recognize me, did you?

BIANCA: No. Your eyes are still... the same as before.

MARINA: But the rest of me... *(They laugh. Marina lifts her glass.)* Gaudeamus, old buddies. *(Radu and Vincent make a comic stab at singing the beginning of the song.)* Those cultured Brahmans! Andropause has done nothing to diminish their sparkling... wit.

RADU: We rehearsed before you got here.

VINCENT: And stop calling us Brahmans. After twenty years, the joke's worn a little thin.

BIANCA: On the contrary. It keeps getting better and better. A good comedy routine, like a good wine, improves with age.

MARINA: Authentic champagne! Say, it's been ages since we've had any of this stuff.

> *A long silence. Katia is ill at ease. Marina continues to stare at her. Radu and Vincent pour oil on the flames by staring just as hard at the two women, each in turn, as if there were a tennis match going on between the two. Katia moves to a different spot, coughs and chokes on her champagne.*

BIANCA: So, how are things for you, now?

KATIA: Not bad. They tell such lies about us in the West. About how badly things are going and all.

MARINA: When in fact the Rothschilds and the Rockefellers would just love to change places with us. They even wrote to us about it, but we turned them down.

VINCENT: We're getting by...

VIOLETA: They say there's going to be a commercial TV station broadcasting any day now.

RADU: *(singing)* "My lady fair, our life is sweet..."

MARINA: You know I'm a doctor?

BIANCA: Didn't you want to be a professor?

MARINA: What a memory. You see, we change. *(Tearfully)* Other people went on to be professors, not me... *(Laughing)* but I'm happy, very happy, euphoric, even. *(She begins searching frantically through her handbag, removes some pills and swallows them at once.)*

> *Marina stares off in a certain direction, remaining silent, and then from this direction Vlad suddenly appears, in his burial suit. He takes a bottle of champagne and pours some into everyone's glass. The other guests don't seem to notice this but Marina holds out her glass to him, continuing to look him in the eye. Vlad turns away from her. He goes to the photo and looks at each person in the room, comparing them all to the picture. All the others look at Marina.*

MARINA: My marriage lasted a month. One night of pleasure, nine months of waiting and a lifetime of alimony! *(She bursts out laughing.)* My husband ran off with another woman. *(Katia can be clearly seen moving off, looking for the telephone.)* I brought up my child all by myself, all the while taking care of my elderly parents. And over here being a divorced mother is worse than being black in South Africa. After that, I got more and more tired, after that I got fat, after that I lost my teeth, and now... As soon as my son is grown, they'll discover I have cancer and I'll finally be able to get some rest. Forty years of constant struggle in what seems like a dense fog and I don't have a clue what it's all about. *(Raising her glass)* Tchin tchin!

> *The sommelier goes over to Bianca. He first passes by Katia to whom he points out the public phone. Then he gives a shiver because, on entering, he passed Vlad who was exiting.*

THE SOMMELIER: The buffet is ready!

> *Silently, Silé enters from stage left and stands off to the side for a moment to observe the others. At stage right, Robescu,*

still in hiding, is the only one to have noticed Silé's arrival. He takes pains to hide himself even more than before.

BIANCA: *(laughing)* Thirty! Well really, I was a bit optimistic!

RADU: *(staring at the photo, to himself)* But who was the thirtieth person?

BIANCA: In any case, I'm putting this one *(She picks up a set of tableware.)* off to the side. It'll be for the one who's not here, who couldn't come tonight... *(With tears in her eyes, she puts the tableware in the center of a table and stands looking at it, as if fascinated.)*

RADU: There are some who died, too.

BIANCA: So soon.

SILE: *(who has been leaning against the doorway until now)* There are infants in maternity wards who die. So why not us?

RADU: Silé!

KATIA: *(hanging up the receiver, then picking it up to redial)* Enter the hero!

VINCENT: So, old pal, you decided to come after all.

VIOLETA: Hello, Silé...

MARINA: Still as handsome as ever, that guy.

VINCENT: *(less enthusiastically)* Say, old man, thought you were at the hospital.

SILE: *(with a malevolent look)* I was...

He shows them his artificial hand. When he gets to Bianca,
they greet each other with a hug that is rather cool, on both sides.

RADU: *(quickly)* You know Ionesco is dead?

SILE: Which one? There were three Ionescos.

VIOLETA: The one we called Sherlock Holmes or "Elementary My Dear." You know, because he always knew how to solve all the math problems...

VINCENT: You'd show him a three page problem, and without even using a pencil, he'd announce in a loud voice, "Elementary, my dear: the answer is pi 4R cubic root of 474,857."

RADU: So "Elementary My Dear" is dead.

BIANCA: From what?

RADU: Elementary, my dear. From drowning!

BIANCA: No!

MARINA: Unbelievable. He, of all people, who hated going into the water.

RADU: I remember our gym classes at the swimming pool. The teacher threatened to give him a grade of zero if he didn't dive in. That was serious for him: he had a perfect score in everything else. If he dropped his average by just one point, he wouldn't be first in the class, any more. But he wasn't going to dive.

SILE: One day, there was a swimming champion who was subbing, a real Neanderthal, and tough. He told us to drag him into the water by force.

RADU: Poor "Elementary My Dear" threw a fit.

VIOLETA: A premonition?

KATIA: *(still on the phone)* No way! It was just a coincidence. Foolish superstitions...

MARINA: The great expert on the human soul has spoken!

VINCENT: While we were pulling him toward the water, he was trying desperately to hang on to the floor, using his fingers, his toes, his nails...

RADU: He left a trail of blood alongside the pool.

BIANCA: But still you went on dragging him?

VINCENT: With gym teachers it's like being in the army, you don't think, If you refuse, it's push-ups for everybody... till you drop from exhaustion.

SILE: *(to Bianca)* You know what beasts men are...

BIANCA: *(pointing Silé out to the others)* Is he picking on me, or what?

VIOLETA: He's just joking.

RADU: It's true you two could never stomach each other.

BIANCA: Don't look at me...

SILE: I haven't done anything to her... yet.

BIANCA: *(salaciously)* And, I'm afraid in your case, you're not going to, any time soon.

MARINA: What I don't understand is how a guy afraid to go anywhere near the water wound up drowning.

RADU: After graduating from Civil Engineering school, first in his class, as usual, "Elementary My Dear" was hired for work on a big, new hydraulic power station. He was delighted.

VINCENT: And one day while he was checking out the dam... Plop!

RADU: Engineer overboard!

BIANCA: He was such a nice boy, Ionesco.

MARINA: *(she is rummaging through her bag. She swallows several pills from a tube. Seeing Bianca's stare)* Tranquilizers... I take so many that I'm addicted... and I've gotten fat... It's since I got out of the asylum I've been taking so many. *(Bianca laughs.)* No, really, it's no joke. I was in an asylum. Good thing I'm a doctor and can swipe all these tranquilizers. No pharmacist would ever give me this many. *(She tries to swallow her medication by taking a drink of champagne.)*

SILE: At least try not to drink any alcohol, on top of it.

MARINA: That's kind of you.

SILE: I'm only thinking of the disgusting contents of your digestive tract... in case there's an autopsy.

MARINA: *(after blowing him a kiss)* I'll have myself dissected in some other hospital.

VIOLETA: They both have the same sense of humor they had in med school.

SILE: *(wistfully)* Oh, to be in the resident students' room, with Marina...

MARINA: Those were the good old days... Stop it now; you're giving my clit an erection.

KATIA: Oh, how gross... both of them.

MARINA: *(returning tit for tat)* There are those who just talk, and those that do.

> *She rises and goes to the phone, running into Katia there.*

KATIA: *(just hanging up)* Here, you can have it. The person... wasn't in. (Returning to the others, visibly upset) Popesco is dead, too.

RADU: Popesco... Eugene.

KATIA: Adriana, too.

BIANCA: Adriana?... How?

> *An embarrassed silence.*

SILE: She died at the hands of the law. Her death was caused by complications resulting from the legal prohibition of abortion.

VIOLETA: Like many others.

KATIA: All that's been terribly exaggerated.

SILE: They ought to ban this type of discussion for all those who can't have children.

KATIA: That's slander.

SILE: No, a violation of doctor/patient confidentiality.

BIANCA: *(to Silé)* That's right, you're a doctor, too...

SILE: That surprises you, doesn't it? Considering you always thought of me as an inferior brand of shit.

BIANCA: Oh, I wouldn't say inferior...

VINCENT: *(to the sommelier who is passing around hors-d'oeuvres)* You'd better keep these two apart, if you want to keep your dishes intact.

THE SOMMELIER: *(with a look and shrug)* Those who tease each other, please each other... *(He continues passing around the food, under the astonished eyes of Vincent.)*

MARINA: *(into the phone)* Hello, Florian? Did you find your dinner in the fridge?

VIOLETA: Silé is a neurosurgeon. He's the only one who's actually doing the work he wanted to do at eighteen.

SILE: *(taking a glass of champagne, showing off his artificial hand)* I doubt seriously if I can go on doing it.

> *Bianca looks desperately from one to another of the guests, seeking an explanation. With silent signals they indicate to her that they will explain later.*

BIANCA: *(to herself)* Vlad, too. He wanted to be an architect. And he was one.

MARINA: *(shouting into the phone)* No, I forbid you to take any money out of the box. I'll be home early tonight... and I forbid you to go out, you understand... you... Hello! Hello?

Florian... *(It is clear that her son is no longer on the line.)* Don't hang up on me like that!

VINCENT: *(pouring himself a glass of whisky)* I remember that Katia wanted to be a professional revolutionary. A sort of local version of Krupskaya!

KATIA: *(bitterly, to Vincent)* And you, you wanted to be an explorer. Well, I guess driving a taxi is an adventure of sorts.

VINCENT: Head of the drivers union!

KATIA: But not an explorer.

VINCENT: An adventurer, that's what I wanted to be, you dumb cluck! An adventurer, not an explorer!

MARINA: *(returning to the others)* As for me, I wanted to be a professor, like my mother. And here I am a doctor. As for my teaching methods, as you've just seen, my son's education has been a complete success. *(She finishes her drink in one gulp.)*

RADU: All I wanted was to be independently wealthy.

BIANCA: No you didn't. I remember, Radu, you wanted to be a diplomat.

RADU: An independent diplomat, powerful, respected... International conferences, hoards of journalists at the conclusion of negotiations... ha, ha... That was all a dream. Might as well try to be a deep sea diver when your home is the Sahara Desert. *(To Violeta)* And you , what was it you wanted to be?

VIOLETA: The mother of a family... *(Laughing)* and I'm a C.P.A.

VINCENT: As for Bianca, she had no problem. She was already a writer.

RADU: The child prodigy of the Carpathian/Danubian region.

BIANCA: That's slander. My dream was always to be nothing... And I'm almost nothing.

SILE: Just try a little bit harder, comrade... You know, for a person who wants to live in the shadows, you're awfully bright and sunny.

BIANCA: I don't have to be especially brilliant to dazzle you.

SILE: See what happens when you're too nice to women.

MARINA: *(in a tone that could be taken as serious, or mocking)* I love it when friends are honest with each other.

VIOLETA: *(passing a tray of hors-d'oeuvres among the other guests)* Help yourselves, these look delicious.

MARINA: Olives à la grecque. I haven't had these since we were freed from price controls.

VINCENT: That was in another lifetime.

Each one munches on an olive or a cracker, with a glass of champagne in hand. They're still a bit stiff, still a bit defensive.

KATIA: Florea died, too.

RADU: So much for the theory that the dumber you are, the longer you live.

SILE: Ionesco, "Elementary My Dear," and Florea... The top, the bottom... *(He crosses himself.)* Ridiculous... We're all going to the same place: the graveyard.

MARINA: Vita died, too. But it wasn't me who operated on her.

RADU: No, it was Prodan.

MARINA: That guy has killed off half of Bucharest!

SILE: He gets sent a lot of hopeless cases.

RADU: He's a butcher.

MARINA: His father is a great doctor. He's the one who made him take up the same profession. Otherwise, Prodan Junior would never even have made it as a stretcher-bearer.

BIANCA: He was a mean, pretentious social climber. Even as a little boy... I remember that cretin used to hide in the girls bathroom and try to corner us.

SILE: Oh, are we allowed to criticize? Even those still alive?

BIANCA: *(hostilely)* Meaning?

SILE: I thought this was a reunion where we only said nice things and where we mourned our dead. I thought we were just going to stand around holding our champagne glasses, pinkies in the air, and exchange recipes.

BIANCA: Is that why you came?

SILE: Of course. To get in touch with my feminine side.

Everyone laughs.

BIANCA: What's so funny?

SILE: *(darkly)* I'm a very funny guy.

VINCENT: *(pouring a full glass of whisky)* Wait till our tongues get loosened up, then you'll get a real earful...

MARINA: *(holding her glass out to Vincent for him to fill it)* It won't be long now.

VIOLETA: Vita left behind three children... motherless. I wanted to adopt them. Silé did the paperwork for me.

BIANCA: And...?

VIOLETA: Their father wouldn't have it.

SILE: He went insane with grief, the poor bastard.

VINCENT: He took a knife and went after Prodan Junior. But when he saw him he changed his mind.

MARINA: I found this out from my colleagues. The father found him with two nurses in the physicians' lounge. When he saw him, he decided Prodan Junior was such a loser that he threw down the knife.

VINCENT: And Prodan, that idiot, instead of saying thank you, even took him to court.

SILE: And the poor guy had to spend a month in prison. Fortunately, Violeta took care of his kids during that time.

VIOLETA: They're so beautiful, so sweet... Wait, here's a photo of them. They look like Vita, don't they?

BIANCA: Very much.

VIOLETA: The father now lives shut up inside with them... like little animals living underground. He doesn't even send them to school.

RADU: *(studying the class photo)* Seven dead.

SILE: *(to Marina)* You shouldn't drink when you're taking tranquilizers.

MARINA *(drinking)* You're so right, dear heart!

BIANCA *(to Radu, appalled)* Seven dead!

RADU: We've lived through a revolution and twenty years of a golden age.

VIOLETA: Eight dead. Leon died during the earthquake.

BIANCA: *(floored by the news)* Leon... We shared the same bench during our last year in school.

VIOLETA: We used to call him the prince consort.

MARINA: You were a widow and you didn't even know it.

BIANCA: Poor Leon.

> *Vlad enters, and, in a very friendly manner, he stands behind Silé, resting his elbow on Silé's shoulder while following the conversation with interest. No one seems to notice him.*

SILE: The earthquake was nineteen years ago. You're not going to start crying over him now...

BIANCA: For me, he's only been dead for five minutes... Give me time to get used to the idea.

RADU: There were at least some people you kept in touch with.

BIANCA: That's just it... There weren't! I left right after the exams. Remember, you'd all gone off to do your military service... You sent me greeting cards for the New Year. I took those cards with me when I went off to the West. I used to cry every night. I didn't know if I was going to stay or come back and, when I was feeling especially homesick, I would read your letters, or Vincent's or Vlad's.

RADU: Vlad, your best buddy, is he coming tonight?

BIANCA: *(tearfully)* Dead...

KATIA: You already know?

VINCENT: But we promised each other to break it to you gently.

RADU: Is Vlad dead?

MARINA: He died this week.

BIANCA: I went to his burial.

KATIA: We didn't see you.

BIANCA: *(bursting out laughing)* I'm sorry... I'm sorry... It's just my nerves... I suppose I got there late... I went to his home first, it took time to locate his neighbors who told me what had happened, it took time to find the cemetery... But that "We didn't see you..." I couldn't help it. *(Laughing)* In Paris, the other day, I was introduced to somebody at a dinner.

I heard them say, "Incidentally, he's Romanian, like you." Well, this guy, a real dyed-in-the wool Stalinist—not that he could help it, of course—he looks me up and down, he doesn't shake my outstretched hand. And then he says, in this gruff, suspicious voice, "You're Romanian? Why haven't I ever seen you at the demonstrations in front of the embassy?" *(She starts to laugh again.)* As if it were a Romanian's duty to be... *(Laughing)*

A long silence.

VINCENT: And why weren't you seen in front of the embassy?

Bianca is stunned.

BIANCA: Because I wasn't there, that's why... I have that right, don't I?

> *There is a general sense of astonishment. Each one mulling over his own thoughts. Silé starts to laugh. The others look Silé and Bianca up and down, suspiciously.*

SILE: *(to Bianca, laughing)* You see, of course, nothing has changed. When you left, people asked you why you weren't at the parades on May Day. You come back, and what happens? People ask you why you're not among the demonstrators outside the Romanian Embassy.

KATIA: *(with great seriousness)* Bianca was never very civic-minded. She's always lived in a universe of her own. And being a writer isn't much of a help in staying connected to the real world.

RADU: Which didn't keep you from electing her class president instead of me.

SILE: Maybe because she had the conscience of a human being.

BIANCA: *(conciliatory, to Radu)* My big moment of responsibility, which came about thanks to you, was when I had to explain to the leadership of the party that if you were playing soccer in the classroom it was not because you intended to smash the president's portrait, that this incident was merely an epiphenomenon related to your lack of maturity and not the conscious decision of a band of dissidents. So you see, Radu, you didn't miss much.

VINCENT: Which portrait got smashed? I don't remember.

SILE: You were the one who did it, you idiot.

VIOLETA: And it was Silé who took responsibility...

SILE: I don't remember any more.

BIANCA: Well, I remember... Vincent had gotten into so many scrapes that he might have been kicked out at the first misstep. We looked for a volunteer and Silé, whose scholastic "police record" was totally clean, offered to take your place.

MARINA: *(swallowing another handful of pills)* When are we going to start eating? When are we going to start drinking?

SILE: *(going over to her, Vlad right behind him, and reading the label on the container)* If you're taking all of these, you're better off not drinking... at least.

MARINA: *(with charm)* Who cares? There's a doctor in the house, a good one.

SILE: With all that crap you've been swallowing, I'll take you to Prodan for resuscitation. By that I mean Prodan Junior!

MARINA: Have mercy. Not, Prodan, please! I have a child to raise... *(Shifting her tone, abruptly)* And when I think that bastard is teaching in a university.

SILE: Nutritional hygiene. It was the least dangerous subject they could give him.

VINCENT: Even at that, he must fuck up a lot. I ran into him at a wedding. He eats like a pig and drinks like a fish. I don't see how he can teach nutritional hygiene, unless it's to other animals.

MARINA: That's what I wanted, a full professorship... teaching, not lancing boils and treating psoriasis.

> *Vlad, seeming bored, draws up a chair and begins to write a letter.*

VINCENT: *(to Bianca)* Did you know I got into trouble when you wrote to me from outside the country? Oh boy, did I get into trouble because of your letters. I was relaxing in the barracks when my NCO called me. I thought, "Uh-oh, it's the guardhouse for me." I was always getting called up for little offenses. But no, this time it was worse. He took me to see my commanding officer. It was "Atten-shun!" and all the rest. He had this knowing look on his face...

SILE: They always have a knowing look on their face.

VINCENT: "So," he goes, like he's real sharp, "Someone's been sending the address of his unit to foreign spies, hey?"

BIANCA: I only realized it later. You sent your army address to me in Bucharest and of course I took it with me... without thinking that I was going from one world to another. Over there, I felt so lost, so all alone, I was waiting for a "come back, come back," and it never came... So I wrote to you.

ROBESCU: *(emerging from his hiding place)* I certainly wrote to you. I told you to come back.

VINCENT: Well, well... The eyes of Moscow are upon us.

RADU: Does that surprise you?

SILE: This goes to show that only the good die young.

ROBESCU: *(to Bianca)* Do you remember me?

Bianca goes over to him and embraces him.

VINCENT: The kiss of Judas.

SILE: No, a kiss for the leper.

BIANCA: Of course, Robescu. Of course, it's true that you wrote me and I even wondered at the time how you got my address.

VINCENT: Don't ask, it's better not to know.

RADU: His daddy had access to all the files. He's the one who compiled them, in fact.

SILE: Do you remember who Daddy Robescu was?

BIANCA: Robescu-the-Good-Lord.

ROBESCU: *(to Bianca)* But my first name, do you remember what that was?

BIANCA: Of course I do, Robescu, who do you think I am? Some old lady with Alzheimer's?... Valentine!

Robescu smiles.

ROBESCU: *(including the others in a sweeping glance)* You see, I took some risks in coming to see you. A lynching party can be quickly organized.

VINCENT: That's why he always travels with four motorcyclists around his armored car, a black Volga.

ROBESCU: An armored black... Chrysler.

SILE: I forgot. We fought a revolution... so as to replace your Volga with a Chrysler.

BIANCA: *(to Robescu)* What's been going on in your life, old pal?

Discreet clearing of throats.

VINCENT: It's a fact she's always been a little scatter-brained. I'm not surprised now that her carelessness almost got me court martialed.

MARINA: *(to Bianca)* You certainly ask some strange questions to Comrade Son-of-Comrade-Robescu-the-Good-Lord.

BIANCA: What do you mean? The secret police have been abolished since the revolution, haven't they?

Everyone bursts out laughing, timidly at first, then quite openly. Robescu laughs the loudest of all. Calmly, Vlad slips his letter into an envelope and hides it in one of Bianca's pockets or else in her purse, and makes an exit.

SILE: The pure-minded see only their reflection in others.

RADU: Or in this case, blessed are the feeble-minded.

VIOLETA: Her head was always in the clouds.

BIANCA: Am I the only one who feels cold here or not?

VIOLETA: *(smiling)* It's... unanimous. *(Indeed, throughout this scene, everyone with the exception of Marina, has kept his or her coat on.)* Saving on electricity...

> *The sommelier enters and passes around glasses of champagne to everyone.*

ROBESCU: I've taken over from my father. I'm now Robescu-the-Good-Lord Junior.

VINCENT: Which explains the posters you saw on University Square that say, "Enough With the Name of the Father and the Son!"

MARINA: Oh my, yes. University Square. You should have been there, Bianca. It was lovely, everyone loved each other.

KATIA: What was that you said? There were nothing but hooligans and gypsies... a handful, at that...

VIOLETA: Ten thousand people!

ROBESCU: Five hundred. The official tally was five hundred.

VINCENT: Ten thousand is right!

RADU: Even more.

VIOLETA: *(looking around at the others and discreetly signaling to Silé)* Stop that talk, now—I mean, politics. We're here to see each other again, not to settle old scores!

MARINA: The most beautiful song of all, do you know it, Bianca?
Better a corpse than a communist
Better a pauper than an activist...

Vincent, Silé, Radu and Violeta sing along with her.

BIANCA: How I'd have liked to be there.

KATIA: What are you saying? It was a just a bunch of losers.

RADU: So you must have gone to University Square, to get a look...

KATIA: No. I saw them on TV.

MARINA: Of course, on the state-run TV... *(To herself)* She's pathetic.

KATIA: All they were doing was drinking and looting... They were doing disgusting things.

SILE: That's perfectly true. Those demonstrators were such clever thieves they even managed to swipe my arm... and hide it under the tracks of a tank that was passing by.

VIOLETA: *(reproachfully, to the others)* I told you...

KATIA: What's the matter... We were talking in general.

Bianca quietly approaches Violeta.

BIANCA: What happened to Silé?

VIOLETA: As soon as he found out that tanks were being used to disperse peaceful demonstrators on University Place, he rushed from his work at the hospital to help with the injured.

A young man had fallen in front of a tank. Silé tried to pull him out of the way, but his own arm got caught in the tracks and was torn off. *(There are tears in her eyes.)*

BIANCA: *(wide-eyed)* Silé did that... But he was always a good-for-nothing. He never cared about anything... except chasing girls.

VIOLETA: *(on the verge of weeping)* You don't know him.

> *Robescu, Silé and the others draw closer to Bianca and Violeta.*

RADU: What do you think of the country... "Twenty Years After"?

ROBESCU: What do you think of us?

BIANCA: I think you're all wonderful!

RADU: Bullshit...

BIANCA: I swear to you, I'm telling the truth. I find everything... so picturesque.

RADU: *(horrified)* Picturesque!

SILE: Why not?

RADU: *(to Bianca)* You get sentimental because you're far away and you don't know the price of meat... It's just like before. *(To the others)* She's never had to worry because she was always shut up in the dormitory, working all day long!

VIOLETA: That's not true. I was in the same dorm room with her...

ROBESCU: She was already writing. She spent all her time in libraries, literary circles and writers' clubs.

MARINA: Don't you remember how she used to go over her lessons on the playground?

KATIA: I'm here to tell you, she never did her homework in math. She copied off of me.

SILE: What drives Radu crazy is that he can't even imagine anything coming easily... He can only imagine work, work, work... Help!

RADU: I only made one mistake in my life, and I'm still paying for it. I should have stayed in Switzerland when they were still accepting us there as refugees. *(To Bianca)* You've had it easy over there... for the last twenty years!

BIANCA: Is that what's eating you?

> *Marina and Vincent start to sing and form a conga line, getting the others to join in behind them. Like a serpent, they work their way around the room. Robescu, the only one not dancing, sits in a chair but joins in the singing. The line sweeps up Radu and Bianca as it weaves and snakes its way around the stage The sommelier enters with a tray of hors-d'oeuvres, but soon, at Bianca's insistence, he is dancing with the others.*

THE SOMMELIER: I used to sing the same song when I was a student...
> Un elefant se legana
> Pe o pinza de paianjen...

ALL:
> Un elefant se legana
> Pe o pinza de paianjen...

*When the line breaks up, Radu, Bianca, Katia and Vincent
are down stage, seated on chairs. The others are serving themselves from the buffet table.*

BIANCA:
>Un elefant se legana
>Pe o pinza de paianjen...
>An elephant was balancing
>Upon a spiderweb...

RADU: I heard you once, on Radio France Internationale.
You were talking about Romania. I couldn't understand a
word, you were speaking in French... but just as fast as
always.

BIANCA: *(impassibly)* Un elefant se legana...

RADU: You have an accent when you speak Romanian.

BIANCA: An accent!

RADU: A foreign accent.

BIANCA: *(furiously)* An accent? Me? You're crazy!

KATIA: No, he's right. I heard it, too.

BIANCA: Well, of course, you would say that. You always agree
with the last person who spoke.

KATIA: Why are you always so mean to me?

BIANCA: Listen, Miss Brown Nose, why don't you just shut up!

VINCENT: Finally, the Bianca we all know and love... I thought
she had lost her revolutionary edge. I even said to myself,

"Well, what do you know? Bianca went to Paris and got herself all civilized."

BIANCA: Not much danger of that. The Balkans are in our genes!

RADU: You have an accent.

BIANCA: Vincent, do I have an accent?

VINCENT: Of course not. You know that Radu and Katia both have a screw loose...

RADU: I may have a screw loose, but she really does have an accent. She has a French "r"...

BIANCA: *(fuming with rage, and rolling her "r"s, to Radu)* I have a French "r"? You can ask anybody in Paris, everyone knows that I roll my "r"s.

RADU: Maybe you roll your "r"s for them, but for us you gargle them.

BIANCA: I do not have an accent! Listen: Un elefant se legana...

RADU: *(looking at the enlarged photo)* That's what we were singing... the last day of school... But who is the missing thirtieth person?

BIANCA: That's right, change the subject, that's a good idea.

RADU: We danced down the street in a conga line, singing that song.

VINCENT: And the principal, that old coward, sent for the cops...

RADU: They thought it was a demonstration.

BIANCA: We started out singing a song and we came back escorted by the police.

VINCENT: You were at the front of the line, with two big white ribbons in your hair. I still have the photos...

BIANCA: I was the one out in front?

KATIA: You were the class president.

RADU: Elected by the idiots here assembled.

BIANCA: How was it that you didn't run against me?

RADU: I was the only one who abstained. To be in the opposition seemed to me too risky... That's what's called being cut out for diplomatic service.

VINCENT: All that fuss over one little incident. They threatened to stop us from taking the finals...

RADU: And to stop us from taking the university entrance exams.

BIANCA: And all because we went a little ways down the street singing a ridiculous song about an elephant balanced on a spiderweb.

VINCENT: What I remember are the smiling faces of people at their windows. Some of them thought for a moment a revolution was starting.

RADU: *(to Bianca)* All the time we spent waiting, you kept telling us, "Don't be scared. They wouldn't dare stop us from taking our finals." How did you know that?

BIANCA: I didn't. I just said that to keep our spirits up. I was scared to death.

RADU: Bullshit! You knew.

KATIA: No one knew anything. Things could have turned out very badly.

BIANCA: How could I have known?

RADU: I have no idea. *(Insinuating)* Unless maybe your parents happened to be communists?

BIANCA: My parents were dead, as you know... I went to the principal to confess that I was the one who got the whole parade started and I offered to be the one to make up for it... in place of everyone else.

KATIA: That's true, I remember.

VINCENT: The thing I remember is Katia saying, in the principal's office, "Bianca is the one who wanted this big parade, I was against the whole thing."

KATIA: I don't recall. I was so young... Do you realize, getting punished like that right before the finals, before the entrance exams in Political Science? It could have ruined my life!

RADU: You seem to forget that we were all just as young... as you.

VINCENT: And that we were all about to take our exam.

RADU: If we'd failed it, it could have ruined all our lives. Twenty-nine other little lives... almost as precious as yours!

KATIA: You've always been mean to me, all of you! *(Crocodile tears)*

VINCENT: Ever since grade school, that's what's worked best for her. She started crying and everybody caved in... I still remember how well she cried when Comrade Stalin died. After that, none of the teachers dared to give her less than a "C". Any little girl who weeps so well for Comrade Stalin must be a good political watchdog... So be careful what you say and do.

KATIA: You wouldn't understand. My father was a communist back in the days when the party was outlawed. He went to prison for ten years. When Comrade Stalin died, in a way it was my own father I was crying for.

VINCENT: We're all child martyrs.

KATIA: I refuse to discuss politics with you.

VINCENT: We're not discussing politics. We're discussing family. Papa Stalin...

KATIA: You don't understand a thing. Comrade Stalin makes you sneer.

RADU: That's not so bad. Before, he used to make us tremble.

VINCENT: We don't say Comrade Stalin any more. We say Mr. Stalin, Sir Stalin, Dottore, Commendatore Stalin, Señor Stalin, Stasta, Stala, J. S....

KATIA: My father was exploited his entire life by your parents, by the fucking petty bourgeois types with their fucking little factories... He was a typesetter, and came down with lead poisoning at the age of twenty. Do you get what I'm saying? My grandmother was illiterate. Does that even exist any more? Who was it taught the peasants how to read and write if not the communists, the Party?

BIANCA: My grandmother went to prison, too, and she died there, like all the rest of my family, which explains my orphanage. She may have owned her own land, but she was just as illiterate as yours.

VINCENT: *(discreetly looking at his watch, as he has frequently done)* A good return punch.

KATIA: Bianca never knows what she's talking about. She doesn't do it on purpose, but she makes shit happen wherever she goes. Even coming back after a twenty-year absence, she has to make shit happen for other people. I'm sorry, Bianca. It's not your fault but that's the way you are... nose in the air.

BIANCA *(truly stunned)* What, my nose is in the air?

KATIA: Yes, way up in the air. If there's a turd in the middle of the street, you don't see it. It's not even something you do on purpose. Your eyes are programmed to see nothing but the sublime and the ideal. Guess you don't give a damn that a kilo of meat costs two thousand lei, and a good average monthly salary is only fifteen thousand. That sort of calculation strikes you as vulgar... You live on idealism like some people live on love, and that's an insult, yes, an insult, to all those poor, downtrodden people for whom the price of meat is of vital, daily concern.

RADU: *(to Bianca)* Pettiness is a constant in the Third World.

KATIA: We're not a third world country! I won't let that go by. We are not a third world country!

VINCENT: No, of course not, my sweet, we're a Super Power.

KATIA: *(stubbornly)* We are not a third world country.

VINCENT: We sell our children and our whores, whenever possible for cold cash. That's a typical third world trait.

KATIA: *(shouting)* Who sells their children? Where did you get those imperialist fairy tales?

RADU: You must forgive her. She's the only one who still uses the old vocabulary: imperialism, Santa Claus, and all the rest of it.

KATIA: *(incensed)* If that's the way it's going to be, I'm leaving.

BIANCA: Katia, I want to apologize. I always thought you were only interested in getting ahead. You were being sincere.

VINCENT: Sincere... but an asshole! *(To Katia)* Farewell, Ophelia, get thee to the politburo.

KATIA: *(sitting down)* My ulcer is bothering me... I've got to take my pills.

RADU: We'd better stop talking about politics... It's bad for our ulcers and all our other open sores.

KATIA: *(drinking a glass of water)* That's better. I hate it when people aren't sincere.

RADU: *(to Bianca)* When I saw your ad in "The Voice of the People," I was sure it was just a joke.

KATIA: What? You read "The Voice of the People?" You really shouldn't...

VINCENT: What a masochist she is. Even when no one's paying any attention to her, she has to take up the fight again.

RADU: And what should I read instead?

VINCENT: "The People's Cause"... like in the old days?

RADU: Wait just a second! *(To Bianca)* Did you place you ad anywhere else besides "The Voice of the People?"

BIANCA: No.

RADU: *(to Katia)* So... Just where did you see the ad?

KATIA: I don't know... Somewhere else...

Vincent chuckles.

RADU: No, she didn't place the ad anywhere else...

VINCENT: Katia, always so pure and virginal, politically speaking...

They all laugh.

KATIA: You're always on my case! Why don't you pick on somebody else this time. Bianca, for example.

VINCENT: Bianca's been a long way off for the last twenty years. Meaning? She hasn't done anything to us.

KATIA: And what did I ever do to you?

VINCENT: Oh, you did a lot. As head of personnel you did a lot of files on us...

RADU: Comrade Robescu pretends not to know you, but we all know that you were the one who compiled the best dossiers for him.

KATIA: I was just doing my job. I never took a penny.

RADU: The worst thing is that's true. She thinks she's behaved decently...

KATIA: I have!

RADU: Each time I was up for promotion as a teacher, it was you who took it upon yourself to point out that I had a sister living in Switzerland and that there were no suitable positions for me...

KATIA: With a spot like that on your record, you can't expect to be able to educate our nation's youth.

VINCENT: And you never failed to point out my three marriages. You got personally involved and went at it with remarkable zeal... If you'd been head over heels for me, you couldn't have been any more eager to dig up dirt...

KATIA: *(gulping down her drink to give herself courage)* I hardly think anyone that unstable should be in charge of the workers in a labor union. Subsequent events have proven me right.

VINCENT: You didn't really give me a chance. And besides the post of union leader was just what Igor wanted.

> *Vlad crosses the stage. Bianca stops him for a moment by grabbing his sleeve.*

BIANCA: This isn't my show any more... I feel like I'm somewhere else, a ghost...

> *Vlad smiles at her and exits.*

KATIA: *(hysterically)* Leave Igor out of this! *(Weeping)* You've never liked Igor...

VINCENT: No, I can't say that I have. I'm a bastard too, but at least I'm honest, from time to time. When it comes to my three marriages, I was honest every time and that's what galls you... you're almost yellow from it. You're eaten up with jealousy... right down to your ovaries. And when you phone your Igor, you discover he's out on the town, looking around for some better bet, someone more in line with the current system. You used to be a good deal for him, but your market value has dropped since the fall of the dictatorship. With your past, you're like a tin can tied to his tail... or some other appendage. Just a weight that keeps him from scaling the heights he wants to conquer.

KATIA: I love Igor. I'd walk through fire for him. I won't let you pass judgment on me, you who let yourself be kept by foreigners... old ladies... *(Weeping)*

VINCENT: *(going over to Katia, trying to be friendly)* Come on, baby. Stop your crying. When you come right down to it, we're both on the same wavelength. Maybe for my old lady tourists, well, I'm their Igor. And after all, no one's judging you. We're all in this together. *(With even greater noise, Katia dissolves into tears. Very surprised, Vincent turns to the others.)* Gee, just when I try to cheer her up a little... What did I say now?

RADU: *(staring at him)* The truth.

BIANCA: Please explain all this to me, slowly and in detail! Don't forget I'm twenty years late. First of all, do you have any children?

KATIA: *(gulping down her drink)* No. And I'm never going to.

VINCENT *(checking his watch)* That's very kind of you. Imagine if you had a daughter just like you and my poor unfortunate son had the misfortune to run into her...

BIANCA: You have a son?

VINCENT: He lives with his mother.

BIANCA: And Violeta, who so much wanted to have children?

KATIA: *(sighing)* She was unlucky.

RADU: The most amazing thing in all this is that the obstetrician in the delivery room was, again, Prodan Junior.

KATIA: She was in pain.

RADU: He almost killed her. Fortunately he had his daddy right behind him, as usual, to repair the damages that Sonny Boy caused.

VINCENT: They saved Violeta, but the child died. She can't have any more and she has to pee in a plastic bag now.

BIANCA: No!

KATIA: *(to Vincent)* Why do you go and talk about things that you know nothing about?

VINCENT: I do know through the union that Violeta has a disability pension. So, true or false?

KATIA: Even though it's the truth, you don't have to go and shout it from the rooftops.

RADU: Bianca, if you were still hoping that there'd been a revolution... now you know.

KATIA: But what revolution? Why a revolution? We were all so well off before. It was hard, but there were laws. If you respected them, nothing bad, or really bad, could happen to you. Often they were unwritten laws but everybody knew what they were. And then suddenly, all at once, shooting, burnings, our society shaken to its core and the world turned upside down. Today, nobody knows where he is any more, or on what side, or even who he is... People get divorced for political motives, parents turn their children in, some of the best people can't get a job, and there's not even a place where they can air their grievances... Igor's at home biting his nails. He doesn't even dare go outside the house. He didn't dare come here tonight. He sent me to have a look, but he's going to be sulky with me when I get back because I only came out of duty to him... I certainly didn't want to show up here and have to run into that lunatic, Marina. She's apt to do anything to me, strike me, throw arsenic in my face...

RADU: Acid.

KATIA: Whatever. I'm surrounded by enemies. I didn't want to come here. I've never done anything that I wanted to do in my life. I just did my duty. My duty! And what happened? Everybody turned against me. *(She weeps and hiccups.)*

VINCENT: *(handing her a handkerchief)* If you think we got the chance to do what we wanted that often in our lives...

KATIA: *(taking the handkerchief, glancing at it)* Thank you.

Downstage, Robescu is making a phone call.

ROBESCU: Hello? I'm sorry to be phoning you this late... Your husband isn't back from the lab yet? My name is Robescu... the same! He told you about me? Yes, it's about my biopsy... I'll give you the number where I can be reached. When your husband gets in, have him ask for Robescu. In the room where the Petresco High School is having their banquet...

It's 59-17-61... Tell him to give me a call as soon as he gets in. To let me know the results. You must see to it that he calls me even if the results are not good... Thank you. You won't forget? It's very important... Good bye... Don't forget to tell him: it doesn't matter how late!

He hangs up and remains lost in thought for a short while. Vlad appears before him. Robescu seems to see him. All the others are looking at the class photo.

BIANCA: We were all young and beautiful. Youth-without-age, do you remember?

KATIA: No.

BIANCA: Of course you do. It's an old Romanian fairy tale. I'm writing an essay about it.

VIOLETA: Isn't that the story of the little prince who cried while he was in his mother's womb?

BIANCA: And he would only agree to come out when his father promised him youth-without-age.

RADU: It's starting to come back to me. He gets his wish and then, like an idiot, instead of taking advantage of the situation till the end of time, he comes home to die. *(To Bianca)* That's your story, isn't it...

BIANCA: Who knows... What would have become of me here?

SILE: The same thing that became of the other literary geniuses in our high school: discouragement, the wear and tear of the daily grind, failure in various forms.

RADU: They don't earn a thing.

VINCENT: And literary glory ain't what it used to be.

BIANCA: If you think it's any different in Paris.

ROBESCU: I always said so.

MARINA: *(to Bianca)* I think that's disgusting. You're killing off the last of our illusions. And without any hope, how will we get along?

BIANCA: What's become of Floriana?

KATIA: Not much.

BIANCA: Is she writing?

SILE: She's all washed up. She married a guy and made him a success. Another one of those highly gifted girls who wear themselves thin trying to realize all their talents. Her husband made a minor name for himself as a poet, something he quickly abandoned to take up a career in real estate... A user and a bum.

SILE: His forgotten wife, very sensibly, went into a depression, then to an asylum, along with a literary sterility which is most likely permanent.

BIANCA: And Caterina?

SILE: I've run into all the brightest lights of our generation... in the psychiatric ward. Caterina married a "comrade in a highly responsible position" within the secret police. You think it's possible to blossom and be creative when you're sharing your bed with a comrade like that? A syndrome of defeat, depression, frustration, alcoholism and all the other symptoms of complete failure.

BIANCA: Failure? She was the most gifted...

VINCENT *(to Bianca)* No, no. You, you were the most gifted...

RADU: By the way, that immense talent we were always hearing about, just where has it gotten you?

BIANCA: To a semi-successful professional life and a failed private one, I suppose... but the game isn't over yet.

ROBESCU: *(holding onto Vlad's sleeve, though he remains invisible to the others)* This is going to be the longest night of my life. Wouldn't you know that those results would come back today of all days, the day of our reunion. I was hard on the others, I'll be hard on myself. If it's not incurable, I'll ask her to marry me tonight, I swear it... I'll do whatever she asks, anything. Twenty years, that's insane...

> *Vlad gestures like an orchestra conductor then kneels down in front of Robescu to make what seems to be an adjustment to his leg brace. We hear music in waltz time. Robescu suddenly rises and steps forward without limping. As if in a dream, the entire stage is bathed in a bluish light. Robescu takes Marina in his arms and waltzes with her before passing her off to another dancer. He dances with all the girls, one after the other, before stopping in front of Bianca whom he solemnly invites to dance.*

This is Robescu's Great Waltz. It's Robescu-the-Good-Lord Junior who's picking up the tab. So everybody fill your bellies, your loins, your eyeballs, your nostrils full of dreams and hopes... Everybody is invited, everybody dance! Even the cripples! This is Robescu's dream: a land where those without arms can be jugglers and those who can't walk, acrobats... I'll be nice, I'll be sweet, I'll be forgiving, I swear it— if she'll say yes. If she'll say yes, I'll be cured... of everything.

It seems to me that a smile from her... just one... I've only dreamed of her once. Just once in twenty years, even though each night I made a point of thinking about her before going to sleep... Once in my whole life, in that dream with her, I wasn't limping. I was walking by her side.

He solemnly comes to a halt in front of Bianca to invite her to dance. But, at the same time, without having seen him, Bianca turns her head to one side, rises and goes over to the photo. The music stops all of a sudden and Robescu, limping once more, follows Bianca up to the photo.

BIANCA: And Igor? What's become of our dyed-in-the-wool Stalinist?

Marina sighs and rises to cross to the phone.

VINCENT: Robespierre? He wanted to move the masses with his oratory. Instead, he's a shitty little journalist. He even tried to take my place at the Taxi Drivers Union. They booed him off the floor.

KATIA: And you, you were ousted by the rank and file this morning. *(She rises.)* Where are the restrooms, please? *(As no one answers her, she exits with great dignity.)*

VINCENT: *(after making sure that Marina, dialing a phone number, can't hear him)* Katia married Igor after getting him to divorce Marina. He left her with a three-month-old baby. After the divorce, Marina went out of her mind. They put her in an asylum. She ran up and down the halls in her nightgown, telling people that the barbarians were at the gate. She looked for Igor in pill boxes and nurses' pockets... They gave her electroshock treatments and she was finally able to return home to take care of her child and her elderly parents. A whole generation, sacrificed.

BIANCA: And the child?

VINCENT: He takes all the dough his mother earns and, when she's hasn't got any, he knocks her around. He's a husky, well-fed adolescent... What makes it sticky is that Igor is in the process of breaking up with Katia who's in disgrace since the revolution and he's leaving her for... Virginia.

RADU: The whore?

VINCENT: Of course, she's got money. Since we're about to enter the era of market economy, the guy is having himself recycled... *(Suddenly anxious)* I wonder what my American lady is up to, why hasn't she called me? Sorry, I'm going to make a phone call.

> *He crosses to the telephone where Marina has just hung up. Marina heads for the buffet table, dragging Bianca and Violeta along with her, though the latter would prefer to stay with Silé and Robescu. The two men remain by themselves, face to face for a moment. They don't say a word.*

MARINA: Poor Vincent... We're all in the same boat. We'd gladly sell ourselves... if we could just find a foreigner to buy us. We first tried to sell off our industries but Katia and a few other hotheads shouted us down, saying "We're not selling off our country!" And then nobody wanted to buy it. Since then, our people, showing splendid common sense, have been selling themselves off as separate items... You know anybody that wants to buy a female doctor who's half crazy, with two old parents and a juvenile delinquent on her hands?

VINCENT: *(into the receiver)* Hello? I'd like to speak with Room 7... Gladys, why haven't you called me? Hello... Gladys, have you been drinking? Is our little excursion still on for tomorrow? I was going to show you some places just outside the capital... You didn't know? Gladys, you're not alone there... That's not the radio! *(He looks at his watch and hangs up the phone, in a rage.)*

Silé rejoins the others quickly.

SILE: We haven't been that close, I know, but to go and leave me alone with the man from Moscow...

Everyone looks at Robescu, who has remained at the buffet table, alone.

MARINA: And how are you? Are you living in Paris?

BIANCA: Yes.

MARINA: How many cars do you have?

BIANCA: I don't have any.

MARINA: Are you as poor as that?

BIANCA: *(laughing)* No... I don't know how to drive.

MARINA: You're pulling my leg.

RADU: What do you think, Marina? That everybody over there is rolling in dough?

VIOLETA: You must think we've changed.

BIANCA: I didn't hear a word from any of you... for twenty years! I would have been doing you a disservice by writing to you.

KATIA: It wasn't as strict as all that.

VIOLETA: It was entirely possible to get the boot if they found out that you were writing to somebody in the West. And if, on top of that, you were writing to a Romanian refugee...

RADU: You must have at least written to your family...

Robescu, who was standing alone at the buffet table, now rejoins the others, carrying his plate.

BIANCA: What family? Don't you remember that I was raised on public assistance? When I came to our high school, at fourteen, it was straight from the orphanage.

ROBESCU: I remember the day you first arrived. You had short hair and your stockings... your stockings were black... very beautiful... black net stockings...

BIANCA: Knit stockings! I was ashamed. They were the cheapest kind. We knit them ourselves at the orphanage. And I dreamed of the soft, sheer stockings the other girls had.

MARINA: Now it's the opposite. You must have so many dresses! What are they wearing in Paris right now?

BIANCA: A little bit of everything.

MARINA: I hear that floral-print velvet is very big right now.

SILE: With bells hanging from each breast and a florescent directional signal over the pubic area.

ROBESCU: And a big wide opening over the buttocks!

MARINA: Robescu is turning into a human being ! Saint-Just must be rolling in his grave...

BIANCA: *(sourly)* Just your average sex fiends...

MARINA: Romanian manhood in flower. Guaranteed rough and primitive. Our neighborhood specialty. Always ready for action... And I'm here to tell you, me, who's had a go at all of them, Silé is the best.

SILE: Marina, you've had too much to drink.

> *Without anyone noticing his presence, Vlad enters very quietly from upstage. He's wearing his burial suit but has taken off his jacket. He sits down on a chair and begins sewing a piece of navy blue cloth on the sleeve of his jacket: it's his school ID number. He seats himself comfortably so as to be able to observe the stage. Only Bianca seems aware of his presence, which she feels but does not fully comprehend.*

BIANCA: Is that you, Marina, the angel of virtue, speaking?

MARINA: At eighteen, sure, I was ferociously committed to my virginity, but later, around age twenty-five, when... I started having problems... I gave them all a shot. All beasts, every one... except Silé!

SILE: You talking about me, sweetheart? Wanna get together for a little action?

MARINA: Now, of course, he's behaving like a jerk, but he's the only real gentleman.

> *Robescu chokes on his champagne.*

MARINA: *(to Robescu)* Don't worry, I won't go into detail. Tonight, I want to be nice. I feel so good being here with you, my friends... It's made me young again. I'm eighteen, for the second time. That was perhaps the last time when we were all happy, and pure, and unique. We teased each other at times but everyone had his place in the world, which the others respected. The Brahmans dreamed of becoming great diplomats and adventurers, we dreamed of our first kiss, Bianca was writing, Katia... was doing her duty, and nobody had gotten on anybody else's nerves, yet... Our fight to the death with life hadn't begun. There was still room for everybody on this earth. This evening, it's a little as if all that had been given back to us for a few hours... Because inside we haven't really changed... inside.

BIANCA: The same dreams...

VIOLETA: The same loves... *(Everyone turns and stares at her in astonishment. Laughing)* That's right. The same loves.

ROBESCU: Violeta is right. She was always full of common sense.

VINCENT: You too.

ROBESCU: Not me! I'm a pressure cooker with an explosive mixture of anxieties and unfulfilled passions threatening to blow the lid off at any moment. I'm the disabled stallion whose frustration transforms itself into cruelty and vengeance, both potent and cynical. I'm so pissed off at God the Father, *(Laughing)* both my own and the other one, that I take my revenge on the human race. Didn't I ever tell you that I came down with polio in Moscow, when my father was starting out on his first foreign assignment? Right off, I had the impression that I had paid my debts. With my leg I paid for the privilege of being the Good-Lord's son... That's why for forty years I've been bustling about like a squirrel in a cage. I have to keep moving so as to be... so as to try to be a little less afraid. But tonight, yes, I feel it too, it's the moment of grace. I'm no longer afraid.

MARINA: Oh, my my my... We have a different Robescu with us. One with a soul...

> *Bianca looks at Vlad who has finished sewing on his student ID number and who is admiring his work.*

BIANCA: *(reading the ID number)* Number 1089.

MARINA: *(thrown off stride for a moment, returning now to her original ideas)* All that really matters in life is a good, satisfying fuck... *(Looking at Silé)* But there are so few real men around.

BIANCA: There are others.

MARINA: *(half drunk)* Just names! Just phone numbers... and fax numbers!

VINCENT: At last we'll find out who Bianca was secretly in love with. We'll know who won the bets we made twenty years ago! Come on, tell us who you think it was.

SILE: It was Vlad...

> *Silently, Vlad signals that, much to his great regret, he wasn't the one.*

VINCENT: Come on... It was that "lecherous old poet of forty." You know, at the time we thought he seemed a hundred.

SILE: Bianca, tell them it's not true.

BIANCA: As soon as I take my nose out of a book, I don't understand a thing.

SILE: I know. If someone kisses you on the ankle, you're convinced they want to take a bite out of your leg.

Bianca laughs hysterically.

BIANCA: What a memory!

SILE: What a defeat, humiliating.

MARINA: *(after a moment's thought, to Vincent)* I'll bet a bottle of whisky that it was Silé.

SILE: Marina, you drink too much.

VIOLETA: Bianca didn't have anybody in love with her.

RADU: Why no, she spent all her time studying and polishing the apple.

ROBESCU: Not true. She had a secret love... It was me, of course. *(The others appear highly skeptical.)* I know from looking at my daddy's files, which, by definition, are infallible. *(Everyone begins laughing.)*

MARINA: If Robescu's showing signs of a sense of humor...

RADU: Strange how this love business always leaves me cold.

BIANCA: Don't you mean "frigid. "

KATIA: *(peevishly)* All you people think about is sex... It's revolting!

VINCENT: *(to Bianca)* Won't you say a word to Radio Bucharest, the answer that our friends and listeners have been waiting twenty years to hear?

Bianca is still looking at Vlad. She begins searching her pockets.

BIANCA: Do you want to see what I've been keeping? I should be congratulated. In twenty years and twelve different moves I've never once lost it.

She takes out a piece of blue cloth with a number on it: her own school ID number.

ROBESCU: *(wistfully)* Number 1047!

VIOLETA: *(aside)* I've kept my ID number, too. Number 1037. Silé had Number 1050.

MARINA: Remember how Virginia used to use snaps to fasten hers on so she could take it off when she went to pick up foreigners in their hotels?

BIANCA: And I was the one who got collared by the police in a hotel. I'd been sent by the president of the Communist Youth League to find Virginia and bring her back.

RADU: And you went in your school uniform?

BIANCA: Of course I did. I was on an assignment.

VINCENT: If you didn't exist, we'd have to invent you!

BIANCA: The worst thing was, I was so absent-minded that I went to the wrong hotel. The cops picked me up, ID number and everything... I had to explain it all...

RADU: Just by looking at you they could tell you weren't a "working girl."

KATIA: I wonder if that filthy Virginia will dare show her face here tonight.

MARINA: Well, a lot of others have dared...

SILE: No cat fights, please. I refuse to stitch anybody up after hours!

BIANCA: I've never understood why they let me go. That same evening, as if by miracle, they stopped shouting at me, they even apologized.

ROBESCU: *(to himself)* No need to wonder...

BIANCA: And they never apologized to anyone...

RADU: You must have furnished them with a few names.

BIANCA: I swear I didn't.

RADU: We know how these things worked. Nobody got released the same night... Especially an orphan with no one to step in and rescue her... Who did you sell out? Tell us, the statute of limitations has expired.

BIANCA: *(more than ready to resort to action)* See this fist? How would you like to see it up real close?

ROBESCU: It was my father who stepped in.

RADU: I don't see why he would have stepped in for some little orphan. Even if she was the president of her son's class.

MARINA: *(looking at Radu)* He's amazing, this guy. Not only does he have no feelings himself, but he's even convinced that other people haven't got any, either... Radu, life must be beautiful for you. You never suffer.

RADU: Yes, I do. When I don't understand something.

SILE: In the future, whenever there's something you don't understand, tell yourself that it must be what is commonly called a feeling.

BIANCA: You actually did that for me, Robescu?

ROBESCU: *(modestly)* Please... Valentine.

BIANCA: Thank you... Valentine.

VINCENT: All this smacks of melodrama, don't you think? The sleazy villain who all of a sudden redeems himself by an act of unverifiable heroism?

RADU: I quite agree with you, my dear colleague, it is rather difficult to prove.

VIOLETA: Maybe you can't see it, but after all, why should you be the ones to decide the matter? I was a boarder at the school, just like Bianca. Where we were, everybody knew there was a plainclothes cop who always checked to see if Bianca came back to the dorm. The night they held her at the hotel, he came in to question us. One of the girls remembered that the president of the Communist Youth League had sent her to find Virginia and give her a talking to. The guy must have phoned Robescu's father and the rest is history...

BIANCA: You never said anything to me about that guy.

VIOLETA: We didn't dare. We didn't even know why he was spying on you... We thought it was because of your background, your family dying in a labor camp and all that. It's only now that I figured out it was because of Robescu...

VIOLETA: Valentine, why did you do that?

SILE: He may be my mortal enemy, but, please, have the goodness not to ask him that question. I'll draw you a picture...

The light dims to a dream-like atmosphere. Marina suddenly begins to dance a sort of wild flamenco. Vlad, like another dancer, claps out the rhythm with his hands.

MARINA: I've so often dreamed of being loved like that... Why don't these things happen to me? I'd know right away who it was. Holy Virgin, you're so unfair. You rain down your blessings on Bianca's head and she doesn't even realize it. What's more, she doesn't even care! All she's interested in is writing her plays. Let her write them, then let's close the book on that subject! And give me her admirers. It's such a waste. Here I am, alone, obese, depressed... Nobody gives me a mink, or posts his daddy's bodyguards outside my door, or gives me flowers. Nobody would even give me a piece of bread if I was hungry. No, I get hit if I don't turn over whatever's in my wallet, I put soup on the table and get a sour look in return, every single day of the year, I'm even abandoned for a dinosaur named Katia. So what if I asked Silé to keep me in mind... After that first night, he never came back... And the worst of it is: he didn't blame me for a thing... None of them ever had anything to blame me for... but none of them ever came back. I have a heart too, you know... Holy Virgin give me any one of them and I'll make him happy.

At the end of this flamenco, Marina ends up in Vlad's arms, bent over backwards in a suggestive tango position. Return to reality. The lights come up and the characters stand about in a circle, as before.

BIANCA: *(looking at her ID number)* Wouldn't it be funny if we all put these on and went out.

ROBESCU: Like survivors from the camps.

VINCENT: Look who's talking about camps!

ROBESCU: Why not? The guards on the watchtowers must have survived, too.

Bianca laughs.

VINCENT: What have you been drinking tonight, Robescu?

ROBESCU: I don't know, but I'll be drinking it from now on... I hope...

Silé returns from the buffet table. He brings Bianca a plate of hors-d'oeuvres.

SILE: At least Bianca is still like before. She never remembered to eat...

BIANCA: But before you wouldn't have fed me... !

SILE: That proves I've become less of a jerk... Eighteen years ago, at the end-of-school banquet, you were wearing a white dress, almost exactly the same.

MARINA: Bianca will never change. Even twenty years ago, when everyone would kill to get their hands on foreign clothes, she went around in her Romanian shirt that cost all of one hundred lei. And now that she's back from Paris, what's she got on? A Romanian dress...

RADU: It's a case of reverse snobbery.

Silé comes back from the buffet table with a plate which he hands Violeta.

VIOLETA: Thank you, you shouldn't have.

KATIA: And what about me? Isn't anybody going to bring me anything?

SILE: In your case, it's Robescu who'll do the honors.

ROBESCU: I've brought you something else... *(Showing off a large ledger)* Our school record book! Containing all your scores!

THE SOMMELIER: This calls for an aria about scoring. *(He sings, as Leporello.)* In Italia novantuna ma in Spagna... ma in Spagna... son già mile tre...

> *Given his ability to imitate the mannerisms of great opera singers, when he finishes everyone gives him a big round of applause.*

BIANCA: *(feeling the weight of the large ledger in her hands, wistfully)* Our last year, section D...

ROBESCU: Correct.

VINCENT: How did you get it?

RADU: *(whispering)* Vincent, don't ask stupid questions.

> *There is much jostling, half-joking, half-serious, as everyone tries to find the page where his or her scores are recorded. They all leaf through it together, talking at the same time.*

VINCENT: Let me see my page!

RADU: Wait! There's enough here for everybody.

MARINA: Put it down on the floor. That way everybody can see.

KATIA: Turn the pages alphabetically!

VIOLETA: For four years I could never bring myself to look at this...

BIANCA: Oh god, that" F" in chemistry! How I suffered over it. For all the good chemistry has ever done me, I should have spared myself the grief.

VINCENT: When I think we would have stooped to any indignity for a "C."

MARINA: That's for sure. You were already sleeping with that woman who taught us science.

VIOLETA: Say, Alexander. Whatever happened to him?

RADU: Smart guy. He left right after college. For the U.S.A.

VINCENT: If all the women over there are like Gladys, I hope he enjoys himself.

BIANCA: *(to Vincent)* Do you love her?

VINCENT: No, it's just to get out of this place! No other country will take us in as refugees. Thank you, revolution. In order to get out, there's only one solution: marry a foreigner.

BIANCA: It's gotten so much better here.

RADU: Why don't you come back if it's really that great?

BIANCA: I'm considering it very seriously.

VINCENT: She's insane.

MARINA: You're really the only one who wants to stay. All we want to do is get out of here.

SILE: What you mean, "all of us"?

RADU: All of us!

SILE: Not me!

ROBESCU: Not me!

RADU: Okay... all those who want to emigrate to the West, raise your hand...

Marina, Radu and Vincent raise their hands...

RADU: *(looking Katia and Violeta up and down)* Hypocrites!

BIANCA: *(looking at the ledger)* Say, Gaia certainly had bad grades! What's become of her?

They all burst out laughing.

SILE: She turned out to be the glory of our class. She's a member of the Chamber of Deputies...

RADU: That's it! I know who's missing from the photo! *(To himself)* It's awful...

BIANCA: *(shutting the ledger)* Well, in the end, except for those who died or moved abroad, almost all of us showed up.

SILE: Survivors... We're a band of survivors.

The Boys by Themselves

Downstage, the five boys are smoking. Vlad is among them. He doesn't smoke but he's seated with his legs crossed. He glances from one to another. He will intervene from time to time and, when he gives the signal, the atmosphere caused by the stage lighting will change, plunging us for a moment in each character's dream. The sommelier crosses the stage.

THE SOMMELIER: Would any of you gentlemen care for an after-dinner drink?

RADU: A tomato juice!

THE SOMMELIER: With or without ice?

RADU: Without. I'm just a little too fond of living, and I happen to know what kind of water you doctor your ice cubes with.

THE SOMMELIER: I personally never doctor anything... *(To Vincent)* And you, sir?

VINCENT: A double whisky with lots of ice... to make it last. *(He laughs, very pleased with himself, he's completely smashed.)*

ROBESCU: I'd like a cognac. A Courvoisier.

The boys give an ironic whistle of pseudo-admiration.

THE SOMMELIER: *(adopting the same tone as the others)* The gentleman is a connoisseur.

ROBESCU: It's a question of training... *(He gives the sommelier a wink.)*

THE SOMMELIER: *(to Robescu)* The gentleman is improving with age... like the Courvoisier... *(To Silé)* And you, sir?

SILE: A beer!

The sommelier turns to Vlad who hands him a candle.

THE SOMMELIER: Very good, sir!

> *He puts the candle in a small candle holder, in the middle of the circle formed by the men and lights it. Then he exits to get the drinks. All the characters stare at the flame as if hypnotized.*

VINCENT: When you come right down to it, we don't get along so badly. I'm not sorry I stayed.

ROBESCU: *(pulling out a cigar)* A wake... *(The boys whistle when they see Robescu's cigar.)* Care to join me?

> *Robescu offers them each a cigar. Vincent and Radu take one.*

VINCENT: What's with you, Robescu? Is it because Bianca's back? First time I've ever seen you give anything away without demanding a commission.

RADU: There must be somebody here who took physics in college... Please explain to me why these last twenty years have gone by like five minutes... Einstein must have had something to say on the subject.

SILE: *(his gaze absorbed by the flame)* Fifteen years ago, when I was a young doctor fresh out of med school, I had to sit up with the body of a guy who failed to make it through a skull operation... my first on-the-job death. It was nighttime, I was the only doctor on duty. They'd turned a section of the residents' room into a kind of mortuary chapel. A cleaning woman had lighted a candle. Then she washed and shaved the dead man. That corpse and I spent the whole night together. And that was probably the one time in my life when I was really face-to-face with myself. All night long, I talked to myself, honestly and directly, because that dead man was there. The next morning, when they came to take him away, I felt as if they'd gotten there too early. Nobody will ever listen to me the way that man did.

ROBESCU: We're all the same... holding a wake for our youth which is dying, and for the dead men we're going to become.

VINCENT: You're getting spooky again, Robescu.

ROBESCU: You're not going to believe me, but... I feel very much at home with all of you this evening! You don't like me... and I feel exactly the same about you. Nevertheless, we share a common history. Each one of us has his own place and his own path, but we'll always be bound together. One day, a thousand or more miles from here, one of us will think of one of the others and that will make him feel more alive. We're divorced from each other but we have joint custody of our children.

VINCENT: *(to Robescu)* Speaking of which... You and Silé were the smart ones... Confirmed bachelors with no ties to anyone.

RADU: And me? Nobody's wants to know what I think. Even though I've got three kids... all highly intelligent.

VINCENT: We're forty years old, forty already, old buddies.

The waiter arrives and serves them drinks.

RADU: Thirty-nine.

VINCENT: There you go again, always getting bogged down with details. And what have we done in those forty years, heh? Nothing. All of us, nothing. Some guys are stuck with the little woman and a few brats, some see their kids every other week-end, like their visits are counted out with an eye-dropper, some work like dogs till at the end they finally drop from exhaustion, and some are just so bummed out they don't give a shit any more... All roads lead to failure... We're not the gods we thought we were when we were twenty. We're back down here with the mortals. In the hive, no, the mole-hill... Brrr, it's gotten cold and dark in our lives.

SILE: After age twenty, you can't help but be a failure... unless maybe you have youth-without-age, as the princess would say.

VINCENT: Damn, that's right. We called her the princess!

RADU: She always had a princess side to her... the princess and the pea. That's why Leon when he sat beside her, was the prince consort. And we were the Brahmans... *(Wistfully)* the highest caste.

ROBESCU: How does she seem to you, Bianca?

VINCENT: Unchanged.

RADU: Her haircolor isn't the same.

VINCENT: Unchanged, I said.

RADU: Of course, over there, how could you possibly get any older or any fatter? *(Wistfully)* With what they have to eat... I've seen the meat in Switzerland. Proteins, not this rancid fat we get. How can you stay slim and fit eating old sausages and salami with soybeans? Whereas in cuckoo clock land... they have gymnasiums, spas, beauty salons... With all that, of course she's unchanged.

ROBESCU: Bianca doesn't go in for that sort of thing.

VINCENT: Oh right, you would know all about her...

ROBESCU: *(smiling)* Not any more, really. I followed her activities while she was in at her university. It was easy enough. We had a man in Paris, supposedly a student, who kept us informed. She was the same as over here, outstanding at her studies, but aloof and rather unsociable. After that, I lost track of her, almost. She didn't show up outside the embassy, even at the demonstrations. She didn't attend the Romanian church...

VINCENT: Where you had your men stationed.

ROBESCU: As you're well aware, having wanted to be one yourself...

VINCENT: Why didn't you take me?

ROBESCU: You won't believe me but I actually put in a good word for you. "A highly malleable subject." Generally speaking, a recommendation from me gave someone a leg up... but the positions were costly items and the protégés seeking them as numerous as the posts themselves. You were on the waiting list and had an excellent chance when you took over the leadership of the unions, and then it was quite out of the question.

VINCENT: Why didn't you warn me that I was so close?

ROBESCU: Would you have believed me?

VINCENT: *(indicates he wouldn't have, downs his drink and shouts)* Hey, waiter, another whisky!

SILE: You guys make me sick. This sounds like a meeting of the Mafia.

VINCENT: Of course, as soon as we stop talking about getting laid, you're bored.

SILE: *(speechless)* You're saying that to me?

VINCENT: It's beginning to get me down... when I get any at all...

RADU: Forty years old, pal. It's about time you settled down.

VINCENT: You never knew what it was like... But when you've known it... Say, Robescu, is it true that you had all the girls in our class?

SILE: Except Bianca!

RADU: No one's expected to achieve the impossible.

VINCENT: Even Katia?

ROBESCU: *(in a voice that means "yes")* I haven't any idea.

RADU: *(very impressed)* Even Katia!

ROBESCU: She doesn't count. She thought going to bed would be useful. I ought not to have made an exception to my rule: anyone who wants a promotion must pay for it. Unfortunately for me, she had no money!

SILE: What a bastard!

ROBESCU: A victim of duty! Try doing it with Katia some time and then tell me if it's a pleasure or not.

SILE: And the moral of the story is: Where there's hope, there's a hard-on.

ROBESCU: In your case it's automatic... I mean, women... are drawn to you...

RADU: The two red hot lovers, Robescu and Silé... They've had them all.

VINCENT: But Silé doesn't have to pay.

SILE: I'm afraid I'm going to have to, soon.

VINCENT: Which one was the best?

SILE: This guy's never going to catch on!

ROBESCU: The best is always the one you haven't had.

RADU: There you go... We're going to start talking about Bianca, again. Why don't you just do it with her and get it over with? You guys all stand around, drooling over her like a pack of dogs in heat. When you come down to it, she's not that terrific. If she'd spent the last twenty years here, working her ass off, she'd be like the others: fat, flabby, coarse and depressed.

ROBESCU: I really don't think so.

RADU: I'm not talking to that guy any more. He's drunk. Not on wine! On love. After twenty years he still hasn't been able to sleep it off. And you, Silé, how does Bianca seem to you? Changed?

SILE: It's hard to say. Twenty years ago I had my eye on the more spectacular ones, like Virginia.

ROBESCU: *(scornfully)* Virginia!

SILE: *(in self-justification)* We all went through that. Up to age twenty, a man is a jerk. He lets himself be led around by his cock. It's only later, after he's gained experience—and weight—that he let's himself be led around by... his hormones.

VINCENT: Damn, you're right! You can't get away from it!

ROBESCU: Silé, you've stopped believing in free will!

SILE: We were twenty years younger... I saw what was there to see: big knockers, short skirts. Bianca wore a uniform that came down to her ankles and didn't even comb her hair.

ROBESCU: That was her charm.

RADU: Her one charm is that if she wants to come back here, I'll gladly take her place in Paris.

ROBESCU: I believe she's seriously thinking of coming back.

RADU: She's crazy! Robescu, is it true you can get visas for other countries?

ROBESCU: We'll see.

RADU: We'll see what?

ROBESCU: How much?

RADU: In lei or in foreign currency?

ROBESCU: Do I look like a dimwit to you?

RADU: Foreign currency... from Europe or across the ocean?

ROBESCU: Stars and Stripes forever.

RADU: How much?

ROBESCU: Between five hundred and a thousand.

RADU: What!?

ROBESCU: That's with the discount I give my friends.

SILE: Why isn't it guys like Robescu that fall under tanks? Then I'd never have put my hand under there.

VINCENT: Is it true that Virginia is back in the country?

ROBESCU: Don't mention her to me. What a headache! A complete bitch. Blackmailer, impossible to get rid of, with just one goal in life: money.

RADU: Is it true it was you who sold her to that African king?

ROBESCU: It was all we could do to palm her off on some cannibal. Alas, he didn't eat her. We sold her to him as a "young Romanian virgin"... for cash: an excellent deal! The state paid for the operation to revirginize her... and that idiot Vincent had to go and screw her several times a day. We were afraid that the whole thing would break and fall apart. Then we'd have had to start the operation all over again.

VINCENT: I remember. Every time she'd shout, "Careful of my hymen, it's brand new!"

RADU: You've got a strong stomach, don't you!

VINCENT: That was ten years ago... Now, I couldn't do it...

ROBESCU: She put my father through hell! The state was paying for everything. It was Prodan Senior who revirginized her... She was sent to our-friend-the-king, he took delivery... No sooner do we start to utter a sigh of relief then that idiot starts to call attention to herself among all the concubines of our honorable, royal friend. They were all willing to sleep with anybody but they were careful enough to keep it a secret, but not Virginia! She even sent us telexes asking us to send her all her so-called cousins, blond men every one, because on top of everything she was a racist. She couldn't sleep with the locals like everyone else. And in the end we had no choice. Official repudiation, apologies at the highest level, millions in commercial treaties at stake... We had to find a replacement gift for our-friend-the-king... My father was already dying of bone cancer and he had to spend his last days making formal apologies for the infidelities of that tramp, what a horror. It was sordid, having to deal with that kind of business... Even today, we're paying her to keep her mouth shut, especially in front of reporters... Now that the press is supposedly free. Congratulations on your revolution: you see for yourself that secrets are being kept as well as ever. Was it worth the effort? *(Tugging at the empty sleeve of Silé's missing arm)* Was it worth the effort, now that you and I are both alike.

SILE: Listen, you grasping little tarantula, the difference between you and me is that you're crippled in the head. You could be a terrific ballroom dancer, with two perfectly shaped legs, and you'd still be a hunchback inside. With me, not having an arm pisses me off, but it would piss me off even more if I hadn't stepped in when I did. I'd have blamed myself for the rest of my life. Up here, *(Tapping his forehead)* where it counts, I'm in good shape. I live and let live. I lose an arm?

I weigh the possibilities. I can't do surgery any more, I'll do something else... a newspaper vendor, that's as good as anything. I'll be doing that tomorrow and I won't mind a bit because everything is in order up here, in the attic. So what if I have to give up my office and my three female assistants at the hospital? That's fine with me! I'll sell my newspapers and I'll screw the local waitresses. I'm not a snob when it comes to class. I'll still listen to the music I love and I'll go down to the delta to watch the birds fly... There's a patch of blue sky in my head, you tarantula. That's something goons like you can never take away... But you, on the other hand, if ever they deprive you of your post at the ministry, you're sunk, you hairy spider. You'll be in free fall because you have nothing to hold on to... except your power. You look at people and wonder what you can get out of them... You can't enjoy yourself, poor bastard, because you're a nobody, you're just a government post, a job... hereditary, at that.

VINCENT: *(quietly, to Silé)* Drop it. He can get his revenge.

SILE: Don't worry. He's already done everything he could do to screw up my life. *(To Robescu)* All those conventions of neurologists in Paris, right? Who was it that regularly black-balled my visa application? An old classmate of mine with a lot of pull at the Ministry of the Interior.

VINCENT: *(to Robescu)* Did you do that to him?

SILE: What were you, born yesterday? They never admit it.

ROBESCU: I admit it.

The Girls by Themselves

MARINA: *(continuing a heated discussion)* Especially since they say that over there women get everything they want from men: furs, alimony... We've seen it ourselves, on "Dallas."

BIANCA: *(laughing)* I thought all the women on "Dallas" were miserable alcoholics.

MARINA: They are... but their clothes are divine!

BIANCA: I went through a stage, too, when I wanted everybody and everything for myself.

MARINA: And...

BIANCA: I wanted a mink? I got it, then a chinchilla, I got that, too. When it came to a sable, I just couldn't... I'd lost the desire. So I stopped.

KATIA: The temptations must be awful.

BIANCA: Just like here. There are things you can have and things you can't. In the end you realize that the main thing is wanting... To still be able to want something.

MARINA: There you go with your reverse snobbery.

VIOLETA: No, she's a romantic.

BIANCA: I'm a satisfied woman... because this reunion was perhaps the last thing I still wanted.

MARINA: Were you married?

BIANCA: I got a divorce.

MARINA: I hope things are better over there because being a divorced woman in Romania...

ALL: *(in chorus)* Is worse than being black in South Africa.

They laugh.

MARINA: *(to Bianca)* Is there someone else... ?

BIANCA: There was... No! No one.

MARINA: Was your husband rich, at least?

BIANCA: Marc, very rich.

MARINA: *(crossing herself)* You're insane. *(She fills her glass up with whisky.)* Stories like that make me sick.

VIOLETA: Bianca has an independent nature.

KATIA: That's what drives the men mad... that and the fact she seems to follow her instincts, come what may... That's easy enough to imitate. Tomorrow, I'm also going to stop going to work, stop doing my laundry, stop running errands, because I, too, am... an artist.

VIOLETA: *(to Bianca)* Robescu is still in love with you, like twenty years ago.

MARINA: I never would have thought him capable of an emotion.

BIANCA: He has a strange fascination, slightly venomous... I've always thought he had a certain sensuality.

KATIA: You're depraved.

VIOLETA: If he knew that, he'd go to his grave a happy man.

MARINA: Watch out. If he finds out he has a chance, he could keep you from leaving the country.

BIANCA: It's too late, now.

KATIA: Do you have any children?

VIOLETA: How many?

BIANCA: I can't have any.

MARINA: You overdid it with the pill, huh?

BIANCA: Not exactly with the pill... but I overdid it.

MARINA: *(very interested)* Really?

BIANCA: *(playing along)* To the max...

VIOLETA: *(to Bianca)* You see, and you were afraid of dying an old maid because you were too shy. Everything comes out right in the end!

Marina's eyes suddenly meet Katia's.

MARINA: It's strange how your worst enemies wind up doing you some good, in spite of themselves... Think, when you come right down to it, it was Hitler who wanted to exterminate all the Jews, and what did he really accomplish? The creation of the state of Israel. I'm the state of Israel that Katia created... I didn't think that I was able to live by myself or raise a child but when Katia took Igor away from me, I discovered so many things were within my reach! I, who never had a single lover all the time I was married, today I have three... One of them is a patient of mine. A chronic case who's never going to get better. I put him under psychiatric care. He fucks like a god. He's got a permanent hard-on.

KATIA: Igor isn't always fun to be with, you know.

MARINA: I know...

KATIA: He's got a temper.

MARINA: You wanted him!

KATIA: I... *(Accepting it)* It's true. I wanted him!

MARINA: *(continuing to drink)* I'm not even mad at you any more. The only thing I mind is that he doesn't visit Florian...

KATIA: I swear to you that I don't try to stop him. Since I can't have a child...

MARINA: *(crying)* If you could see how he takes after Igor... *(Laughing)* It's a good thing that tomorrow I'll be seeing my pal, the good one, the one with the permanent hard-on.

VIOLETA: *(laughing)* Tomorrow, I'll be doing my washing, my errands and my yearly accounts.

MARINA: *(in admiration)* Virginia's come out on top!

KATIA: That tramp!

MARINA: *(wistfully)* Big alimony payments, huge house full of Oriental vases.

VIOLETA: And no one will go there for fear of being investigated.

KATIA: *(rising)* It's getting late. I've got to phone Igor.

VIOLETA: I'll go back with you.

MARINA: Damn! They're all afraid of getting yelled at by their men. Another evening of not having any fun!

Vincent sneaks up from behind to tease her.

VINCENT: Want me to take you home, doll?

MARINA: *(delightedly)* What kinda car you got?

VINCENT: A Lada, but for you I'll drive it like it was a Ferrari.

MARINA: Casanova! Well, ciao, girls... We only go around once! *(She gestures toward Katia, on the telephone, with pity.)* Poor creature... Ciao, ragazzi! *(Going toward Bianca)* Sorry to be rushing off like this. Now about your play...

VINCENT: What play?

MARINA: The one she's writing about us... You know perfectly well. She stares and stares, and then she writes a play about us. She's always done that to us. *(To Bianca)* About your play, the revolution and all that, everybody contradicting everybody else... I was alone at home, sitting in front of the TV and I wanted to kill myself... Ciao and... write a good one!

   She runs off laughing with Vincent.

KATIA: *(on the phone)* But you weren't there, Igor, I called you... I swear... There are plenty of people there who can confirm it... It's true, you're not on speaking terms with them...

   Downstage, Bianca is alone with Violeta.

BIANCA: Silé isn't married?

VIOLETA: No... It's hard to find a wife as good as he is.

BIANCA: You're looking at him through the eyes of love.

VIOLETA: Silé... Silé... there's a man.

BIANCA: Why don't you try approaching him?

VIOLETA: I'm going to tell you something I've never told any-body. When Vita died, I knew that I couldn't have any more children. So I tried to adopt the children she left behind and, in order to get the adoption papers, I went to Silé for a doctor's certificate. Glad to have the chance to see him again... I went to the hospital... I'd spent a month's salary on shampoo and perfume which I got on the black market... to try and make myself pretty. I ran into him in the hallway with his assistants trailing behind, wearing his white jacket. At the hospital, he's really himself... very warm, very human but very strict, too. No "hi-there-glad-to-see-you. " The hair cut short. His chin, you know how he holds it, up in the air, like this... kind of aggressive. I told him what I wanted but he had to go into the operating area. Since it was urgent, he told me to come back later that evening. I didn't leave. I stayed in the waiting room. I wandered up and down the halls like a little mouse. It's not hard for me to go unnoticed, I look so ordinary... I saw him go into the operating room. He was handsome. Serious. A little smile now and then when he was comforting a patient. Silé, you know, he's a white knight. I saw him go in. He came out three hours later. Exhausted. Dark circles under his eyes. Handsome. Three solid hours, all the while he was operating, I was with him, sweating, breathing hard, my heart pounding. I was con-nected to him, sending him my energy. Then I went to his office... eight in the evening: he was worried. A young nurse was fluttering around him, her blouse open to show off her cleavage. She was very pretty but he didn't notice her. He talked with me about his patient. A child with a tumor. He'd done his best but he was afraid the kid wouldn't pull through... Then he started filling out the forms for me. The nurse finally left, in a snit, and Silé said, "I haven't eaten since this morning. I never eat before an operation. How about us having dinner together?" Just thinking about it, look at my arm, I've got goose bumps... In my wildest dreams, I hadn't imagined it... him taking me out to dinner.

BIANCA *(ironically)* To his place?

VIOLETA: Oh, of course you wouldn't understand. This took place seven years ago, during one of the worst periods of "The Golden Age." There was no light in the streets, not a single restaurant open. To spent the evening with friends, you had no choice but to invite them over. And Silé's place was so attractive. Everything was clean, white, simple. He took some things out of the fridge, things his mother had fixed for him. He heated me up some meat balls and said, "Don't move a muscle. I love doing these stupid household chores. It gives my brain a rest." *(She shows Bianca her arm quivering with emotion.)* You see? Just hearing his voice again in my head... Silé didn't know what to do to kill time until the next day when he could finally find out the condition of his young patient. He set the table. When I think, he set the table himself and my husband would never do that in a million years... my husband, who isn't handsome, who isn't smart. *(Her eyes are misty with the memory.)* "I'll take care of everything but please be kind and tell me a story; that'll relax me, Scheherazade." He called me "Scheherazade." So I told him... everything. My botched operation, the sterility, Prodan Junior, even my marriage, as I'd never told it before. Nothing but the truth. How I'd gotten married just so I could have children and how I'd gotten myself in a fix... Afterwards, he phoned the hospital. Still no word. I knew that if I went home at that hour, after eleven, I'd get a bashing, but I had only one desire. For Silé to keep me with him. And also, he was so nervous about his patient, I was proud to be able to help him wait it out. He began to smoke, then to drink, he was somewhere else... in the recovery room. He said nothing to me about it and he didn't need to. I know him so well... At this very moment, look at him talking to Robescu. He looks polite and relaxed. But he's champing at the bit, trying to control himself, because inside he's boiling with rage. Robescu, strange as it seems, is a little like him... It's funny how often they've been with the same women. But Robescu is a fallen angel who'll never forgive Silé for having maintained his grace.

BIANCA: *(twinkly)* I suppose that the angel wound up by taking your hand and looking into your eyes...

VIOLETA: You don't know him! I was the one who took his hand, and I was the one who looked into his eyes and asked him if he wouldn't be too repulsed by the idea of going to bed with an old classmate, one who's always been in love with him, but who now has to pee into a little plastic bag... He answered saying, "Not in the least. I'll show you two or three medical discoveries to take advantage of the situation." And afterwards, Bianca, afterwards... *(Wistfully)*

BIANCA *(feigning fascination)* He had two penises? Three!?

VIOLETA: You're making fun of me.

BIANCA: I only hope that oaf is worthy of the torch you're carrying for him. It borders on mystic devotion.

VIOLETA: When people say you only really get to know a man in bed, they're right. I thought I already knew Silé. I knew that he was special, that he understood everything there was to understand but, in fact... After a night like that in a woman's life... she can die in peace. Even the next day, while my husband was giving me the worst beating of my life, I was still smiling. The memory of that night was stronger than the blows. I was smiling and I was weeping for joy... silently. That actually made him stop. He must have decided that he was hitting me too hard and that I'd started going crazy. I still live off the memory of that night... and have for seven years.

KATIA: I've got to get home. Igor is having a fit... but I was glad to be here.

BIANCA: You can invite Igor to join us.

KATIA: Oh no, I'm afraid you don't know him... This is probably the last time we'll ever see each other and I don't know what to say to you, Bianca. You haven't changed... I don't even know what that means. Okay, I'm going. Nobody will notice I'm gone... as usual. *(She exits.)*

VIOLETA: *(watching Katia leave)* Poor thing.

BIANCA: *(to Violeta)* You never tried to see Silé again after that night?

VIOLETA: I called him a few weeks later, at the hospital. He was happy, so happy. His patient had recovered. He asked me for news about my adoption. I never knew if he was pretending to have forgotten because I hadn't pleased him or if he really had forgotten. I think he was so worried about that sick child and he'd had so much to drink that night. He didn't remember... he didn't remember... *(She cries.)*

BIANCA: That asshole!

VIOLETA: He didn't remember. To be kind to me, he even mentioned a new technique for artificial insemination. I asked him if it was possible with my plastic bag and he answered, "You wear a urine bag? I didn't realize that... " He had forgotten. It was the happiest day of my life.

THE SOMMELIER: A phone call for Mrs. Dobresco!

VIOLETA: That's me... *(She rises and goes to the phone.)* That's it. The dream is over... *(Into the phone, in a voice of extraordinary sweetness)* Hello, darling?... Of course, I'm coming... You're right, it's very late! Forgive me!... You're in front of the restaurant? All right, darling... I'm leaving right now... Yes, darling. I know you'll make a scene if I'm not down there in five minutes... I know, sweetheart, I'd better not be late or else you'll punch me so hard it'll make my head spin... Right away, darling. *(She hangs up and smiles at Bianca.)* You were saying that your private life's a failure? I think you're being too hard on yourself. *(Bianca takes her in her arms, squeezing her tightly; both are crying. Violeta breaks away, gently.)* I've gotta go, otherwise... *(Violeta crosses to the group of men.)* Good bye, boys! *(She blows them a kiss; stopping in front of Vlad, she looks at him tenderly and makes the sign of the cross above his head.)* May God keep you...

SILE: *(rising)* Don't you want to stay a while, Violeta? You've gotta tell us what's been going on in your life...

VIOLETA: *(smiling to heaven)* Next time... I have to go now but I'll think about you... I'll think about all of you boys, every day. *(Violeta, exiting, passes before Bianca.)* We two haven't changed. We're still without armor... We suffer as much as ever, but you're lucky, you've got a few prejudices to shield you... I'll leave my secret with you... in your heart. I know it'll be safe there. Oh, and when you think of it, live as if you were living for me a little... I want to thank you. You don't know what a gift you've given me, inviting me here tonight... I'm going! My five minutes are up. Back to reality... Good night! *(She exits.)*

BIANCA: *(to the sommelier)* I'd like the check, please.

THE SOMMELIER: Those gentlemen have already taken care of it.

BIANCA: Who has?

THE SOMMELIER: The two invalids... *(Realizing what he has just said)* Forgive me, I'm so tired... They both came up to me. Each one wanted to pay. I managed to get them to do something jointly. It wasn't as easy as you'd think. They weren't speaking to each other.

The Last to Leave

BIANCA: *(going towards them)* Valentine, Silé, thank you... You shouldn't have...

RADU: Did they send you flowers?

BIANCA: In a manner of speaking... And to you, too, Mr. Tight Ass.

RADU: A vulgar expression... by which I recognize our own Bianca.

ROBESCU: Her choice of words suits her well.

SILE: She doesn't always know what she's saying.

BIANCA: That's perfectly true.

RADU: You know who's missing in the class photo?

ALL: Of course. You.

RADU: You didn't notice my absence... Even I didn't notice it. For twenty years, I thought I was in it, I thought I was him...

BIANCA: Of course not. That's Vlad. His back is almost turned, but it's Vlad.

RADU: I just now realized. *(Wistfully)* A diplomat... that's what I should have been. Always able to move gracefully, to speak gravely, to comport myself in the prescribed manner, important and, in the end, nonexistent. Never interrupting the flow of things with a vulgar display of emotion. *(Rising with difficulty, like an old man)* Emotions... Ugh! *(Heading towards the exit, he stops in front of Bianca.)* I've always found you vulgar, princess; that's why I can't stand you. You're so alive that I can see your glands secreting hormones. I see your blood rushing to your face through every vessel whenever I accuse you of having a foreign accent. You're transparent and so alive. Too alive, princess! That's exactly what the others like in you, seeing the wild copulation of your cells, their damnable "life," shamelessly on display... It turns my stomach... I'm a cold-blooded reptile. A reptile has no emotions, and he's so clean! But that doesn't make an impression, not even on a photograph... any more than a ghost would. Forgive me. I've had too much to drink and this cigar is making my head swim. The reptilian diplomat, or the diplomatic reptile, leaves you with his greeting. We are living in a marvelous world and we're still only al mezzo del camin... *(He exits, staggering, passing near the waiter.)* Nature loves diversity... unfortunately...

Bianca remains standing, between Silé and Robescu. Behind her, Vlad watches.

SILE: He had too much to drink.

ROBESCU: Or not enough.

Bianca sits between them.

BIANCA: At last, men among men.

ROBESCU: You're more beautiful than twenty years ago.

SILE: You're unchanged. As pug-ugly as twenty years ago.

BIANCA: *(laughing)* When things go wrong, I'll come visit you. You two cheer me up...

ROBESCU: Your real favorite was perhaps the couple we formed, Silé and I!

SILE: That way you had the bastard, the decent guy and, inevitably, everything in between.

ROBESCU: Silé and I are alike.

SILE: *(ironically)* You pay me too great an honor!

ROBESCU: It's not by chance that we find ourselves the last to leave. We're the kind who pursue the dinosaur as far as we can... The valiant knights and the princess. Of course, everyone's dinosaurs are different, but we're the only ones who've gone so far, each within his own jungle...

SILE: *(ironically)* So pure, aren't we?

ROBESCU: *(to Bianca)* Are you happy?

BIANCA: *(laughing)* I missed out on half my life... *(With a forced laugh)* But there's still the other half... I'm counting especially on that portion between the ages of seventy and eighty.

ROBESCU: Are you happy?

BIANCA: The only people who are happy are people in love... That must strike you as funny, no?

ROBESCU: You see, I'm not laughing.

SILE: If I'm in your way, I can leave now and let the two of you bill and coo to your hearts' content.

BIANCA: Why did I have to have a talent, a vocation? I only wanted a great love affair between the sheets.

ROBESCU: I always knew it.

BIANCA: That's pretty remarkable. I didn't know it myself at the time.

SILE: *(to Robescu)* It's easy enough to say, after the fact.

ROBESCU: *(stubbornly)* I did always know it.

BIANCA: Maybe I've been happy but when it's over, I forget. I have no memory for happiness. I'm not a woman. *(Ivanovic's waltz, "The Waves of the Danube," can be heard.)* We're the same... How is that possible? It's like a geological fault line. Deep inside, we're unbroken.

The sommelier comes up to Robescu.

THE SOMMELIER: A telephone call for Mister Robescu!

ROBESCU: *(archly)* Excuse me, my destiny calls. I shall return.

SILE: I'm afraid so.

Robescu takes the receiver.

ROBESCU: You did well... *(Then he listens in silence, his posture progressively more slumped.)* All right then. Tomorrow morning... *(He sinks into a chair where he remains prostrate and haggard.)* Why did it have to be tonight?

> *The sommelier offers Robescu a glass of water but he doesn't see it. Vlad gestures, and the light changes. There is a dreamlike atmosphere and the same music as that of Robescu's Great Waltz, only now he is limping. Slowly, he exits while dancing, his arms around an imaginary partner. From far upstage, Vlad and the sommelier watch the two other characters.*

BIANCA: Only us two...

SILE: No point now in arguing.

> *Bianca searches through her handbag, takes out the letter that Vlad had slipped into it and reads it. She gazes at Silé with infinite affection.*

BIANCA: You're so kind to me, sometimes...

SILE: *(obviously understanding nothing)* I can drive you home. It's too late for you to go back by yourself. Where do you live?

BIANCA: *(laughing)* I didn't have a chance to even think about that. I don't live anywhere... or else number 49 rue Saint-Sauveur, in Paris, the first arrondissement.

They laugh. Vlad, like a hypnotist, motions with his hands to the sommelier, who, like a medium in a trance, obeys. Slowly, Vlad draws him over to a place between Bianca and Silé.

THE SOMMELIER: I have to go now, but since I find you both such nice people, I can leave you the key. Just hide it behind the flower pot when you leave.

SILE: I don't want to cause you any trouble. I can catch the subway in another hour.

THE SOMMELIER: *(Vlad continues to direct his movements from a distance, like a puppeteer pulling his dummy's strings.)* Rest here, why don't you. I'll put these two banquettes together. It's a little chilly, the coldest moment of the day... But the dawn is breaking: I can put the lights out... I was delighted to make your acquaintance, Miss. *(To Silé)* This lady reminds me so much of my fiancée, Blanche... I've been deeply in love with her all my life. Once... in the last century, I went so far as to touch her on the ankle, in the park with the fountain... But she was the most beautiful, the best behaved and the shyest girl in all of Bucharest. She read Hegel in the original. She went off to study piano in Paris and there... They took her to a camp at the beginning of the war. She disappeared. Poof... Gone! As if by magic! Generally, that's done with white rabbits... I've never forgiven myself for letting her go... Good luck, young man!

He exits, at Vlad's silent command. Then turning out the light so that the stage is bathed in the first rays of dawn, Vlad, too, makes his exit.

SCENE 6: WALTZ, BUCHAREST, DAWN

BIANCA: Brrr... It's cold...

SILE: The Romanian winter!

BIANCA: *(laughing)* The Balkans...

> *Silé lights a candle which he holds in his hand. They are stretched out side by side in order to keep warm, bundled up in their coats.*

BIANCA: *(moving closer to him)* I'm only doing this just to get warm... *(Silé gazes at her. Embarrassed, Bianca wants to break the silence.)* What are you thinking about?

SILE: "Just to get warm..."

BIANCA: Oh God, I feel ill at ease. I've always been ill at ease around you.

SILE: Me too... intimidated, not ill at ease!

> *Bianca snuggles up to him.*

BIANCA: *(laughing)* Just to get warm, the Balkans, the Carpathian/Danubian region and all that stuff, understand?

SILE: It's true you haven't changed. You always felt you had to apologize for every spontaneous impulse. It seemed as though you were apologizing for being alive... Let me assure you, it's perfectly legal to be alive... and very good for your health.

BIANCA: *(overly dramatic)* I'm just a poor orphan girl. I apologize for outliving my parents.

SILE: That story about the ankle the sommelier told... It stirred up something in me. Do you remember? The 30th of May... 1973... The park with the fountain... We went for a walk after they took the photo. You sat on the grass... and you were wearing those little clogs of yours with the wooden soles and the apple-green tops. The ones in the photo. I was sitting near you, there were five or six of us, a small group just hanging around until it was time to go home... You were talking, as usual. I was listening to the music in your voice, not even noticing what the words meant... when I tried to kiss you on the ankle.

BIANCA: You didn't try... you did it!

SILE: You immediately stopped talking... A silence fell around us... deep as a well... Everyone was still.

BIANCA: You and I are the only ones who remember it.

SILE: You turned toward me, abruptly. With such a surprised look, your eyes wide open... as if you were seeing me for the first time.

BIANCA: I'm trying to recollect the faces around us... The prince consort was there, Vlad, not Violeta. She'd be sure to remember...

SILE: Robescu was there.

BIANCA: I don't recall.

SILE: He's always remembered it... my kissing you on the ankle. I'd never done that to anyone. And I've never done it since. Not that I'm proud of it. I never wanted to after that... After that first glance which—finally—escaped the rigid censorship of your cerebral cortex... I received the *coup de grace*. The class Romeo made to look ridiculous in the eyes of all assembled when kissing the ankle of the inaccessible maiden who, predictably enough, topped it off by withdrawing her foot in evident disgust.

BIANCA: It wasn't disgust.

SILE: If you could have seen the look on your face. A star looking down on a snail half crushed in his own slime.

BIANCA: I thought that you understood... with all the experience you supposedly had. That look... It was something stirring... for the first time... an intense, physical stirring, deep down inside.

SILE: Why didn't you say anything to me about it?

BIANCA: I was waiting for you to do it again.

SILE: You're just saying that to make a cripple feel better.

BIANCA: I dare you...

> *Silé looks at her for a moment, then he kisses her on the ankle. Something stirs deep within her; in him, as well. She draws closer and kisses him, passionately.*

BIANCA: You took your sweet time...

SILE: My arm... I'm not used to this yet. This is the first time since... the accident. *(She silences him with a kiss.)* For twenty years... I've dreamed of making love to you, of kneading your breasts with my two hands... two!

BIANCA: I fell in love with you, not with your hand...

> *At the same time, they both blow out the flame of the candle. But the stage remains lighted. Dawn has already arrived. They laugh and embrace.*

A Waltz from Twenty Years Ago

Slowly, silently all the other characters return to the stage. They wear the same uniforms as in the photo. The girls are in long, sleeveless, navy-colored, smock-like dresses over light-blue blouses. The boys are in suits with navy-blue jackets and similarly colored ties. All of them wear a patch with their school ID numbers on the left sleeve. We hear a syrupy Italian melody from the 60's: "Tu, il mare, io, amore, sempre e tutti quanti." Marina is speaking in a stage murmur with Violeta when Silé joins the other characters. Marina tries to persuade her friend to go up to Silé but Violeta's gestures indicate that she doesn't dare. Wishing to prove to Violeta that the situation is not all that complicated, Marina asks Silé to dance. They begin to dance just as Bianca, in her "civilian" clothes, enters on stage. Silé gives a start. Bianca shoots him a disdainful look and goes off to sit in the corner with Katia, the wall flower at the dance. As soon as Bianca sits down, Katia begins to talk to her. Bianca nods in agreement from time to time. We sense, however, that she hears nothing of what Katia is saying. Radu and Vincent are conferring in a corner. Robescu enters. He sits down next to Bianca. When the dance ends, another syrupy song begins. Silé moves toward Bianca but she, as a form of retaliation, goes up to Vlad and asks him to dance. Silé finds himself standing in front of Katia, whom he invites to dance. As they dance, they project an air of profound boredom. Radu dances with Violeta and Vincent with Marina. From time to time a dancer will clap his hands together and everyone will change partners. In this way Silé finds himself dancing with a delighted Violeta, Radu, pompous as ever, with Katia, and Vlad, joyously, with Marina, while Bianca dances with Vincent. As Vincent holds Bianca a little too close, Vlad and Silé exchange looks. They clap their hands and, in the ensuing change of partners, no matter who dances with whom, they see to it that Bianca

*is always partnered by one of them. Robescu watches these
maneuverings in wonder. The music, growing ever livelier,
ends in a waltz, the recurrent "Waves of the Danube" by
Ivanovic. Bianca waltzes with Silé in a passionate, harmo-
nious fashion. Still, an air of violence, mingled with sensuality, seems to emanate from this couple. The others move aside
to clear the center for them. Robescu rises and hobbles over
in their direction as if he wanted to stop them. But he stops
short, as if nailed to the floor by the whirlwind they create.
This waltz is both a premonition of, and a metaphor for, their
first night of love. Suddenly, everyone assumes the melancholy
solemnity of those wan, graceful figurines who move about to
the sounds of their music box. Bianca and Silé separate,
returning to their banquettes. The others exit gravely, like a
funeral procession, all the while dancing.*

After Love

Breathless. Visibly after love. Entwined.

BIANCA: I'm not cold any more.

SILE: I'm not afraid any more... We both made out all right
on this deal.

BIANCA: A boorish remark, typically macho.

SILE: True. I'm a boor... (*He kisses her on the hand, with great
ceremony.*)

BIANCA: If I'd been born a man...

SILE: Which would be a real waste...

BIANCA: I would have been just as sweet... as sweet as you, I hope.

SILE: I'm the man you would have liked to be... *(He kisses her on the forehead.)* What are we waiting for, why don't we make some duplicates copies?

BIANCA: I can't have any children.

SILE: Not all by yourself, you can't. But if you're very good, I'll explain to you how it's done.

BIANCA *(laughing)* But I can't.

SILE: I kissed you on the ankle one day, and the feelings it stirred up in me have lasted for twenty years... That kind of desire doesn't belong to the everyday world. We're in the realm of magic!

BIANCA: We're in the Balkans!

SILE: If you really want children, anything is possible in our magical region...

BIANCA: This is a doctor talking?

SILE: Exactly. I'm perfectly placed to have lost all illusions concerning the omnipotence of the real world, but I've had a glimpse of the possibilities which the magical can offer. They're limitless... For example, now, twenty years later, in this magical region, what would you say to me?

BIANCA: That I've always loved you...

SILE: You see? In the magical region you can speak the truth, the truth you always denied in the real world.

BIANCA: And how would you respond?

SILE: That I've never stopped loving you. I even remember the first hostile look you ever gave me, when you saw me for the first time. That was the day classes started at Petresco High School.

BIANCA: We were already scowling at each other.

SILE: In the real world, yes. In the realm of magic, we were already in love.

BIANCA: That day in May, the day of the photo, I remember it perfectly.

SILE: So do I.

BIANCA: I remember everything you said to me.

SILE: So do I.

BIANCA: You made me an offer.

SILE: Really. ?

BIANCA: After you kissed me on the ankle, you got up and ran away.

SILE: Ran away? Me? Come on...

BIANCA: Exactly. You ran away, but an hour later, you came by the dorm and asked for me and you spoke to me.

SILE: Don't remember that.

BIANCA: I came back right away because I had a feeling you would show up... or rather, I hoped you would! When you arrived you were out of breath, and sweating.

SILE: After I left you, I ran until I was out of breath... to punish myself.

BIANCA: What for?

SILE: For not having kidnapped and ravished you, for not asking you to marry me... How should I know?

BIANCA: That's it. At the entrance to the dorms, you offered me all that.

SILE: And you ran away while I was talking. What good does it do to go over all this again?

BIANCA: If the offer still good, my answer is yes.

SILE: I live in a hundred and twenty square feet, I'm crippled, I only make twenty thousand lei a month, and I support my elderly mother.

BIANCA: Will you be able to make love to me every single day?

SILE: Will you be able to get by without a cleaning woman... or make do with having one only once a week?

BIANCA: Will I be able to write in Romanian again?

SILE: You'll write in French. There always was something far away about you.

BIANCA: *(taking him in her arms)* Why do you say that?

SILE: Because you had on almost the same dress twenty years ago...

BIANCA: I think I've finally become a woman.

SILE: How do you know?

BIANCA: I'm finally beginning to remember happiness. I still feel your hands on my body... Finally, I have roots in the present.

SILE: So when do we get married? I suggest the first significant date, March 5th! It's my birthday.

BIANCA: *(frightened)* No! Not March 5th!!!

SILE: Is that a problem?... You're not going to tell me that you believe in omens, are you?

BIANCA: You can't have been born on March 5th.

SILE: You want proof? Here, here's my passport! *(He takes out a green passport and shows it to her.)*

> *Bianca takes out her own passport, garnet-colored, and hands it to him. Each of them looks inside the other's passport.*

SILE: *(stunned)* March 5th!

> *There is a musical interlude.*

SCENE 7: STARTING FROM SCRATCH, PARIS, DAWN

*Bianca is seen, wearing a kerchief to hide her shaved head,
writing or rereading, before she sends it, the following letter.
Nevertheless, the most appropriate thing would be to have a
slide projection of a photo showing Bianca, with shaved head,
smiling and happier than ever before. And at the same time,
her voice would be heard, from offstage.*

My darling, when you took me to the airport you asked me
if I would be able to tolerate, once again, an existence
deprived of material comforts, after the splendors of Paris
and the lifestyle I was accustomed to with my previous almost-
husbands. I didn't give you an answer because I love you and
one can't lie to one's beloved, even in haste... I wasn't sure.
Living in a city plunged into darkness, having occasional hot
water, eating bananas only once a year, perhaps these were
major obstacles, after all... Since my return to Paris, three
days ago, I've slept... three days straight... during which I
dreamed as much as in an entire lifetime. Dreams in
Romanian, mixed with dreams in French. Sometimes you
were twenty years old, other times you were forty... I even
dreamed we were together in an old folks home.

By the way, I don't understand how anyone who loves me as
much as you claim to can go so long without writing or phoning me! It's true you've sent me seven letters and two faxes
but the last news I had of you was a thousand years ago... that
is, two whole days.

When I emerged from my three days of sleep, I awoke with
a clean conscience... I went to the hair stylist... and had him
cut off all my hair. If you run your hand over my head one
way it feels like the cocoon of a silk worm; do it the other
way, it feels like a hedge-hog. They say it will grow out soon...
I don't really know why I did it...

I have a dim memory of having my head shaved when I was six years old and going into the orphanage ... This must mean that a new life is starting... starting from scratch... I'm a late arrival in this story, because you've been in love with me for twenty years and me, only since... we first met... but as a welcoming gift I'm sending you some of my curls which I'll put in the envelope... All this to let you know that bananas once a year and no hot water hold no terrors for me. So I'll return very soon... to your side... and we'll get things started all over again... at the scene of the crime... in a hundred and twenty square feet... The baby is Romanian and must go home... If you really loved me, you should have stopped me at the airport. I know perfectly well that you let me go out of respect for my expressed wishes, but even so... The last time you respected my wishes, it cost us twenty years!

I've let this letter lie around on my desk for days and days. I couldn't bring myself to finish it... I miss you so much and words are so inadequate... I think of you every moment and every moment I miss you... What's more, I didn't feel so well... I received your letter and the airline ticket. Paris to Bucharest, one way... I had to laugh... I'm finishing up my work on youth-without-age, then I'll give it to the publisher and I'll be there. I know that you keep your promises. Do you remember what you promised me? That you're going to give me three children... Last night, I dreamed I saw my illiterate grandmother again, and all the rest of my deceased family. They announced that they had an heir... This morning I took the test. I've been pregnant for a month. We're in the realm of magic and I love you... *(She winks as she seals the envelope.)* The baby is Romanian... and going home... and French will be the baby's mother tongue.

Leïla Sebbar

My Mother's Eyes

Translated from the French by
Stephen J. Vogel

UBU REPERTORY THEATER PUBLICATIONS
NEW YORK

Leïla Sebbar was born in Algeria to an Algerian father and French mother. Both parents were teachers. She studied literature in Aix-en-Provence and then in Paris, where she has been living since 1963. Her original work focused on the myth of the "good Negro" in eighteenth century colonial literature and on education for girls in the nineteenth century, until she turned to fiction. She contributes to several literary revues and to programs of the French cultural radio station, France Culture. She has published essays, short stories, most recently *La Jeune fille au balcon,* le Seuil, 1996, and novels, most recently *Le fou de Schéhérazade,* Stock, Paris, 1991, and *Le silence des rives,* Stock, Paris, 1993 (Kateb Yacine Prize). Several of her essays and novels have been translated into Italian, Dutch, and English and a number of her short stories have been translated into Arabic, German, and English. She has contributed (texts and commentaries) to several photo anthologies, expressing the conflictual relationship between the Northern and Southern shores of the Mediterranean and the diversity of immigrant life. *Les Yeux de Ma Mère (My Mother's Eyes),* her first play, was broadcast by France Culture on April 4, 1994. *Une Enfance algérienne,* an anthology of works by seventeen writers of secular, Jewish, and Muslim background born and raised before Algeria's independence, has been published by Gallimard in 1997.

Stephen J. Vogel has previously translated Anca Visdei's *Always Together,* Daniel Besnehard's *Passengers* and *The White Bear,* all published by Ubu, as well as two other plays by Daniel Besnehard, *A Simple Death (Arromanches)* and *The Child in Obock. The White Bear* was produced by Ubu Rep in 1992. *Always Together* was published by Ubu in *Plays by Women III* in 1996 and produced by Ubu twice to critical acclaim in 1996. Other translations for Ubu Repertory Theater include *All It Takes Is Something Small* by Martine Drai (France), published in Ubu's Anthology *Monologues; The Prophet and the President* by Jean-Luc

Raharimanana (Madagascar), published in *Afrique II; Intelligence Powder* by Kateb Yacine (Algeria); and *The Daughter of the Gods* by Abdou Anta Kâ (Senegal), which was included in the first *Afrique* anthology now out of print. He is co-translator of Raymond Queneau's *En Passant* presented at the French Institute/Alliance Française as part of Théâtre de la Cabriole's *Be-Bop at Saint Germain-des-Prés*. He recently translated *Class Photo* by Anca Visdei (Beaumarchais Foundation grant) which is also part of the Ubu anthology *Playwrights of Exile*.

My Mother's Eyes, in Stephen J. Vogel's translation, had its first staged reading at Ubu Repertory Theater, 15 West 28th Street, New York, New York, 10001, on March 10th, 1997.

CHARACTERS

THE GIRL
THE WOMAN COP
THE YOUNG FIREMAN
THE FIREMAN
TWO COPS

SETTING

A glass information booth in the Paris métro.

Inside a glass information booth in the Paris métro are a girl and two firemen. The girl is sitting behind the formica-covered desk, opening up packets of information pamphlets which she then hurls at the firemen on the other side of the booth.

THE GIRL: Go on! What are you waiting for! Go on! Hit me! What are you here for? Are you keeping me here? I don't need to be watched. You're afraid I'll run away. You're waiting for the cops with the handcuffs. I didn't do anything. I don't know why I'm in this booth. Like behind the window of a storefront. I'm not a whore. I've seen them in Amsterdam behind their windows. Low-class immigrants, every one. You know where they come from? Are you listening when I talk to you? Why are you here? What are you waiting for? You're pleased with yourselves because you stopped a girl on the platform... I wasn't about to throw myself under the subway train. Not that. Never... I'd rather die. You don't say a thing. I'm used to it. It's happened to me before. I know what happens next. But you'll never get me. You hear me? You'll never get me...

She shouts, getting to her feet and throwing the pamphlets in the face of the younger fireman who forces her to sit down again.

THE YOUNG FIREMAN: Take it easy!

THE GIRL: *(shouting)* I am taking it easy. You see how calm I am. You're the one that hit me.

THE FIREMAN: Nobody hit you.

THE GIRL: So, what's all this? Look. You can't see a thing in this booth. I have bruises on my arms. Look. You don't see them? Firemen always carry flashlights. My brother told me that. He wanted to be a fireman, the jerk... In that case, he might be here instead of you... That would be funny, wouldn't it? I've got bruises all over. Who did it, if not you?

THE FIREMAN: We didn't do it, and you know it.

The girl rolls down the sleeves of her black leather jacket. She continues her work, very methodically. The pamphlets litter the floor of the booth.

THE GIRL: Why am I here, shut up in this stinking booth. Why, if you didn't do it? The cops say the same thing, we didn't do it. So who did do it? And that time they tied me up in the café. I hadn't done anything. I was with a friend of mine, a girl. We were having a few beers on the house, waiting for some friends of ours who never showed up. The owner called the police 'cause we got laughing a little too loud. He was scared of us. My friend studied martial arts, like me. She didn't go in for belly dancing, like some of those little bimbos with shit for brains. The owner got scared. We weren't doing anything wrong, though. Sometimes, we were bad. One day, or I should say, one night in a café, with some friends of ours, we trashed everything in sight. The owner got out this club from behind the counter. That guy didn't have a police dog. We wrecked everything in sight, tables, glasses, bottles, the front window. We ran like hell. He never saw us again. But that other time, me and my friend, the karate kid, we didn't do a thing. They showed up, a police van full of 'em. My friend takes off and I wind up in handcuffs. I found myself in some kind of little cell I don't know where it wasn't the hospital. A little room like this booth but without the windows and it smelled of piss, with nothing in it. I sat down on the floor. Here it smells like feet. It must be you with your crummy boots. Okay. I want to get out of here. Let me go. I didn't do anything.

The girl stands up . She throws herself at the shorter of the two firemen. The other fireman brings her under control. She sits down again and continues to hurl pamphlets which start to spill out of the booth.

THE FIREMAN: You got a family?

She lifts her head and shakes her frizzy hair

THE GIRL: And you? Have you got one, a family?

THE FIREMAN: Sure I do. But they're not in Paris. I'm not from around here. I come from Lille.

> *The girl looks at the younger fireman. She parts the tight curls covering her eyes.*

THE GIRL: So, you know Roubaix? It's right next to Lille. I was born in Roubaix. Later, I lived in Saint-Denis. You know it?

THE FIREMAN: Roubaix. I know it. Not Saint-Denis. Your family is in Saint-Denis?

THE GIRL: Yes. Why?

THE FIREMAN: We're going to call them.

> *The girl cries out.*

THE GIRL: No! No! Don't call! They don't know where I am. They don't know anything. They think... No! No! If my father sees me here with the cops, he'll kill me, and my brothers, too. You don't know them. No! Don't call. Give me back my papers. You have no right to take them away from me. If I don't have my papers it's your fault. They're false papers. A false name. Everything is false. The picture is mine. Not the rest. Call, you'll see...

> *An emergency team of police officers arrives at the booth. There are four of them in all, including a woman cop. She enters the booth with two of the men. She leans over the girl.*

THE WOMAN COP: We won't hurt you. Don't be upset. Be reasonable...

THE GIRL: No! No! I don't want to go to the hospital. I won't go to the hospital. Never... No! No! I don't want to. The hospital is awful, no, no...

> *The girl clutches at the edge of the formica tabletop. The woman cop speaks to her, gently.*

THE WOMAN COP: Oh no, it's not so awful. They'll take care of you there, you'll see. Things will get better. If you don't follow orders we'll be giving you an injection, we'll have no choice, it'll be your fault. Calm down now.

> *The girl sits up straight.*

THE GIRL: Anything, but not the hospital. They put me in with the weirdos... I'm not a weirdo... Okay, I shoot up, so what? I do what I want... Not the hospital I'll run away. I'll jump out the window. I did that once already. Afterwards, they shut me up in some special ward. Nobody was allowed to go out. We watched TV and ate chocolate. Old ones, young ones. I stayed cooped-up I don't know how many weeks. Nobody came to see me. A male nurse told me my father wouldn't let my mother come and see me. We were locked in. Men, women. Everybody looked like a bum, crazy clothes, worn-out slippers, dirty skin, some of them, spiky hair in all directions, real ugly, you know... I was the youngest one there so of course they all looked at me, they stopped prowling around like those mangy wolves at the zoo, I used to watch them for hours with my sister behind the iron fence, you see them even from outside, they stopped right in front of me and stared at me, the men, some of the women, too, finally I just stayed in my room, I wouldn't let anybody in, one time I asked one of the male nurses to lock me in because there was this guy that always wanted to talk to me and I didn't want to. He was circling me, I could tell, people think it's so big, the ward, but it's small really.

He was an Arab. I could tell right away. He had gray skin and a black beard, black hair with greasy curls, his eyes were black and oily, like olives, I didn't like him watching me with those eyes, I had the feeling I'd get to be like him, soft in the head, pitiful, almost slippery and slimy like his eyes. He always wore this trenchcoat, the same as Colombo, you know? You've seen him on TV? My little brothers never miss that program and I watch it with them, he's funny, Colombo, but that guy, always following me around with his trenchcoat covered with grease stains and a dirty collar... He was always smoking, his fingernails looked like they were in mourning, where I come from we say that's the devil hiding under your nails. I thought he was disgusting. He came up to me slowly, like nothing was up, as if I couldn't see right through his little trick, he talked, you couldn't understand his words, what language was it? Not Arabic, not French, not Kabyle. I would have recognized it... A mix, no, a mish-mash, and he smoked right down to the butts, he burned his fingertips, he had no feeling in them, maybe? I wonder. It wasn't that I was afraid, he was nice, quiet, I don't know why he was there... They had me shut up there and I was no weirdo. I'm talking to you, I know what I'm saying, I'm not just imagining things like other people that say whatever comes into their heads, it's funny at first later they repeat themselves, you don't want to listen anymore. With him, I just never understood his gobbledygook, not that I really tried, it was like with the other one, the little Korean or Laotian, I don't know which, who used to smile at everybody, all the time, he used to say the names of these cities in Asia, I forget which ones, he spoke this unknown language, I think he made it up, he was all alone, nobody to come and visit him, just like me, he'd escaped a massacre by pirates, one of the nurses told me, but at least he didn't pay any attention to me, like the other one did...

He looked like my father, my father is tall, not stooped over
like him, once by accident I saw him when he was standing
up straight, he was just as tall, my father is handsome, in our
family we say he's handsome, brown-haired with tight curls,
dark, dark eyes, wears a mustache, a solid build, not all bent
out of shape, he was never crippled like other men in our
neighborhood who stay at home keeping an eye on their
daughters and their wife... I think he fits the image too much,
like the guy in the ward, some people mistake him for a Turk
or an Iraqi but for them it's the same thing, meaning he's
an Arab, how could I say he's not. I don't know if my father's
handsome but he's certainly rough, he's rough with us his
daughters, we have to obey him, he's the one who makes all
the decisions even at home, home is the woman's place, my
mother told him, but he keeps saying he's the one who gives
the money and he's the one who's in charge, he's a tyrant.
So even if it is true that he's handsome... this man who
doesn't look like a tyrant, you can't tell any more if he's handsome or not, and it seems to me he's like my father. That surprised me when it first came to me, because it's not at all
obvious... Shut up in my room, I didn't see him any more,
my stomach wasn't tied up in knots as much... I was well-
behaved, the good little girl, all quiet and everything. I asked
to take a walk with one of the female nurses, a fat one from
the Antilles who liked me. I ran away. She couldn't run. I
was already far away when she got back to the ward, the poor
thing... No, no, not the hospital...

THE WOMAN COP: If it isn't the hospital, it's the courtroom.

THE GIRL: I know the courtroom. I'd rather go to the courtroom... But why the courtroom? I haven't done anything.
Nothing at all. Those other times, sure, but now, I haven't
done a thing.

A COP: That's not what we were told...

THE GIRL: So what were you told?

THE COP: You know. Why do you ask questions? You know very well. We know all about you. Girls like you... If it's not you, it's your sister...

THE GIRL: My sister. What are you saying? Leave my sister alone. You know my sister? That would really surprise me. She's dead, if you really want to know, my sister is dead... *(She stands up, tries to upset the table with the formica top, and shouts.)* Why are you talking about my sister. Leave her where she is. She's dead, I tell you, dead... Oh, shit.

THE COP: Take it easy. I didn't know. I'm sorry, I wasn't talking about your sister... It's just an expression... You know, just an expression. Sorry—let's not talk about it any more.

> *The girl is sobbing. One of the cops is calling from a phone booth in the métro, opposite the ticket counter. The girl is crying. She is almost inaudible.*

THE GIRL: She's dead, yes she's dead. You don't believe me. It's true. I didn't believe it either, that she was dead. It was when I saw her body. They called my home, from the morgue. They told my mother that she had to come down to the morgue to identify her daughter's body. My mother was the one who told me. I was hiding out. From time to time, I'd call home from wherever I was without saying the name of the place, my father and my brothers were looking for me. That day I called. I wanted to talk to my mother. She was crying on the phone. She was alone. It was in the afternoon. I didn't understand right away. I couldn't hear well, the phone I was using was a piece of shit. I stayed calm. I told my mother to repeat it. She talked about the hospital, I didn't know why, my sister wasn't sick. She used this word that I didn't understand, she repeated it several times. Finally, I understood. A guy I was friends with, they found him like that in the toilet of some little café, an overdose, it was his brother who told me, he was crying too. We had a few beers, afterwards it was better. I didn't want to explain to my mother over the phone. I told her, "Wait for me, I'll be there," I hadn't seen her for six months or more. She was waiting for me. All by herself. She wasn't crying any more. She was sitting on the sofa, her hands on her dress, a typical Arab woman's dress. She didn't move. She was wearing the same headscarf with the fringe, she buys them on Boulevard Barbès. She didn't get up. She didn't give me a kiss. She said, "Is that you, daughter? Well, what is it? Tell me, do you know? What's all this about, this message from the hospital? Is it serious?" I didn't answer her. I didn't explain anything. I told her to go get her street clothes on. She asked me, "You know where we're going?" I said, "Yes, I know, they're waiting for us." She took her papers. She didn't know where my father was working. He used to change jobs all the time. And my brothers, she never knew where they were hanging out, if they were working or not. The little ones were at school. She thought the morgue was the hospital. I took her by the arm. We didn't speak. She showed her papers. They understood. They told me to explain things to her. They couldn't just take her into the room like that, if she didn't know anything. I sat down next to her. I held her hands. I spoke softly to her. In Arabic. I found the words, that surprised me.

I never wanted to speak Arabic at home. I preferred to learn Kabyle with my girlfriends in our building. I'd rather say that I'm a Kabyle or a Berber, it doesn't scare people as much. I don't say that I'm an Arab. As a matter of fact, I'm not an Arab. My mother didn't understand. I refused to answer her in Arabic, it was her language, with my father, they used to speak in Algerian, she always used to speak to us in the language of her country, with me it was sometimes in French, sometimes in Kabyle, that used to get her so mad. She told my father, one night; he beat me several times, but I didn't give in, he was the one who said to my mother, "You made this daughter, I don't know her." And he never touched me again. At school I was smart, the teacher used to say she was proud that a little Arab girl was her best student in French. One day, why was it? I started being a bad student. I didn't want to keep hearing it all the time, I was even held up as an example, "She's an Arab, a little Algerian girl and in spite of that..." In fact, afterwards, they said, "She has difficulty because she's an Algerian, at her place they must speak Arabic or Kabyle... That's the reason why..."

With my sister, in our room, before she stopped speaking, we made up a language, just for the two of us, it was like a secret cabin and nobody was there to watch over us, even if we weren't all alone there, we had to share the room, it was as if we were all alone. Up until school age, my mother used to speak to us in Arabic. My father enrolled me in an Arabic class, you could study Arabic in school, a teacher from my father's country came just for that. The principal was willing, I told them no. I took a look at the Arab teacher, I didn't like him. I said no. My mother cried because my sister also said no. She wouldn't allow me to watch TV until I agreed to take Arabic. I didn't watch TV for six months. The others put up a fuss, my mother gave in, but she shut my sister and me up in our room when certain programs came on. Afterwards, she forgot about it.

My mother thought that all this was an attack on her and my father, on her country, but that wasn't it. I didn't know how to explain to her. I was next to her. I could feel her warmth and her fear, too. She was like a little girl. And I knew, I was going to explain everything to her. I spoke to her in Arabic, as if I had never spoken another language with my mother. She shivered, even though she wasn't cold, she squeezed my hands, I was talking, talking, sweet words came to me to comfort her before the words of truth, the hardest for her, but she listened to what the language of her mother was saying now in her daughter's mouth, sometimes soft and I could hear her breathe easily, sometimes stiff and she began to pant. She listened to me, to the very end, without a word. Tears fell without stopping, one after the other, my mother stared straight ahead and her tears fell, I no longer recognized her beautiful eyes, famous on both sides of the sea, in our families and beyond, her eyes bright and soft, soft, not always, they shot out flashes sometimes, like the sharp edge of a battle-ax, her eyes fixed straight ahead didn't see me, they were frozen in sorrow. I wiped her tears with the corner of her headscarf, I know she was listening to me, her hands were warm in mine, not like her eyes. She was listening to me, but I was afraid she would start to shriek. *(To the woman cop)* You know how women shriek?

THE WOMAN COP: Oh yes, I know. My parents are Italians from the south, Calabria. You know it?

THE GIRL: No. I don't know it. Except for my neighborhood, Roubaix, Saint-Denis and my mother's town, out in the sticks, I don't know anything... No, that's not true. I've done a lot of traveling, but I don't talk about it.

THE WOMAN COP: That was where I heard the village women, those old hags in black who look so wicked, like witches, almost. They come to your house and shriek over a corpse. I didn't like that when I was little.

THE GIRL: *(interrupting)* Well, neither do I. My mother was crying. I was afraid she was going to start shrieking. I'd heard her do it before, several times, once in her village, another time in our neighborhood with the other women, in the room where they meet, next to the one where they wash the corpse. That was in the village, in our neighborhood they don't wash the corpse, they send him directly from the hospital to the Moslem burial ground or back to his country, in a lead coffin, I know, I saw one they sent by plane, it was an old man, he died in the hospital, but in the village some of the women came to the house, the ones who wash the corpses, that still happens over there, they're scary, they shut themselves up with the corpse, that time it was a woman. A young woman, her baby lived, she didn't. My mother was one of her cousins, she cried and shrieked with the women. My sister and I ran away, we hid out in a little clump of cork trees, not far from the village. I didn't want her to start shrieking, not my mother, not in the waiting room of the morgue. She didn't shriek, fortunately.

I spoke to her in Arabic, softly, after a moment, I was still speaking, she looked at me, her eyes had lost their color, my mother has blue eyes, I told you, that's why my father chose her instead of her sister, she told me that herself, if she comes, you'll see, she'll come, you promised me that, I'm here with you waiting for her, I'll be calm, I'll be calm, her eyes, blue sometimes like stormy seas, sometimes like the clear sky that migrating birds cross in summer, a blue that shimmers in the heat, you see what blue I mean? Her eyes are blue.

THE WOMAN COP: *(keeping an eye on the cops at the telephone)* Yes, I see. Summertime in Calabria, the sky is like you described.

THE GIRL: My mother looked at me, I was speaking in Arabic, it was as if she was listening to me with her eyes, the blue was intense, a stormy color and at the same time soft, I don't know how to explain it, can a person's eyes be hard and tender at the same time? My mother's gaze when I spoke in Arabic was like it was filled with love but I knew she was unhappy then, lost, how could she believe it, that her daughter was dead, far away from her, I couldn't believe it either. Even today I still think she's not dead.

Two cops enter the booth.

A COP: We're taking her in.

The girl backs up to the window, her arms protecting her face as if they were about to beat her.

THE COP: We're not going to hurt you. You come with us. It's easy. Otherwise... It won't help to get all worked up. Lashing out in all directions, like that. It's no use. Get up. Otherwise...

The girl struggles furiously. She screams.

THE GIRL: And those? What're they for? I've seen things like those before at the nuthouse. Leather wrist restraints... They're to tie me up. I'm not crazy, I told you. I don't want to go to the hospital. I want to see my mother.

THE COP: Okay. All right. Sit down. If you calm down, we'll call your mother. She'll come. We'll wait for her.

THE GIRL: Is that so? My mother is coming to get me? She'll take me home with her. I want to go home... I want to see my mother...

The woman cop, standing next to the girl, signals the young fireman to hide the wrist restraints.

THE WOMAN COP: She'll come, your mother. We're calling her. She'll be here soon. We're going to wait for her here with you, calmly and quietly.

THE GIRL: Will she take me home with her? Is she coming to get me? All by herself. Tell her over the phone, tell her to come all by herself... Otherwise, I'm staying right here. I'm so tired... I want to see my mother, all by herself, all by herself. We'll leave here together. We'll go to her little house in the village, beside the sea, you go down a path and there it is, the sea. With my sister we used to go there when we were little, we tossed knucklebones, like dice, under the fig tree in the courtyard and we went down to look at the sea. We didn't swim. My grandfather used to tell us scary stories about monster-women hiding behind the rocks, he told us that the sea is dangerous, that evil spirits could kidnap us under the waves, we believed him, we were little.

He used to say that his daughter's children, schooled in France, would be lost to him, to the country. He told my mother, his daughter, that as long as he was alive, he would do everything in his power so that we didn't become lost children. At the hour when he should have been taking his nap, he called us together, my sister, myself, two of our brothers, they were still being obedient back then, we sat down around him, cross-legged, he gave each of us a thin board that he had cut and carved himself, modeled after the one that he'd kept from the days when he went to Koran school, and to write with, a reed, carved to a point, which he called a "calam." He made ink out of burnt sheep's wool, we really liked all that, we weren't used to it, but when it came to learning suras from the Koran and making the letters of the Arabic alphabet, before writing out sentences from memory... Well... My grandfather had a long switch made from olivewood that he would beat us with if we didn't listen. How many times my sister cried, I didn't cry, I ran away. To punish me, my mother kept me from celebrations, from long walks to see the marabout, my sister begged me to stay with her while she studied the Arabic of the Koran, my brothers shouted insults at me in Arabic, in Kabyle, they had Kabyle playmates back in our neighborhood in France, in French, I said no, and I took a nap like the other children stretched out on a mat in the shade in the bedroom, at that time of day. My grandfather told my mother that my sister was a good student and she should leave her in the country with her sister, she would go to school with her cousins, she would learn the language of the Ancestors, not like me.

My mother wouldn't have said no, my sister said that she was willing to stay, if I stayed, too. I said no. My grandfather asked my mother if by any chance I knew how to say yes. I would have said yes to going back because of the sea and the birds, I used to hunt them with the boys, with a sling, a sling made out of pomegranate wood, I wasn't allowed, I knew it, my mother kept telling me it wasn't a game for little girls, but me, playing house with my dollies in the courtyard, always shut inside, that, never.

I never saw the sea again, or my mother's country, either. My father threatened to send me to a tribal village, which tribe, I never heard mentioned, he brings up the tribe every time things go wrong at home, and the old uncle who can bring back the honor of the sons and daughters who've lost their way in France... I ran away before the trip back to the tribe... I'd like to have a look at the sea. My father said no, no summer camps by the seaside, because of the bathing suits, even for the swimming pool at school he wouldn't let us, and because of the boys. Summer camps for girls only, that doesn't exist any more, my father didn't understand they put the boys with the girls and the girls undress, he said to my mother that with a bathing suit, even a one-piece suit his girls would be completely naked. He never wanted that. Later on, it was too late. I haven't seen it now, the sea, since my summer over there, I was seven years old. We don't go over there for our vacations any more. My grandfather died last year, my mother didn't have the money for the trip. She cried for her father but she stayed in our neighborhood. We kids had forgotten him.

With my mother, she's coming here to get me, we'll go back to her house, in the village, it's my mother's house, now, nobody can stop us. My mother will take me back to her house. Both of us, my mother and me, in her house.

The cop who telephoned her family enters the booth.

THE COP: Nobody's there. Once it was busy. Afterwards, nothing. I called I don't know how many, three, four times, nobody. What do we do? We bring her in or we wait some more? I'm trying. If there's nobody there...

THE GIRL: *(to the woman)* I'm calm. You see. Not like a little while ago... I could have smashed everything in sight. I insulted the firemen, they were hurting me, they ran after me on the platform, they wrestled me to the ground. They hurt me —insulting law officers—give me a break... We'd all be behind bars... I'm calm. You're my witness. I'm waiting for my mother. She's going to come, right, she's going to come... She can't leave me like this... At the hospital they won't want me to talk, even with my mother. She's going to come. I'm waiting, I'm calm, I'm not shouting, here in this office there aren't any more pamphlets to throw. I'm waiting. You too?

THE WOMAN COP: *(checking the time)* Our shift will be over pretty soon. They'll be sending our replacements. I'm not going to be staying much longer. Don't worry, they'll find your mother for you, she'll come.

THE GIRL: I'm waiting for her. I know she'll come. She'll say she has no luck with her children, her daughters, her sons, they get by, she doesn't know how, she doesn't ask questions, they never say anything, she keeps saying she doesn't want any police at her house, that's all. Now, she's going to be afraid, if the cops phone, she's going to think that I'm dead... What I think she does, my mother, is just pretend she doesn't notice anything. They say that blue eyes, not all of them, some, hers for sure, can see right through secrets and metal doors, her eyes are made of diamond, it's true. She acts as if... She covers her head and her eyes with the veil which she never wears in France, in her country, yes, but she's gotten out of the habit and she says she doesn't see anything bad, she doesn't hear any of the evil things people say. The vicious gossip, you know? Where you come from, in Calabria, there's a lot of vicious gossip going around?

THE WOMAN COP: Where I come from, vicious gossip goes around whenever people are bitter. That kind of gossip is never about anything good, never, and it likes the sound of its own voice, you know what I mean...

THE GIRL: *(interrupting)* Do I ever... In our neighborhood, it kills more than any weapon. The girls especially. People talk about the boys, but it's like when they get in trouble it's something to brag about. I know some of them. I know all of them, I can tell you that almost every one, except for the youngest, is mixed up in something sneaky, some kind of shitty business... They call that being on the job, believe it or not. If they were really on the job they wouldn't get themselves arrested all the time... They're pathetic, little thieves, little pushers, little pimps, they're completely useless to anyone and then later they whine and snivel about other people being racist or whatever. I know all about them. I'll never work with them. They're just a bunch of poor Arabs and if they get treated like dirt that's tough. They're just a bunch of assholes. You'd never catch me with one of the guys from my neighborhood. I've never been to bed with an Arab, and I never will... Why am I telling you all this... Because nobody's listening in this booth and we're all going to die of asphyxiation...

THE WOMAN COP: *(leaning over the girl)* I'm listening to you.

THE GIRL: Whatever you say... It doesn't matter. I'm not talking for your benefit. I'm talking because, that way, I can wait for my mother. She's going to come. I'm waiting for her. I'm talking, that way I'm calm and I won't go to the mental hospital.
With my mother we waited. My mother is patient. Not me, but that time I was patient. For my sister, she didn't know where she was, she'd never heard of the morgue. I explained

gently, for a long time... I was so afraid she'd shriek. She didn't shriek. Finally she understood. She got up, she waited for someone to take her into the refrigerated room. She held me by the hand. What I saw... I saw my sister under a big white sheet. Where we come from the corpse is put in a shroud, white, like that one, all wrapped up and we tie a knot at the feet and the head, I saw that once in the village, I was little, I went into the room, I wasn't supposed to, I hid and I watched.

My mother looked at my sister, laid out under the sheet and she said, "It's my daughter, yes, it's my daughter, it's her." She stood there for a long time, without moving. I took her by the arm. We went out. She didn't cry. She didn't talk. They only let her see the face. The man in the white jacket wouldn't let my mother see her daughter's body. She complained. He told her to get out. They wanted her to identify her daughter, that was all. My mother didn't know that the medical expert had already performed an autopsy, they told me so, but for my mother it was as if her daughter had lost her soul, if you open up a body, the soul flies out. The body must remain intact otherwise the angels won't claim the soul. My mother told me, I've never forgotten. Angels, great numbers of them, wrench the soul from the veins, the nerves, the blood, they draw it up through the throat and with the last gasp of breath, one of the angels carries it off on the tip of his spear. For my sister, it was the spear of light. That's what my mother thinks, she doesn't know she committed suicide. My sister committed suicide, I know, they told me so. I made up some story for my mother's sake. Where we come from, suicide is forbidden. My mother would have thought my sister's soul was impaled on the angel's spear of wrath. Suicide is shameful for the whole family. I told her she was in a car accident and that she died instantly. She believed me. I loved my sister. Always together, since we were little, everywhere, all the time. People thought we were twins. My mother dressed us alike. She was the one who made our dresses, our skirts, almost everything. The rest she bought at Tati's. And then, one day I never knew why, we were sort of separated. At school we were in the same class, at the same table, we asked to be, they put us next to each other everywhere, even in the lunch room. At camp too we slept side by side... We did everything together. Why did it happen? What caused it? I never knew. Nobody could understand it. All at once, just like that, my sister stopped talking. Mute. From one day to the next. My mother took her to all the hospitals, and to the marabouts too, finally my sister refused. The doctors couldn't figure it out or else they didn't want to tell us anything, I don't know. Things didn't work out with the marabouts either. My mother spent a lot of money on them. My sister refused to go out. She stayed shut up at home, silent. She helped my mother, she took care of the kids. She watched TV. I used to bring her books from the library. She didn't speak. I cried for days and days, afterwards I didn't cry any more. I told her to write me little notes, but even that she refused to do. She didn't talk, and I talked to her all the time when I was still living at home. There came a time when I didn't want to live at my mother's any more, sharing a room with my silent sister. I was suffocating, I couldn't take it any more. I was afraid of myself... of what I might do to my sister to get her to talk. Once, I almost beat her up... I could have killed her, I was that enraged... And my mother, she'd planned everything out for her, right before misfortune struck. Because no matter what the women next door said about the advantages for a man, a husband, in having a silent wife at home... they say it helps keep peace between husbands and wives... my sister's fiancé abandoned her when he found out. Would my sister have even wanted him? My mother had helped her embroider her entire trousseau. I never wanted that, sewing, knitting, embroidering, cooking, all that stuff... My mother never tried to get me a husband... for my sister, yes. She was docile, attentive, skillful. She embroidered sheets, pillowcases, napkins, satin negligees,

dishcloths, bathrobes, tablecloths, she crocheted table mats...
I admired her, I couldn't have done it. She made some for
me, I just giggled, I said I wouldn't be needing that, me, married?... She said and so did my mother, "You'll see... You'll
be very happy..." But I didn't really give a damn.

THE WOMAN COP: *(interrupting)* My mother and my grandmother also embroidered my trousseau and I learned how.
When I got married, I had everything. Your mother was right...

THE GIRL: *(continuing)* My sister kept the linens for her
trousseau in a big metal trunk, my mother bought it for her
on Barbès, hand-wrought and silver-plated, it's so pretty, it
was her hope chest, it looks like a coffin. Once she showed
me the dishes she was hiding among her embroidered night-
gowns. My mother had bought everything a young married
couple needs, it was lovely and useless. I wasn't jealous. My
mother said she was first going to marry off her oldest daughter, that was the custom, then the younger ones. My sister
was older than me, it was normal, my mother taking charge
of my trousseau without consulting me... I told her I wasn't
even interested. She wouldn't listen to me. Together we went
to the bridal department at Tati's to pick out the wedding
gown. We had a good time. My sister tried on all the gowns...
and she wasn't the only one, everywhere there were mothers with their daughters, they came in from the sticks. My
sister is beautiful, like my mother, more beautiful than me,
the customers and the sales clerks just gaped at her, dazzled,
I'm not lying, the girls who still hadn't found husbands were
so envious, she'd make a magnificent bride, but the Arab
women, I don't know if it was just a coincidence, but they
were all Arabs, they came from far away to the bridal department of Tati's, they didn't make too big a fuss, not too loud,
not too shrill, my mother would've shut them right up,
because of the evil eye. The girls were planning to get married in white with lace and a veil like my sister. My mother

chose a long veil which covered her like the veils where we come from, but transparent, a light gauze. The future husband was somebody my sister didn't know. He was a distant cousin, a man of the tribe, as my father put it, he had studied medicine over there, he was coming to France for his internship, my mother had planned the whole thing for a long time, she had received a photo from the photographer's studio, my sister didn't say a thing when she saw the photo, she didn't say no to the marriage. She had her diploma in dressmaking, she'd go and live over there, in the capital, they were looking for seamstresses to start some high fashion salons. My mother had arranged everything. My sister never said no to my mother's plans for her. Everything was perfect. I saw the photo of the fiancé, we used to talk about the fiancé who would soon be arriving, I didn't like his looks, but he was my sister's fiancé, not mine... He was older than her, but that was normal, fifteen years, I think or maybe ten, I guess... He had a nice job, an apartment, my sister wouldn't be living with the mother-in-law, a car, he was a good Moslem, his beard was kind of reddish but maybe the picture didn't do it justice. My mother was happy. She kept saying she couldn't have found anyone better and besides, the other candidates she'd seen just didn't measure up. Not one of them.

My mother's eyes had never been so blue. My father commented on it. He said to her, "Who's the one getting married, you or your daughter?" "Why do you say that?" My father said laughing, "It's your eyes that are talking, not your mouth." It was true. Her eyes were singing the color blue, the sea, love.

And my sister, suddenly, stopped talking. My mother wasn't worried about it at first. Disaster couldn't strike like that, so harsh, so ruthless, in the midst of so much joy. The fiancé came to our home. He saw my sister, he liked her but she didn't speak, not a word. My mother reassured him, asked him to be patient, he stayed with an uncle, longer than planned, almost six weeks, my sister remained silent. He went

away, he said we'd deceived him, that he'd lost his honor and that one day... Throughout the neighborhood vicious rumors circulated. People said my sister was no longer a virgin, that it was all a trick. My mother had told us about marriage, about customs, about the wedding night, she described her own wedding, blue and happy, like her eyes. The blood on the sheet she could describe with perfect ease... I understood right away. She explained it to us, I found it barbaric, I told her, I kept saying, "It's rape," even though my mother slapped me for it. My sister said nothing. She wasn't outraged like me. My mother talked some more about tradition, honor, the tribe... I'd stopped listening. My sister made no sign of protest. My sister was a virgin, I'm sure of it. Vicious gossip is what killed her that's what I think. She was a virgin. Not like those girls who have themselves sewn up again, I know some of them, because the man's family wants a blood wedding. And the doctors who do it they're all bastards and the girls who get themselves sewn up again are they virgins or whores? The fiancé went away. My sister didn't cry.
I know she committed suicide. I didn't tell anybody. Here I am telling you, I don't know you, or you. I'm talking. You're listening to me, you're not listening to me... it's the same thing. I'm waiting for my mother. She's going to come. She's never once abandoned her children. I know some girls, older than me, they abandoned their child at birth. Would you do a thing like that?
Where we come from, people don't like illegitimate kids. If a girl who isn't married has a child, she makes him disappear, any way she can... I mean, she kills him... or she leaves him somewhere. In our neighborhood, a neighbor is raising her daughter's son. She ran away like me, and one day she showed up at her mother's house with a child, no father, he'd disappeared, the girl never saw him again. Her own father didn't want the kid, even though it was a boy, and he only had daughters, they tell us often enough that having daughters is a great misfortune, seven daughters... He said he was

going to take a second wife in order to have a son, he didn't
do it, think maybe he had another wife back in his country
and seven sons over there? He said he was building a house
in his village, he never wanted to take his wife and his daughter there. The mother kept the child in spite of her husband,
she kept repeating that he'd come from her own daughter's
womb, that he was part of the family, her grandson, she wasn't
going to deny him. She loved that child more than anything.
He wasn't her daughter's son any more, he was her own son.
The daughter left home. She came back from time to time,
but her son no longer knew that she was his mother, she, not
his grandmother. He called her Imma—and his mother when
she came to see him, he didn't call her anything. He sensed
that his grandfather didn't love him, he avoided him, never
in the same room, it was the grandmother that told my mother
all that, they'd known each other since the beginning of the
neighborhood, they moved in at the same time. They're the
same age, I think, married over there, at sixteen... younger
than me... I'm about to turn eighteen... legal age... My father
says it's twenty-one where we come from, but I'm not living
back in the tribe... Here, it's eighteen... A child, the first, at
sixteen... I won't be having a child. It's better that way. My
mother has seven. She says it's over now. She's not old. I think
she's not even forty. Maybe forty-two, she doesn't know exactly.
Okay. It's stifling here in this booth. How many of us are there
in here, two firemen, a cop, you, me...
Can I go out for a breath of air?

She gets up. The firemen force her to sit down again.

THE WOMAN COP: Easy, take it easy.

A FIREMAN: You don't know how strong she is. She's a bundle of nerves. You'd think you were pinching her nerves.
She's tough, she's wired... I don't know how we're going to
get her into the van...

THE OTHER FIREMAN: We're going to tie her up. Like a deer, hanging by her hands and feet from a strong pole, carrying the pole on our shoulders like a hunting party, when you come back with the animal wounded or dead, and still warm...

THE WOMAN COP: *(interrupting)* What are you talking about? You think that's going to calm her down? You just say whatever comes into your head, don't you? Leave her alone.

THE FIREMAN: Whatever you say... You'll see what happens if she breaks loose...

> *The girl presses her face against the glass, as if to breathe in the air coming in from the métro. Suddenly she gives a start and runs to the desk to hide underneath. A young man passes by without looking toward the booth, he jumps the turnstile, the cops being busy elsewhere.*

THE WOMAN COP: *(bending down to talk to the girl)* What's going on? What wrong with you? You're shaking. Are you sick?

THE GIRL: Has he gone? Can you still see him...

THE WOMAN COP: Who do you mean?

THE GIRL: The boy in the leather jacket and the jeans, is he still wearing those worn-out cowboy boots?

THE WOMAN COP: Who is that boy?

THE GIRL: Is he there?

THE WOMAN COP: No. I don't see any boy like that. Of course, they all look alike. Over by the news vendor, there are three of them, you can't tell them apart. Jacket, jeans, sneakers, all the same. Except for the hair, and if you look closely, their skin color. But seen from here, they look like shadows through this dirty window...

THE GIRL: So, he's gone then?

THE WOMAN COP: I don't see one with cowboy boots. Who was he?

THE GIRL: That was my older brother. I know he goes out looking for me, when he has time. He doesn't make a big thing out of it, like my father did at first, but if he ever finds me... well... it won't be the hospital, or the courtroom, it'll be right back to the sticks... And once you're back there, forget about ever leaving, everybody's watching you, you've got no papers, no way are you going to escape. I don't want to die in some prison over there. Not that, or else forced to get married to some awful guy, shut up inside, and when you go out, there's the desert. It happened to a friend of mine, one of her cousins told me about it, it's pure hell. She hired a private detective to steal the girl back, a really fantastic story. Over here, the men in the family had kidnapped her and smuggled her off to a village in the south, the desert is all around like you're on an island in the middle of a storm, all the time, and big scary rocks... It's fine if you want to die, you walk a little in the dunes, you get lost and you die because nobody goes looking for you. She wasn't even penned up. The whole village kept an eye on her. So, a detective to sneak the girl back here... She wanted to be kidnapped again not by the same ones of course, and with a whole different destination. Did she really stand waiting behind the iron bars on her window, like they say in the stories? Maybe the detective disappeared with half the money he was supposed to get, the other half he'd get if the operation was a success. The cousin paid him a lot, where did she find the money? As for the girl, I don't know what happened to her. I haven't seen the cousin, maybe she's a prisoner too in some little place out in the desert... That's how they are, over there, they're crazy, worse than here... That's why my brother, the older one, the other one isn't so bad, he'd help me, but he doesn't dare because of our older brother, if he ever finds me...

THE WOMAN COP: You can sit down. We're calling your home. We're trying to get your mother on the line.

> *One of the young firemen is playing with the wrist restrainers. The girl watches him, as if fascinated. She speaks, her eyes staring straight ahead, barely audible.*

THE GIRL: I got there. I wasn't all by myself. There were three of us. We didn't know each other. We were in the same police van, and later in the same cell. A cell for one person, there were three of us inside. Pure hell. We fought all the time. A sink in one corner for washing, washing ourselves, washing our underwear, the toilet in the same place with just a board waist-high to hide your ass, for the rest people turn their backs, a tiny cupboard, things falling out of it, a wobbly table, narrow, no drawers, we put everything on the beds and to top it off they were bunk beds... Everything, ha!... what little we had in our suitcase shoved under our pillow. We could never decide on a TV program, I had no money, nobody came to see me, I no longer had a sister... My mother, my father didn't want to. I saw the lawyer, but I didn't like her. I went out for sports activities, to the library, even if it wasn't to read, at the end I read a little, I really liked love stories that took place in faraway countries, I found a few of those. I used to read. In the cell, the light is poor. Somebody loaned me a reading lamp, a friend I knew from sports, but the other girls always wanted to sleep after watching TV. What I was looked for on TV was news about my neighborhood in Saint-Denis, where they were always rioting. We saw other neighborhoods torn to pieces but not mine. Finally one day, we couldn't stand each other any more, we started shouting all three of us, we hurled insults, called each other every name in the book...

I was coming back from the library, and what do I see? Rimbaud ripped in two, his eyes poked out, his hair scribbled over with soot, like when you write with a piece of burned cork, we used to do that on the walls in our neighborhood, the names of the girls we didn't like right next to the name of a boy, the worst punk we knew. If the girl's father knew how to read, he'd tan her hide... When we'd hear her screaming, we'd burst out laughing. It was fun. There was a little group of us, my sister didn't want to come along, we were into combat sports and boxing, my sister chose dancing, this was at the Young People's Center, one time we got into a fight with some guys who were out to rape us, we trashed everything, my father never found out about it... I would've really gotten it then... I walk into the cell and I see Rimbaud slaughtered. First I didn't say anything. I just stood there next to the poster. You've seen that picture of Rimbaud before, the one where he's so handsome, so young... You know Rimbaud?

THE WOMAN COP: *(smiling)* Who doesn't know Rimbaud? That's all people talk about, you see him everywhere, that same face, everywhere, there must be only one picture of him, not like other people... Oh sure, I know him. He's very pale, he's in black and white but his hair must be like straw and his eyes are light-colored.

THE GIRL: *(interrupting)* He has the blue eyes of Nordic people. His hair is blond, gold-colored, soft and fine like a little child's. Have you read his poems?

THE WOMAN COP: No. Never. I haven't had the chance.

> *The woman cop keeps a sharp eye on the corridors of the métro. The girl's mother may arrive at any moment.*

THE GIRL: Well, I learned two poems by Rimbaud at school I know them by heart, if you want, I can recite them to you, I'm never going to forget them. My mother wanted to teach us prayers, my mother is very devout, she prays five times a day, she taught my sister, I pretended, for a while, later I didn't want to. My mother gave my sister a little prayer rug, to me too, I rolled it up under my bed. After school my sister went with my mother into her room with her little rug, she put on a head scarf, like my mother and they both prayed, sometimes I sat on the edge of the bed, I stroked the pink satin bedspread with the swansdown lining. My mother had bought it on Barbès with us along, she'd saved for years, she'd dreamed for so long of this bed spread worthy of a trousseau. Well, I thought it was awful, I didn't say so to my mother. It's smooth, satin. I stayed seated while the prayer was going on, I listened to them, I was happy enough, but I didn't want to do it, to learn those verses by heart. It was Rimbaud I recited, like my mother and sister recited prayers. "Wandering" and "Romance" were my favorites. I read others too, some very, very long, I liked the titles, but I didn't catch on too well, I didn't learn them by heart. "A Season in Hell," that's a beautiful title, don't you think?

So, I was calm, I come back from the library, real calm, and my poster... Calmly, I strolled over to the poster that belonged to the girl who didn't like me, hers was Madonna, her hair is black she spends all her money at the hairdresser's in prison to make herself as blond as Madonna, she dresses like her, she makes her own clothes like what she sees her idol wearing on TV and in the magazines she collects, she wears the same make up, nobody has the nerve to tell her she's overdoing it... I told her once, she took her revenge on Rimbaud. I pulled her poster down, I stood right square in front of her and her friend both sitting on the edge of the bed, they didn't move a muscle, and I tore it up slowly, into little pieces that I scattered all around the room. The other one, her friend said, "Stop, stop, don't touch James Dean."

Hers was James Dean. I didn't touch her little American faggot. I simply said, "Your faggot, you can wipe your ass with him." That's when they jumped me, both of them. The Madonna one shouted insults at me. I knew the Capo would be there soon, the sadistic nun we called her the Capo but I couldn't hold off any more... The one I didn't like accused me of having AIDS, I know some girls get AIDS, everybody knows it, young kids, Arabs, junkies, the Arabs, I know them, I don't go out with them. We don't get along. I told her, "Say it again." She said it again screaming like a maniac, I threw myself at her, I wiped the floor with her, she was smaller than I was... I could have killed her. The guard arrived, she opened the door, she saw me going wild, I hit her with my fists, she screamed, she rolled around on the floor. The guard called for help, other people came running. They put me in solitary, and after the hearing, in a prison cell. That's when they put the wrist restraints on me and tied me to the iron bed bolted to the floor. They gave me a sleeping pill. I woke up... I asked to be by myself. But they told me there wasn't enough room, that was only for political prisoners. I asked what you had to do to be political. They didn't answer.

A cop enters the booth. He speaks to the woman, telling her that he finally got hold of the mother, that she was home alone, that's she's on her way. But since she isn't familiar with Paris, she'll be bringing a friend along, a woman who lives nearby. The girl hears none of this. She says nothing to the cop.

THE GIRL: You know how long I've gone without seeing my mother? You won't believe me. If I told you where I've been, what I've done... The slammer, the nuthouse, that's nothing by comparison... You think I'm bragging, that it's all in my head, like some movie I saw, it's no movie, it's real. I'm young, I know it, but I'm old, too. You're a cop, you see a lot of bastards, bums, cops, losers, crazies, whatever, well I've seen even more than you, a hundred, a thousand times more. I know

you won't believe me even if I tell you, I haven't got any proof, here in this glass booth I made a mess of, that's nothing next to what I've seen, and what I've done. I've pulled some fast ones, I won't go into details. I've gone a long way, about as far as you can go, in all kinds of shitty business, sex, money, coke, as far as you can go away from here, too, so as not to hurt my mother or my sister. I don't give a damn about the others, but my mother's home, that's sacred. So, as far away as possible... because I've been with the devil, and I've been the devil. My mother knows nothing. If anybody ever tells her, I'll kill him. If you or some other cop tells her... I want my mother to act like my mother, not to reject me, to say to me, "You're my daughter, you know you are, a mother whose daughter came from her womb, that's her daughter she won't curse her. You are my daughter. My little girl, my big girl, you know you are, I haven't forgotten it, and you won't forget that I'm your mother, your only mother," I'm going to see her, she won't be afraid, even if she sees me dressed like this, I know she doesn't like black, or mini-skirts or black stockings. Where we come from the girls don't dress like this, except for whores, but they keep themselves hidden you don't see them in the streets over there... I know my mother doesn't approve of girls who wear black leather jackets, or wear leather bracelets with metal studs, or have tangled-up hair that covers their eyes, she's going to think I'm a girl who's not a girl, just a street punk, but she won't say that I'm not her daughter, that she won't say. She'll say, "Come home with me, don't be afraid, I'm here."
I haven't seen my mother for so long. She'll never know that I've been in porno films, she doesn't even know that they exist, she won't know that the emirs in their palaces had secret rooms built that are more beautiful than those in the stories of the sultana Scheherazade... You know "The Arabian Nights?"

THE WOMAN COP: Sure, I know about it. I go to a restaurant where they serve grilled meat, it's Lebanese, I think, it's called

"Sharazad." The maître d' told us about the Sultana and "The Arabian Nights," that's how I know about it, but I haven't read it.

THE GIRL: Me neither, I haven't read it, it's my mother who told me. If she only knew that I've lived in those heavenly palaces... It's really true that it's like being in heaven, the indoor gardens, the fountains, the mosaics, the exotic birds and the gazelles... the red pomegranates and the peacocks... everything they tell you about is true. The women who come from far away, women of every color, but they prefer blonds... and they like them very young... I'll tell you when it comes to virgins they're wild about them, and they're ready to pay any price... But you'd better not try to fool them. I saw a girl get beaten who'd lied and she was kicked out without a centime... You don't believe me? Tough. What I'm telling you is the truth. My mother doesn't know how much I sold my virginity for in a bridal chamber, honored, celebrated, I wasn't mistreated, just the opposite. The emir who chose me over the other girls, the ones more beautiful than those models you see on magazine covers, he wasn't so old, he must have been around my uncle's age, maybe thirty, thirty-five. I could have stayed. He gave me jewelry that I sold to buy coke when I got back. I had a wardrobe fit for a princess... My sister's trousseau, by comparison... I thought about her, about what I could have given her, but I didn't have time to give any gifts. The emir wanted to keep me even though I wasn't a virgin any more, I was the only brunette among those blonds that I thought were so beautiful, much more beautiful than me. But one day he conned me into taking part in an orgy. He threatened me, I gave in. I was living in a kind of harem with the other girls in these private apartments. We had black women, former slaves, who served us, we chatted away in every known language and women's body language is the same all over the world... It was fun but the orgies with other princes, they were princes, they sure didn't

act like princes... I didn't really care for that. One day, I ran away, I spent a few days at the house of a black woman, a servant, in town and I came back here, where I was born. I was rich, rich. It didn't last long... The life of a slave after a glimpse of heaven... You don't believe me, I can tell. You're a cop and you don't know a thing. You know your beat and that's it. I've traveled all over... Desert palaces, do you believe me? You believe me, you don't believe me, I could care less... It's my mother I want. My mother, her eyes, they're unique, I told you, even the women in the far north don't have eyes like that maybe because their skin is too white and their hair is too blond, their eyes fade away when I think of my mother's. I miss my mother's eyes. I missed them before. Who would have imagined, my mother's eyes are as soft for me as her arms were when I was small, and she used to sing to me in her language, I was alone, she sat cross-legged on the thick carpet of red and black wool, I was small but not very small, she cradled me, not for long, because my sister was waiting for her turn, her thumb stuck in her mouth, and her voice was light and clear as if she were singing with her eyes. Well, I want to see my mother, her blue eyes that sing even if she's angry, because I'm in this glass booth, shut up with some cops, even if she sees me dressed like this... I won't tell you the rest, it's no use, you think it's not the same and it's always the same, the same bastards, the same shit, the same old story of sex, money, coke. It's the country that changes, but not for long, and then you clear out. I want to see my mother.
I want to see my mother and my sister. My mother and my sister. The others, I don't want to see. Only my mother and my sister.

THE WOMAN COP: *(looking at her, astonished)* But, your sister... you told me, a little while ago...

THE GIRL: What did I tell you?

THE WOMAN COP: You said that your sister...

THE GIRL: I talked about my sister?

THE WOMAN COP: Yes. You said that she's dead.

THE GIRL: That's not true. I didn't say that. Why do you say such awful things. My sister, dead? Since when? You're talking nonsense...

THE WOMAN COP: It was you, just a while ago... You've forgotten...

THE GIRL: I haven't forgotten anything. Nothing at all. I know what I'm saying. My sister isn't dead... You'll believe anything. I told some stories. That's what I like to do, tell stories and have people believe me. You know what? They do believe me. It's true. I tell everything as if it were true...

THE WOMAN COP: So... It wasn't true...

THE GIRL: My sister, she's going to come with my mother. You're going to see her. I know they'll both be here. I'm waiting for them. You too?... The prison, that's false, the princes from the Gulf States, that's false... It's all false, false... I tell you this stuff as a joke... I'm waiting for my mother. Everything I told you is bullshit, everything. My mother has blue eyes, that part's true. I'm waiting for my mother and my sister.

THE WOMAN COP: I'm staying right here, long as they haven't sent our replacements. Those are the orders, we wait.

THE GIRL: If you're still here with me, you'll see her, my sister. She's alive. I swear it. I was bullshitting you a while ago. She looks like my mother, a younger version, of course... I'm like my father, that's what they tell me, brown skin, black hair, too frizzy, once I shaved it all off. I don't want to look like my father, but if they say so... my mother is a real beauty... yes, she's so beautiful, my sister, too... Not like me. I look like an Arab, too much so... I've sure got the face of an Arab, don't you think?

THE WOMAN COP: I don't know... Maybe a little...

THE GIRL: Sure I do. If I didn't, I wouldn't keep getting arrested all the time. Okay, sure, what I wear... I get noticed. My hair is too frizzy, I don't cut it any more, a real mop-top. You noticed?

THE WOMAN COP: It gets in your eyes, a little... doesn't that bother you?

THE GIRL: No, not at all. For me it's like the veil. When I need it, it comes in handy. I hide behind it. I like that. Especially when they ask me questions. You can't see my eyes... They don't like that... Like a good little girl with lowered eyes... Like a woman behind her veil... The good Moslem woman... *(She laughs.)* Somebody called me a foolish virgin and my sister a wise virgin... I don't know who, but I still remember it. It cracked me up at the time. A foolish virgin... If my mother only knew... My poor mother... If she only knew. But I don't go to bed with Arabs except for money, the ones from the Gulf States, and the rich ones from the Côte d'Azur or from London... I know them all, I despise them with their pinkie rings and their shirts custom-made because they have lousy bodies, they have their initials embroidered, they're just pigs... My mother told me that pork makes you sick, it's true, she says you'll go to hell if you eat it... I don't eat it, but those big tubs of lard, they've got so much cash and it's so easy.. . Some of my friends are Arabs, not all. Arabs, I don't go to bed with. Once I said no to a guy, he turns to me and says, "It's 'cause I'm an Arab?" I said yes. He hit me, but I hit him right back, they had to pull us apart. He called me a

whore, a harki*, daughter of a harki, granddaughter of a
harki, he insulted my mother, he said I only went with the
Cheese, that's what they call Frenchmen, and that I stink like
they do... If I'd had a weapon... Ever since I carry a switch-
blade. If my mother knew all that... She'd start to shriek and
scratch my cheeks like the women do where we come from...
They're completely insane. My mother, I don't want to make
her go insane. I don't tell her anything. Only the things that
are good for her. She believes me, my sister too. They're
going to come. My mother and my sister. They're the ones
I love. Only them. The others... I don't want to talk about it.
I think she's really beautiful, my sister. Not me. She doesn't
seem as much like an Arab as me. Her hair is long, curly, not
frizzy. Light brown. So many times I've combed it out. It's
soft and heavy. She let me do what I wanted. We both
laughed. I created different hair styles using satin ribbons,
flowers, bridal jewelry that my mother loaned us, she told
us to be careful, that that was our dowry, I laughed at all
those stories about trousseaus and dowries... I made fun of
her, she said, "You'll understand later on." We didn't understand anything, we didn't have to understand, not her, not
me. Now my mother's stopped telling my sister to put on a
head scarf before she goes out, she just asks her to braid her
hair, because long hair like hers, she says it attracts men and
brings misfortune. Maybe she's right... If she comes, I'll tell
her to undo her hair, just right here in this booth, you'll see.
My sister's the most beautiful. She has light-colored eyes.
A little strange. One is green and the other one is blue. When
I'm with her in the métro or in some place kind of... We
never get arrested. She protects me. People take her for a
real Frenchwoman... She has white skin, not like me, you saw
my hands, their color, it's like gingerbread, almost, hers isn't,
sometimes I think it's too white... I'm afraid she's getting
sick... We don't look alike, standing beside my sister, but people have always taken us for twins, not real ones, of course.

*Algerian who fought on the French side during the Algerian war of independence.

She's my sister, she's going to come with my mother. They'll take me away with them. We'll go, the three of us, to my mother's house. Her childhood home. From the village, you can look at the sea. I don't know it. My mother told me about it. She told me she has a photograph but she never showed it to me. When I ask her about it, she tells me, "Later on, I don't have time, I'm going to pick up the kids at school." Afterwards she forgets and so do I.

> *The girl is tired. She remains silent. She rests her head on her arms, folded in front of her, as if to sleep. The woman shakes her. The girl raises her head. Approaching the booth is a tall, stout woman, beautiful to behold, her face bearing faint tattoos, her hair covered with a floral-print head scarf. Her eyes are blue. She is alone. The girl stands up suddenly.*

THE GIRL: *(shouting)* Imma! Ya Imma! Ya Imma! Here I am! It's me, your daughter... You're here! Imma...

∽

Noureddine Aba

Such Great
Hope

or
The New Song
of a Lost Country

Translated from the French by
Richard Miller

UBU REPERTORY THEATER PUBLICATIONS
NEW YORK

Noureddine Aba was born in 1921 in Sétif, Algeria, where he completed his secondary education. After a year of studying law at the University of Alger, he was drafted into the army from 1943 to 1945. At the end of the war, Mr. Aba took up journalism and followed the trials of the Nazi war criminals at Nuremberg. He then became a regular contributor to the well-known magazine, *Présence Africaine,* from the time of its founding. Mr. Aba progressively turned to fiction writing. In the intervening years, he published a great number of stories, poems, and plays. Starting in 1979, Mr. Aba won several awards and prizes for his work. In 1985, the Fondation de France presented him with the Prix Charles Oulmont for lifetime achievement. Several of his plays—*Montjoie Palestine* (1971), *La Récréation des clowns* (1982), *Le dernier jour d'un nazi* (1986)—have been performed in Paris or broadcast over the networks of France Culture and Radio France Internationale. In addition to his writing, Noureddine Aba was a regular participant in the lecture circuit in European, Canadian and American universities. He also taught Algerian literature at the University of Illinois, Urbana-Champaign. In 1990, Mr. Aba created the first private and secular foundation in Algeria. The Noureddine Aba Foundation awards yearly prizes to French-language or Arab-language Algerian writers, who while remaining true to their identities, embrace tolerance and brotherhood. Noureddine Aba was a member of the Académie des Sciences d'Outre-mer, and in 1996 became a member of the Académie Universelle des Cultures, presided by Elie Wiesel. In 1992, he was awarded the Prix de la Francophonie de la Société des Auteurs et Compositeurs Dramatiques. He died in 1996.

Richard Miller has translated many works of fiction and nonfiction, from Balzac to Barthes, as well as a number of plays for Ubu Repertory Theater. His translations of Aimé Césaire's *A Tempest,* Paul Emond's *Talk About Love!,* Tilly's *A Modest Proposal,* and Julius Amédée Laou's *Another Story,* were staged at Ubu in 1991, 1993, 1994 and 1995 respectively. He has recently translated *Women and Men* by Bernard-Henri Lévy and Françoise Giroud, published by Little Brown and Company. He presently lives in Paris. His translation of *Huis clos (No Exit)* commissioned by Ubu Repertory Theater—the first translation approved by the Sartre Estate in fifty years—was produced to critical acclaim by Ubu in 1996.

AUTHOR'S NOTE

When a poet chooses French or Arab to express his frater-
nal vision of the world and when fanatics who, hostile to his
choice, assassinate him, at the same time as they kill him they
are also killing the humanism produced by great and age-old
cultures.

It is as a witness to this dual murder that I cry out here. It is
my hope that intermediaries in either of the two languages
will not let this cry be lost in the wilderness.

NOUREDDINE ABA
1992

CHARACTERS

At the hospital:
   YACINE, *an offstage voice*
   THE DOCTOR
   A NURSE

At the eagle's nest:
   YACINE
   HALIMA
   AN OLD BLIND MAN

At the eagle's nest, with chorus:
   YACINE
   SAHIRA
   THE OLD BLIND MAN: WISDOM
   TOLERANCE
   JUSTICE
   CHARITY

In the park:
   YACINE
   SAHIRA
   THE OLD WOMAN
   CÉSAR
   ANTARÈS
   FIRST BEARDED MAN
   SECOND BEARDED MAN

At the eagle's nest:
   YACINE
   SAHIRA
   WISDOM

At the hospital:
   YACINE, *an offstage voice*
   THE DOCTOR
   A NURSE

NOTE

Although there are thirteen characters, the play should be performed by six actors—not out of economy but because of the symbolism inherent in the dream sequences; this will become clear in the reading. In addition, the structure of the play is laid out to meet those requirements: only the characters Yacine and Sahira appear in every scene, whereas the other protagonists appear in dispersed scenes and never at the same time.

Only one set is needed, which must be adaptable to three minimal scene changes: photographs or flats could be employed to represent a hospital room, the "eagle's nest," an area in a public park with a bench. The action begins in the hospital room and returns to it in flashbacks during and after the scenes at the eagle's nest and in the park.
In the first and final scenes the Nurse and the Doctor wear white jackets. In every scene, Sahira wears blue-jeans and shirt, with a blue scarf on her head that also conceals part of her face. Yacine wears light-colored trousers and a shirt. The men in the chorus wear white burnouses, and the woman wears a large, vividly colored shawl.

In the park, the Old Woman wears an Algerian costume of faded striped material, belted at the waist. Her head is covered with a vivid pink scarf. César is dressed very nattily, in a nouveau riche way. Antarès wears an ordinary suit. The two bearded men wear the khamis, the long white shirt favored by Islam fundamentalists, which covers them to the feet; they wear sandals.

SCENE ONE

A hospital room. A patient lies in the bed. A Doctor is standing next to the bed, checking the intravenous drip. A Nurse enters.

NURSE: Doctor, there's a woman here to see the man who's been wounded.

DOCTOR: That's impossible.

NURSE: She's an old friend. She heard the news flash on the radio.

DOCTOR: It was on the radio?

NURSE: The man who was shot is a well-known poet. They said that the fundamentalists shot him at the airport as he was boarding the plane for Paris.

DOCTOR: He hasn't got a chance—two bullets in the neck. The fracture on the right side looks bad.

NURSE: Won't you go speak to this woman? She wants to see him.

DOCTOR: He's in shock, he's sedated.

NURSE: She wants to know if he's going to pull through.

DOCTOR: *(with a shrug)* They just brought him in, it's too early to tell. We're going to do all we can. *(He sighs and continues in another tone of voice.)* I'll go see the woman. Stay with him. They'll be coming to X-ray him.

The Doctor exits, the Nurse sits down by the bed. A pause. Then we hear Yacine's voice speaking, offstage.

YACINE: *(offstage voice)* So, Doctor, here I am again, in your hands. The light has grown dim, dim light for the wolves, the wolves with their beards black as ink. Are they about to attack me? Will they wait until my body has gone cold? But Doctor, you are here... The magic of words is keeping me alive... and I fear them. Yes, I fear that one of them could kill... One word, like a bottomless pit. Help me to remember... I was standing at my window back in Ménilmontant, wasn't I? The mob was gathered down below, waiting for me... They were massed together down there, they reminded me of a thick grove of cypress trees. Am I delirious? No, not delirious. But my mouth is on fire, as if my lips had touched a hot iron. I could hear voices shouting: "Mohammed, give up!" My name is Yacine, but the mob kept shouting, "Mohammed, give up! We won't hurt you. You'll be returned to Algeria!" All those voices, like stones being thrown up at me. It was then that I called for you to help me. I said: I don't stand for my country only, the whole world is my country! And then I realized the true meaning of my name: mankind. Not Mohammed, not Yacine! My name is mankind... mankind! I must shout it out to the skies, from the mountain top. *(The scene changes to the eagle's nest.)*

SCENE TWO

A flat shelf atop a mountain. One or two rocks and, if feasible, a view of other mountain peaks in the distance. Yacine stands gazing out toward the horizon and then suddenly cries out.

YACINE: My name is mankind! *(Sound of echoes. He repeats.)* Mankind! Mankind!

An old man enters quickly.

OLD BLIND MAN: Who dares come here to this eagle's nest at the world's end? You who cry out, do you not know that this is known as "The Place where Rocks Fall from the Sky?" If you are not as blind as I, you must be able to see all those peaks hanging from the heavens. Look out on the right, there, the drop is endless, there is no bottom. Who are you?

YACINE: My name is Yacine. And you?

OLD BLIND MAN: Here, you put aside your name and find another one, one to match your soul.

YACINE: So what is your new name?

OLD BLIND MAN: Wisdom! What are you doing here?

YACINE: I lived in this eagle's nest during the war. It was our sanctuary.

WISDOM: And now you're here on a pilgrimage?

YACINE: Yes, old man.

WISDOM: Who are you?

YACINE: They say I am a poet.

WISDOM: I was Boussaâdya, once.

YACINE: You were a strolling entertainer?

WISDOM: Yes, and a story-teller as well. Scheherazade had nothing on me! So you're a poet?

YACINE: I am also the prodigal son...

WISDOM: *(interrupting)* God, what self-importance!

YACINE: I am only a prodigy when it comes to loving. I am a prodigal son who is returning home after a long, long, a very long, exile. A child born of the dawn.

WISDOM: How long was it, your exile?

YACINE: More than thirty years.

WISDOM: How many twilights does that make?

YACINE: I don't know. Why do you ask that?

WISDOM: Because for more than thirty years this country has been living in a twilight time, under a darkened sky, an endless twilight with no hope of ever seeing daybreak, the dawn.

YACINE: What kind of nonsense is that, old man! Night is always followed by dawn.

WISDOM: Not in this country! That is its punishment.

YACINE: You speak in riddles, old man. What do you mean?

WISDOM: I suppose you came here directly, without stopping in the city.

YACINE: There was no one for me to see. There were only two survivors of our group, Sahira and I. Sahira died last year.

WISDOM: Who is Sahira?

YACINE: She was a nurse, for the group. For me...

WISDOM: For you she was a great deal more?

YACINE: Sahira's arms were like a haven, a promise of land on the horizon, of colors, of sounds.

WISDOM: You loved her?

YACINE: Ah, old man! I seemed to hear my heart beating all around me, below me and above me, the sound seemed to leap around me like deer. And that feeling when we embraced, the feeling that our bodies were ablaze like a forest!

WISDOM: *(dryly, brusquely)* Did you have to come back?

YACINE: Why so aggressive all of a sudden?

WISDOM: Answer me!

YACINE: I was suffocating back there, in Europe. In those countries, everything feels superficial. Exclamations, joys, grace, people keep all those things bottled up inside them. And I was homesick for the dawn that gave me birth. I wanted to recapture the feeling of precious stones raining down on my face!

WISDOM: That's twice you've said that you are the child of the dawn. What dawn are you talking about?

YACINE: The dawn of the first day of our country's independence! Perhaps you've forgotten it!

WISDOM: Listen, my boy, that dawn you keep talking about was drawn and quartered by predatory men only a few days after independence, it was lynched!

YACINE: Your bilious words repel me.

WISDOM: To tell the truth, I despair of this night that has fallen over the land. I am afraid it will be split asunder by a thousand and one bolts of deadly lightning!

YACINE: You're breaking my heart. Tell me, what is happening?

WISDOM: In a moment, I'll summon the chorus. They will tell you how your dawn was lynched.

YACINE: I don't believe you. You're lying, or you've lost your mind.

WISDOM: Neither. I have been to Mecca, I have purified myself in the sacred mosque and before the Holy Kaaba. The chorus will confirm it.

YACINE: So bring on this chorus, let them speak!

WISDOM: I am Wisdom. First, I have to take a few security measures. I must know precisely who you are and what this dawn you talk about was like.

YACINE: What do you want to know?

WISDOM: Everything, since your childhood!

YACINE: Ah, old man! My childhood! It was a blue stream running through green plains. Everything most people lack, I had! I am one of those creatures—rare in this country—whom destiny did not fix in its sights, one finger on the trigger.

WISDOM: You were born rich?

YACINE: My parents were. As a child, life welcomed me and happiness smiled on me...

WISDOM: Did life at least give you what you wanted?

YACINE: For the first ten years, yes, in profusion. Afterwards, no.

WISDOM: Why not?

YACINE: I managed to surmount my fate. But there was great sorrow all around me. If it hadn't been for that, I'd have spent my life explaining to flowers the erratic behavior of bees. I'd have spent my life flushing out the bird that had sought refuge in the woods from the wind... or in trying to guess which twig on a branch might still retain the warmth of a passing squirrel...

WISDOM: In short, you had every reason to be happy?

YACINE: Every reason, but I was not.

WISDOM: Why not?

YACINE: We were living in a time of colonial darkness, a time of speech suppressed, of sleep interrupted by little smartly-dressed white men and a colonial caste that was all puffed up with pride.

WISDOM: Ah, those blessed days!

YACINE: How can you dare? We clung to our sorrow for support as you would cling to a tree! Night and day, we spelled out in solitude our bitter anger. An entire people, petrified for all eternity, like mummies! How can you dare? Why did we take up arms and win back our mountain crests? Even here, where we now stand, our weapons once glittered like mirrors in the sun!

WISDOM: What did you dream about, back then, as you rested between battles?

YACINE: In our own country the landscape was strange to us, the land, the seasons! We used to dream of kites that could soar up to the stars toward a new childhood in the pure air. And we used to dream of returning to our roots, purely, in the crystal snow. We used to dream of a country open to all the peoples of the earth, as the earth is to sea's embrace. (In another tone of voice) Now, old man, you must leave me. I need to be alone, to remember in peace.

WISDOM: To remember Sahira?

YACINE: Her, and another friend to whom I owe a great deal.

WISDOM: A comrade in arms?

YACINE: Yes. He died not far from here.

WISDOM: What was his name?

YACINE: The only name I ever called him was his alias: Cardinal.

WISDOM: Cardinal, and for a Moslem! What sacrilege!

YACINE: He was a pious man, and his virtues were many!

WISDOM: Name one virtue that can justify such sacrilege!

YACINE: He was a man of means, of encounters, of forgiveness.

WISDOM: So he was truly a holy man.

YACINE: He was the leader. Often, he would tell his men: if you want to die without shame, deserving of being called a man, you must fight for your rights as just men fight, not as slaves seeking vengeance. *(A pause.)* It was here, on this mountainside, at this turning of the path, that I saw him for the last time, as the sun was setting below the horizon... It was here that I called his name for the last time. I cast it out like a stone into the silence, and the echo sent it back to me from the distance...

WISDOM: The distance of forgetfulness...

YACINE: No, old man! He is still with me, I can feel him present here like an impalpable shadow. He is here, somewhere among these wild peaks that nothing it seems can conquer... save for the vastness of the sky!

WISDOM: Tell me of the dawn that gave you birth.

YACINE: It was on the first day of independence. A dawn unlike any other dawning since the beginning of time. We had been waiting a hundred years for that dawn, for that arc of light reaching up into the sky. The night before, I had not slept.

WISDOM: Why not?

YACINE: Because I had wanted to be there, at daybreak, to see it.

WISDOM: It must have been beautiful, watching the sun rise after seven years of suffering?

YACINE: Yes, old man, it was beautiful! I came to catch the dawn, to watch it rising over Algiers, to see it touch the walls, the first morning faces.

WISDOM: And were you happy?

YACINE: It wiped out in an instant all the suffering I had endured throughout the long night of colonialism.

WISDOM: What could you have endured, a rich man's son with soft skin. Surely...

YACINE: Stop there, old man! Soft skin, perhaps, but always sad! Sad because of the suffering I saw all around me.

WISDOM: Because fate had spared you!

YACINE: Me, yes, but not my people! I saw them without hope, forgotten, shut up forever in slums like lepers used to be shut up in walled and forbidden villages.

WISDOM: I thought...

YACINE: *(heatedly)* You thought what? That my soft skin made me unfeeling? Do you want me to tell you how my pride was humbled when I saw all my ragged brothers passing by me, locked into such utter solitude that it was as though they had become dead to the world? Do you want me to tell you about the shock to my arrogance when I would see groups of beggars like skeletons crowding around a bakery door, their hands held out to the petty white squires in their Sunday best?

WISDOM: I believe you.

YACINE: It is because of all those things that I decided to be a poet and the intermediary of my people, can you understand? The poet go-between!

WISDOM: No need to shout! *(A pause.)* Tell me about the dawn that gave you birth on that first day of independence.

YACINE: I experienced that great day, a day so pure that it made the heart ache with joy.

WISDOM: Not mine.

YACINE: I experienced that great day of popular excitement, when thousands of voices rent the air! I experienced it without Cardinal, who had died the year before. If you only knew the words of regret that choked me, if you could only know how I tried to hold myself aloof from that great hodgepodge of emotions, without him, without all the companions who had died that we might experience that day. That joy made up of the laughter and the tears of a dazed and transfigured people, a people who had come together at the site of a true miracle, at the geometrically exact conjunction of hope and love!

WISDOM: I imagine that the joy of a people achieving freedom must be like an earthquake. An emotional upheaval.

YACINE: Yes. The streets seem to give way to its power, to the shouts of triumph, the cries of joy.

WISDOM: I can imagine the tumult, the voices flying like arrows through the air.

YACINE: And now even your voice has grown softer, old man.

WISDOM: When the chorus tell you how your dawn was destroyed! Oh, my poor mudjihaddin! *

* Warrior

YACINE: Your "chorus" intrigue me. Summon them!

WISDOM: Be patient. Tell me more about the dawn.

YACINE: What more is there to tell? I experienced that exalted
moment when nature and mankind breathe through the same
mouth, when light, mankind and nature seem to understand
each other—no, more than that: seem to communicate with
each other. It was as though, before, the people had been victims of some mass amnesia and then, all at once, they had
regained their memory... all their memory of all their age-old
past! *(With a change of tone)* Now, summon the chorus!

WISDOM: Let me share in your happiness, I beg you, even
if it is lost.

YACINE: Why "lost"?

WISDOM: The chorus will tell you. Do not be impatient. Tell
me more about that dawn. I can imagine it was a bright day
filled with sun, a nation returning to life. A triumphant day!

YACINE: Yes, old man. The streets were filled with history, it
took us by the hand.

WISDOM: As one takes the hand of a blind man to help him
from one path to another.

YACINE: Yes, history was in the streets, radiant and sacred, as
the Book was for our forefathers.

WISDOM: Now I understand why you say that dawn gave you
birth.

YACINE: Now, summon the chorus!

WISDOM: Do not be in such a hurry to summon misfortune. The chorus... *(Having second thoughts)* You will see. *(With affection)* Look at my face. It is nothing but a mass of wrinkles. My body is all dried up. I did not see that dawn, go on telling me about it.

YACINE: The dawn was filled with hope and love. You cannot know... I suddenly felt absolved of the primal sin that had been weighing for over a century on my fate! And all at once I took my country in my arms, I held it so tightly that it took my breath away. And then I heard myself shout: Hail, Earth! Yesterday, you were bereft of hope...

WISDOM: *(interrupting)* Tomorrow, you will know abundance!

YACINE: Hail springs! Hail rivers! Behold, there are flights of swallows, flights of doves to welcome your rebirth! Hail, all those eyes awakened in the ocean's foam!

WISDOM: *(in similar vein)* Hail the first cry of the Muezzin under his umbrella pine, uttering his first prayer and his first pardons of all those wounded in the war!

YACINE: You can read my thoughts, old man!

WISDOM: Since I can no longer see I am better at reading voices. And yours, so different, lifts my heart. *(With a change of tone)* Why did you not stay in the country, afterwards?

YACINE: I am the poet-intermediary of my people.

WISDOM: Could you not have stayed and been their intermediary here?

YACINE: Why? They no longer needed me. I wanted to be free to wander. I wanted to see new faces. I wanted to tell our former enemies that we had fought without hatred, that amid all the madness and horror we had not lost either the warmth of our souls or the plain words to express it.

WISDOM: You should have stayed.

YACINE: But I tell you again: No one needed me.

WISDOM: And Sahira?

YACINE: I wanted to take her with me, but she refused to come. *(After a pause, irritated)* But Sahira too was a child of the dawn. In the resistance, she was always in hiding, caring for the wounded, helping others to die. *(Abruptly)* Why do you speak of Sahira? Everyone knew that independence meant that each of us had to seek out our country's fabled treasures wherever they had been dispersed, like the rich treasures to be found on sunken ships!

WISDOM: What did you have that was so precious that you should abandon your own people? Your own destitute, naive, good people?

YACINE: Naive and good, yes! But not destitute! I had left them in good hands. I was sure that they would wipe out poverty, that it would disappear without a sound like an intruder feeling himself out of place in the new order. I knew that the brothers in whom we trusted would allow us the wild pleasure of lining all those things—indifference, selfishness, greed, chauvinism—up against a wall and executing them all!

WISDOM: My poor boy!

YACINE: I am not your poor boy, and stop speaking to me in that tone of voice.

WISDOM: You should not have left!

YACINE: Listen, old man, my former fury had been assuaged, my former bitterness was forgotten, I did not seek recognition.

WISDOM: And there were so many others who were more than ready to warm their boots at the revolution's hearth!

YACINE: What do you mean by that?

WISDOM: I mean the upstarts and parvenus who had only waited for independence so that they could gain some advantage, big or little. When the chorus tell you...

YACINE: *(irritated)* Always the chorus! Get it over with and bring them in! Just what are the chorus going to tell me?

WISDOM: They will tell you that thirty years after independence nothing has changed. There is still contempt, there is still poverty.

Halima enters.

YACINE: I don't believe you!

WISDOM: By the Lord of Lords, it is the plain truth!

YACINE: I don't believe you! *(A change of tone)* First, how did you get here, to this eagle's nest that only Sahira and I, the last two survivors, know about?

WISDOM: We fled the foul city. We have come here to pray.

YACINE: Yes, but how did you come upon this place?

WISDOM: Halima brought us here. I believe she was Sahira's friend.

HALIMA: That is right.

WISDOM: *(introducing the young woman)* This is Halima. *(A pause.)* I will see if the chorus are ready. *(He exits.)*

YACINE: So you are Halima?

HALIMA: Yes.

YACINE: You were Sahira's friend?

HALIMA: Yes.

YACINE: Why did she tell you about this sanctuary?

HALIMA: There were no secrets between us.

YACINE: Why did she never tell me about you?

HALIMA: Because I knew her after independence. You are Yacine.

YACINE: I see that she told you about me.

HALIMA: She spoke of you all the time. When she spoke about you she sang like a nightingale, with...

YACINE: So? Go on.

HALIMA: I am afraid I will set off an avalanche of painful memories in your mind. *(In another tone)* And I do not want to talk about her, or you! *(She makes a move to leave.)*

YACINE: Halima! Please... I beg you! *(She turns back.)* First, look at me. Why such delicacy, here?

HALIMA: It's not out of delicacy that I draw the veil. The air here is so pure, so fresh, that it burns the throat... and mine is very sensitive. *(She draws away.)*

YACINE: Halima! Don't go!

HALIMA: *(turning back)* You did not love Sahira!

YACINE: Don't say that!

HALIMA: What did she matter to you?

YACINE: She was the bee, the flower, the sparrow, the isle of bliss.

HALIMA: Poet's talk!

YACINE: She was incorruptible self-respect and the sword of courage, when sometimes mine faltered out of fear.

HALIMA: I repeat, you never loved her.

YACINE: I loved her with my entire soul, with all my senses, with every tenderness.

HALIMA: Then why didn't you stay with her?

YACINE: I had a duty to perform.

HALIMA: *(in a sudden outburst)* That great duty of the child of the dawn! You set out on a white ship that had set its fresh new sails for glory! And on its mast you flaunted your hunger for new faces and new horizons! You preferred them to Sahira!

YACINE: I left with her blessing. She wanted me to carry out that mission.

HALIMA: And what did you say, in all those cities scattered around the globe? What did you say, that enables you to have a clear conscience today?

YACINE: But she urged me to go!

HALIMA: You wanted to leave so badly, your need was so great, that she loosed the bonds that bound you to her!

YACINE: I had to go. After independence, I felt as though I were being carried away, as if I were on a galloping horse. I did what I was supposed to do, I did what I had to do.

HALIMA: *(with sudden aggressivity)* And what exactly did you do?

YACINE: I went off bearing in my arms the dawn, to show it to the world, to tell everyone everywhere that we had fought, not to force our truth on others but only to make it known where it had not been known before. Because for us it was essential that all men look into themselves and understand that each one of us contains the others' fate, it was essential that all men learn that each of us contains the others' indivisible flame within, at the precise, geometric juncture of hope and love.

HALIMA: *(bitter)* You're nothing but a poet! A poor poet taken in by the magic of his own words! You've made that deceptive and false independence into some kind of phosphorescent flood that will burst the dam of heaven with the weight of a million stars! You deceived yourself, Yacine! And now you are going to recant your error, and recant it before the whole chorus!

The chorus enters quickly and takes up the cry with the same tone, in perfect unison.

CHORUS: You deceived yourself, Yacine, and you are going to recant your error!

The scene switches suddenly back to the hospital room. Dim lighting. A male nurse crosses the stage pushing an X-ray machine on wheels, and the scene immediately changes back to the eagle's nest. This reminder of the real world can be repeated as required.

SCENE THREE

The eagle's nest, some time later. The sun is lower on the horizon. Twilight. Yacine stands as though lost in thought. The chorus stands around him in a half circle, as if in prayer. A pregnant silence.

YACINE: *(suddenly)* I can't do it any longer!

WISDOM: You haven't meditated long enough!

YACINE: But I've been standing here for an hour, surrounded by these statues.

WISDOM: They're praying!

YACINE: They say long prayers!

WISDOM: Praying is conversation with God. He hasn't yet dismissed them!

YACINE: Yes, God can be long-winded!

WISDOM: A fundamentalist would have already had your tongue out for those words! Beware of your disobedient mind!

YACINE: Excuse me, but I'm finding your recantation rite a bit long. Couldn't we speed things up a little?

WISDOM: We are waiting for Halima to come back.

YACINE: Yes. Where is she?

WISDOM: She is preparing the candles.

YACINE: Why candles?

Halima enters, a candle in each hand. During the following speeches, Halima slowly exits and enters, returning each time with two candles, which she sets in a circle around Yacine.

WISDOM: You shall see. That is also part of the ritual.

YACINE: You're really subjecting me to an unbearable ordeal!

WISDOM: It would have been even more unbearable if I hadn't been here to speak to you.

YACINE: And why aren't you praying, may I ask?

WISDOM: I? I am to lead the ceremony!

YACINE: Ah. And why is a ceremony being held for me?

WISDOM: Recantation is no light matter. Indeed, it even involves some risk for you.

YACINE: Does it? What risk?

WISDOM: This is not the moment to tell you.

YACINE: *(to Halima, who is completing the circle)* Halima, what are these candles for?

WISDOM: How far have you got, Halima?

HALIMA: *(to Wisdom)* These are the last. *(The chorus stop praying.)* They are ready, Wisdom.

WISDOM: Yacine, the chorus have now become a tribunal. *(Pointing them out one by one)* She is Charity. He is Tolerance, and he is Justice. The Dawn whose child you claim to be spoke untruly, it was mistaken, it gave false witness. The judges must now find you innocent or guilty. Halima will execute the sentence, if you are so unfortunate as to be sentenced to death.

YACINE: A death sentence? *(Laughing)* What will you use, Halima, the lash, the robe, the stake?

HALIMA: Perhaps the pit. It would not be too hard to make you stumble up to its brink. And your body would fall into empty space, your death cry would echo from the depths up to the clouds. But you need only recant your error!

YACINE: Well, let me speak plainly: don't count on it!

JUSTICE: You know nothing of what happened after independence. Wait until you find out how it was slain!

TOLERANCE: At whose hand!

CHARITY: And why independence was nothing but a decoy!

JUSTICE: Why the revolution never occurred!

CHARITY: Recant!

HALIMA: On the first evening after your departure, Sahira lit a candle. And the second evening another. Every evening, another candle. And every year a candle. Over the years, more candles, until she had used up every candle on earth and had been consumed in the candle flames!

YACINE: You're lying. She died of a heart attack.

HALIMA: That's what your mother told you! She had been

warned that all those candles burning in her room were madness, in her room, throughout the house, everywhere, lit
in your memory. One evening, one unfortunate movement,
and the whole thing went up in flames!

WISDOM: Halima, it is not your place to start, that is up to the
judges. You will speak later.

JUSTICE: Yacine, recant your error!

YACINE: I have seen too many soldiers die with one last soft
word to their mothers, a last smile for the comrade-in-arms
at their side. I have seen too many men die as soldiers of the
people, so that the people might again have a voice, so that
the people no longer know contempt and have the right to
sing of the human adventure along with other men.

JUSTICE: Then weep, Yacine, because they all died for nothing!

YACINE: What do you mean, "for nothing?"

CHARITY: The dead you knew, abandoned, unburied, the
dead who were struck down, all those who have gone into
the night, some perhaps in fear...

TOLERANCE:... some perhaps with their country's name on
their lips, with the vision of glittering stars in their eyes, some
humming the refrain of an old song long buried in their
memories, before death, without pity, snatched them up.

YACINE: They did not die for nothing! *(All burst out laughing.)*
Do not laugh! I can prove it to you!

WISDOM: Then prove it!

YACINE: I returned to this country to tell its ragged veterans that in the eyes of the world they were a life-giving example of noble courage. To tell them that their bravery had made them the apostles of all the peoples still struggling against the deadly abuse of tyrants and against the industrialists of death who sow hatred among men!

JUSTICE: He can't escape from his myth! He's become its prisoner!

TOLERANCE: Yacine, you're dreaming, you're dreaming. In fact, your dawn was nothing but the dim, brief light of a shooting star!

YACINE: It glinted on the rooftops, on the walls, on those first eager faces...

CHARITY: *(interrupting)* It was all make-believe, a hoax. Some great trickster had strewn the world with ground glass!

JUSTICE: You must recant. Your fate depends on it!

YACINE: And the November uprising, what about that? Was that just a meaningless spark, without rhyme or reason?

CHARITY: The uprising was real; what was unreal was Algeria's independence!

YACINE: But I witnessed that dawn! I experienced that great wave of laughter, of celebration! I heard them singing hymns to the end of humiliation, the end of contempt, the end of poverty!

HALIMA: You promised Sahira that spring would return, its hands red with the juice of ripe pomegranates. You did not keep your promise.

WISDOM: Let's save some time: recant the false dawn, the deceptive dawn...

YACINE: *(breaking in)* A while ago, old man, you believed in it as well!

WISDOM: Yes, I believed you! That's why we want you to recant. Because you will use any kind of sorcery. We do not want others to fall victim to the same witchcraft. Recant your error!

YACINE: That dawn gave meaning to my life, it was its justification. I will not deny it!

> *From this point onwards, the scene takes on the atmosphere of an unfriendly police interrogation. The questions to Yacine are shouted out as if to overpower him and break him down.*

JUSTICE: How many times do we have to repeat that your dawn was lynched?

YACINE: By whom?

CHARITY: By the very ones to whom you who entrusted it before your departure.

YACINE: You mean the NLF?*

WISDOM: The NLF. You said it was to wipe out indifference, selfishness, greed, chauvinism, fanaticism.

HALIMA: You knew the NLF would not do that! Once you were gone, Sahira became a ghost, locked up in a dream to which you had the keys! A ghost surrounded by candles!

---

* National Liberation Front. The leading movement which fought and won Algeria's war of independence, then became the ruling party for 30 years.

TOLERANCE: Tell him what happened a few days after he had gone. It will make it easier for him to recant.

YACINE: What happened?

JUSTICE: That's when the lynch mob showed their lynching faces!

CHARITY: The tribes of the tribes! The faithful of the NLF!

TOLERANCE: One day they emerged, hordes of them, a storm of them!

CHARITY: Pawing at the ground with impatience, jostling each other like a heard of panic-stricken buffalo.

WISDOM: I told you: a host of pretenders who all wanted to warm their boots at the hearth of the Algerian revolution. All dreaming of what they could gain from our deaths!

JUSTICE: There were some who saw themselves as fathers of the revolution, some who even set themselves up as its brave grandfathers.

CHARITY: There were some who called themselves the rightful historic leaders of the revolution, some who vowed that they would not be history's bastards!

TOLERANCE: And then came the ones who treated them like impostors and proclaimed themselves the sole heirs of the November uprising!

WISDOM: And after them came leaders who hurled deadly insults at each other.

HALIMA: And during all this time Sahira, suspended between

night and day, between a state of grace and madness, was lighting her candles and praying for your return.

WISDOM: And then came the turn of Si Mohammed, of Si Ahmed, of all the other Si's, Si this, Si that!

JUSTICE: And then came the turn of Sidi Mohammed and Sidi Ahmed and countless other Sidi's this and Sidi's that!

CHARITY: And then it was the turn of Ben Mohammed and Ben Ahmed, and all the countless other Ben's this and Ben's that!

TOLERANCE: And they were followed by a multitude of just plain Ben's, men who bragged of being friends or relatives of the one great Ben whose charlatanism had made him famous and who had claimed to be able to change pebbles into pearls.

HALIMA: You were well aware that Sahira's roots were planted in you like a tree planted in the earth. You were well aware that your departure had removed the grounds of her only certitude: her inexhaustible love for you!

WISDOM: And after the Ben's there came with great ceremony the NLF's representatives from overseas, from Cairo, from Tunis, from Damascus, from Riad, Baghdad, Geneva, Moscow, each of them with his list drawn up, his organization of the nomenklatura!

JUSTICE: And last of all there came the hangers-on, the yes-men, the drudges of the revolution, each brandishing his certificate of patriotism.

CHARITY: There were the ones who had distributed pamphlets, the ones who had delivered letters, the body guards.

TOLERANCE: Some were even fairly picturesque and unexpected, old men who had once acted as lookouts came limping up to claim recognition for their part in the revolution. And so they came, so they came...

WISDOM: You began to wonder if anyone had actually been killed during the Algerian war!

YACINE: I don't believe you!

JUSTICE: And so, over the heads of the stricken populace, over the heads of the ravaged countryside, over the dead and the martyrs tortured by the Ku-Klux-Klan, whether uniformed or civilian, they all began to implement their perverse demagogy.

WISDOM: Worse, we went through the delirium tremens of the policies of politicians!

JUSTICE: There were some who supported socialism Algerian-style!

CHARITY: Some wanted socialism on the Cuban model!

TOLERANCE: Others thought that the pro-Cubans were fakers and purely and simply called for a return to Islamic law and an obligatory belief in God!

WISDOM: Some proposed replacing man's exploitation of man with woman's exploitation by man!

YACINE: You're lying! I don't believe in this madness, these gesticulating hordes of impostors without memory!

JUSTICE: Yes, without memory of the ideal that had inspired us.

CHARITY: Without memory of the courage of those who had fought against the shadows.

TOLERANCE: Without memory of their sacrifices, without memory of the martyrs.

WISDOM: Without memory of the oath they had taken to restore dignity to the people!

YACINE: I don't believe you!

WISDOM: We have told you the truth, Yacine. Recant! Don't make us force you. We are not fond of violence.

JUSTICE: But we are not prepared to allow you to spread your lies about that so-called glowing dawn...

YACINE: *(interrupting him)* But what did all your impostors want?

WISDOM: What did they want? Good God, they wanted the seat of power, the throne! As they say in the souks, they wanted it all!

JUSTICE: They were all candidates for the seat of power! They all dreamed of being president, a minister...

CHARITY: *(continuing)* An ambassador, a bank president, a corporate head...

WISDOM: They all dreamed of some high office, no matter which office, no matter which branch. They all thought themselves born to power!

TOLERANCE: They were not men like other men, oh no! They had become men born to power! Men born to rule, men who had sprung up out of nowhere on a solid-gold planet!

HALIMA: But Sahira, who had on this very spot lifted her fist to the sun, like you, who fought, fought to the end—Sahira shut herself up at home with her candles! Recant, Yacine!

YACINE: I cannot!

HALIMA: Do you know that they even refused to recognize her as a mudjihaddine?*

YACINE: They did not recognize her as a freedom-fighter?

HALIMA: No one wanted to be reminded that she had shared in the hunger, the thirst, the fear, the sound of gunfire!

YACINE: I don't believe you!

HALIMA: *(addressing the chorus)* Continue! Exorcise him! It hasn't been enough!

WISDOM: After the lynch-mob that destroyed the dawn came the abortionists of the revolution.

JUSTICE: We watched them strutting through the streets in the midst of their advisers, their chief of protocol, their make-up artists...

YACINE: *(unable to hold back)* Their make-up artists? Why do you call them make-up artists?

CHARITY: Do you think that the lynchers of the dawn, the abortionists of the revolution, would let us see their true faces?

TOLERANCE: Why make-up artists? Because they needed them to cover up the murderous eyes, the shifty smile, the contemptuous sneer, the little hint of something that might

---

* A former freedom-fighter

give away the ordinary greengrocer underneath...

WISDOM: *(continuing)* ... or the pimp, the whirling dervish, the common shop-keeper.

JUSTICE: Artists who were experts at improving a face managed to turn a man who looked like a hustler into a one who had noble blood, a retardate into a senator, a man with the face of a shark into a man with the face of an angel!

CHARITY: We had a war of faces. One of them keep shouting that it was admired by De Gaulle and Kennedy!

TOLERANCE: There was one that claimed that King Feisal of Saudi Arabia thought very highly of it!

WISDOM: There was one that enjoyed the support of an army colonel who had been known as Sitting Bull during the war, one that was close friends of the head of the secret police, better known as the O.K. Corral!

JUSTICE: And then there was the one with the saintly expression who cured cripples and made sterile women fruitful!

CHARITY: We were favored with tales of their unparalleled deeds of courage, of all the achievements of a revolution we had viewed a simple thing but that was turned into something surreal by their accounts!

TOLERANCE: And the words "martyr," "glory," "nationalism," "arabism," were debased by all of them, right and left!

CHARITY: And we had speeches against predatory colonialism, against France-the-loathsome, France-the-accursed!

WISDOM: And there were calls to take up the struggle against a bourgeoisie that was native, bloated, miserly, all-pervasive.

JUSTICE: There was a call for a jihad* against the infidels, the renegades: death to bad Muslims, to the drinkers of wine, the eaters of impure flesh.

TOLERANCE: Down with emancipated women! Throw acid on brazen women who dare show their face in public, who dare to laugh, to sing, to dance, to tan themselves in the sun!

HALIMA: In her dreams she sought your body, in her dreams she felt it stir within her like an unborn child.

WISDOM: Do you realize that the people were betrayed, Yacine? Recant that accursed dawn, admit your error!

YACINE: And my people, tell me about my people!

JUSTICE: The real people were not aware that those in power could alter their faces, like objects that could be converted to serve different circumstances, different needs.

CHARITY: The real people were living a long, enchanted dream of a thousand and one nights! Imagine, Scheherazade sat there at their bedside, in their huts! How they relished all the smooth talkers who promised them the moon, all the hucksters with their endless speeches!

TOLERANCE: The speeches took the place of action: Do you want dignity? Here's a speech! Do you want greatness? Have a dose of verbal diarrhea! Words were thrown around like confetti at carnival time!

HALIMA: And there were nights, in that jungle, when Sahira

* Holy war

would literally shake with fear. Fear entwined itself around her solitude. In the midst of her forest of candles, she trembled, like a secret fearful of discovery!

YACINE: So if I understand rightly, all that happened was a transfer of power?

WISDOM: Precisely! A transfer of power from the long-time European settlers, who were on their way out, and the smart new men, the brand-new men!

YACINE: And what happened next?

JUSTICE: The revolution was laid to rest in a sumptuous pantheon.

CHARITY: The lynchers of the dawn and abortionists of the revolution created the State Party and a secret, underground NLF.

TOLERANCE: And then the State Party imposed obedience to the strict party line.

WISDOM: And political language was purged and strictly controlled, and mouths were kept firmly shut.

JUSTICE: And then any poor relation, anyone who lacked powerful protection, was strictly excluded.

WISDOM: Once the dawn festivities were over, the people bent their heads and became sleep-walkers. Now, will you recant that false, deceitful, lying independence, that lynched dawn?

YACINE: You're making me dizzy! I can feel the earth slipping away beneath my feet. How could that have happened? Here, in this very place, where I uttered my Algerian selfhood with bullets...

HALIMA: *(continuing)* ... and here, in this very place, between two skirmishes, Sahira laid her head on your shoulder, laughed on your shoulder, wept on your shoulder. And when the night sky towered over these rocks, it is here that you told her she would always be the end of your exile, your safest refuge! You were lying to her, weren't you?

YACINE: No, I was not lying to her! I didn't know, I couldn't have foreseen that the dawn we had dreamed of, for which we had hoped for over a hundred years, would be destroyed in its early hours.

HALIMA: Leave us alone! *(The chorus immediately exit.)* You didn't know? You couldn't have guessed?

YACINE: How could I have guessed?

HALIMA: Ah, Yacine! Poor Yacine, who never imagined the host of people starving to be noticed, to be recognized, all those who were burning with impatience, who wanted so keenly to possess what they had never been able to have during their rejected, disdained and ragged lives lived in the shadows.

YACINE: When I imagined independence, it was like the taste of almonds on my lips. And my whole being sang of vast horizons, like waves beating upon a shore!

HALIMA: Poor Yacine! You never thought that those new men were eaten up by their desire for revenge? And that that desire would become so great that they would turn to revenge against their own poor people?

YACINE: No! Stop there! Have pity! You make me dizzy, my ears are ringing! I can't take it any longer!

HALIMA: Once, you told Sahira: A'mri ki A'mrak, your life is mine... Do you remember that?

YACINE: Repeat what you just said!

HALIMA: A'mri ki A'mrak! Your life is mine!

YACINE: How can you know that? It was our secret code.

HALIMA: Yes. I know.

YACINE: We promised never to tell anyone? How can you know it?

HALIMA: (very slowly, after a pause) Because I am Sahira.

YACINE: What did you just say?

SAHIRA: My mother told you that I was dead. In fact, I was only dead for you, dead to the world.

YACINE: And that death by candles?

SAHIRA: The candles? For years, I lit them every evening... And each time, I would call for you...

YACINE: (with a gesture to her) Lift your veil and let me look at you.

SAHIRA: (drawing back) No! Not so quickly!

YACINE: Lift the veil, let me see my Seagull!

SAHIRA: My poor love, it is going to frighten you. I am no longer your Seagull.

YACINE: Sahira... I beg you!

SAHIRA: One evening, as I was on my way home, three religious fanatics caught me in an entryway. First, they beat me, spit on me...

YACINE: Why?

SAHIRA: Because I was out alone, free, my head uncovered. And then...

YACINE: And then?

SAHIRA: They threw acid in my face!

YACINE: My Seagull! That's insane!

SAHIRA: Today your Seagull's face is burnt. Red as a traffic light.

YACINE: Sahira! Sahira!

SAHIRA: I keep telling myself I am still alive, that my love has kept me alive, but every time I see a mirror, I see myself as dead. *(She lifts her veil.)* Look, Yacine.

YACINE: I see only your eyes looking at me.

SAHIRA: What do you feel?

YACINE: A burning, as though I were being branded.

SAHIRA: Oh, my warrior with the silken hands, what have they done to us?

YACINE: That evening when I told you: Your life is mine... I was so thirsty for your body.

SAHIRA: I too. There were so many words I could not speak, words that were on the very tip of my tongue.

YACINE: *(gently)* I can still feel that thirst.

SAHIRA: Despite this ruined, ravaged, broken face?

YACINE: Let me hold you!

SAHIRA: My beloved, spare me the humiliation of your disgust.

YACINE: I am more in love with you than ever!

SAHIRA: Despite this face?

YACINE: Love can be wonderfully stubborn, my Seagull, my Seagull!

SAHIRA: Do you remember the first time we met, in that park?

YACINE: I am surrounded by memories of you.

SAHIRA: Do you remember that on that day I told you that you had just brought me into the world?

YACINE: You were the one who blessed me.

SAHIRA: I?

YACINE: When I met you, I wasn't yet caught up in the struggle. I was still hesitating. You are the one who gave me the strength to become a part of it.

SAHIRA: You never told me that.

YACINE: Sahira, you were beautiful. I couldn't love you in a country where hunger and contempt were a part of daily life.

SAHIRA: The hunger and the contempt are still here, but now we are the ones who have created them!

YACINE: I couldn't love you in a country where every morning the beggars used to gather at the bakery door.

SAHIRA: Now the beggars gather at the doors of bakeries, of cafés, of mosques.

YACINE: In the winter I used to see them cowering in doorways, trembling in fear, like stowaways in the holds of ships, fearing discovery!

SAHIRA: Now they sleep in rags, racked with hunger, on park benches. If you could only see them, huddled together, like drowned men cast up by the sea.

YACINE: I could not stand the cynical laughter that used to cut deep gashes in my self-respect, when I would hear them calling you Fatima!

SAHIRA: Now no one calls me by any name at all. No one even knows I exist!

YACINE: I wanted my people to act for all the people still in chains!

SAHIRA: Your people are still in chains, still dreaming of freedom and dignity, just as they were thirty years ago!

YACINE: I wanted Islam to be the advance guard of universal brotherhood!

SAHIRA: And yet in its name they are murdering poets, they are stabbing doctors, they are strangling professors, they are hanging some poor devil, burning barns, destroying seagulls.

YACINE: Sahira!

SAHIRA: Help me!

YACINE: I'll do anything!

SAHIRA: Help me to raise my voice!

YACINE: Go on! We will raise our voices together!

SAHIRA: I deny this eagle's nest of which I was once so proud! I deny this landscape, I am finished with this sky, this earth! This is my farewell to those who lynched the dawn, this is my hymn to those who aborted the revolution! I am breaking every bond that still binds me to this land! I am shredding the shroud that once covered us!

YACINE: Farewell once-white Algeria, farewell bruised country! Farewell to your name, now oozing blood. Farewell to your shores, your blue waters, your jagged mountain peaks. Farewell to your cemeteries with their throat-slit corpses!

SAHIRA: I hate you, scenes of my childhood! Down to the hearts of your loveliest roses, down to the rays of sun glittering on your rivers, down to the smallest pebbles on your beaches, I hate you!

YACINE: Farewell, your innocent birds frolicking in the light! I deny you with my whole body, cut off from Sahira, with all my broken heart, like Sahira's heart that denies you too. I reject you with all my soul, land that burns seagulls, my soul casts you out.

SAHIRA: No, Yacine, your voice is still too gentle! Make it more bitter, do not murmur your words, throw them like stones, spit them out! Do as I do, throw them like daggers to the winds, to the echoes! What has this land given us, tell me! A youth crushed by contempt, an adolescence filled with instability and prohibitions, castaway in cities with open sewers, ruined houses, courtyards devoid of sun, with mobs of ragged, snot-nosed children, their eyes running and covered with flies! I hate men with turbans and rigid principles! I hate their cloistered women in their shuttered parlors!

YACINE: I hate them, men and women both! I hate their being sleepwalkers, their being their own submissive executioners, their rotten fatalism! Inch' Allah, as God wills! As God wills, bring down storm and lightning upon them! They accept everything with stony resignation, and like miserable serfs they ask for more.

SAHIRA: We will go, we will leave you to your poverty, to your fantasies, to your bloody hungers! Through you we have come to know every disappointment, every kind of betrayal, every pain, every disgust, every rage and nausea!

YACINE: Accursed land, land of fissures, land devoid of joy, of song, of laughter, for as long as I can remember you have been hoarse, leprous, filled with sulfur and vomit! Land that gave me but one Seagull and then destroyed it with fire!

SAHIRA: Tell me, beloved, back there where you've come from, do they rip love and justice to shreds there too?

YACINE: There too, you have furious glances, you have murderers in monocles and top hats. There, every day is not easy. There are those for whom the Arab means a bunch of onions, the Black means a face to be struck with a whip, the Jew a piece of meat for the oven.

SAHIRA: So you were not happy, there?

YACINE: No, not always. But there they have boxes of sandalwood, they have skies like sapphires, I managed to smuggle them, but I had to make myself as small as a thieving bird to do so.

SAHIRA: But then do you realize, Yacine, that you, that I, have just cursed our own land? Do you realize that we are the ones who have given voice to our hatred? My God, what are we to do?

YACINE: My tongue tastes of salt and bile. I do not know!

SAHIRA: Nor do I. But perhaps we haven't known how to look? Perhaps there is still something in this country that has not changed, and we can return to it?

YACINE: What if we were to give it another chance?

SAHIRA: That's what I was going to suggest. Let's go back to that little park where we first met!

BLACKOUT

There is a rapid vision of the hospital room to remind us that Yacine is seeing these memories in his delirium.

SCENE FOUR

A sunny day, a bench in a public park. The first four speeches of Sahira and Yacine are spoken offstage prior to their entrance.

SAHIRA: *(off stage)* Here we are.

YACINE: *(off stage)* Look! Our bench is still there!

SAHIRA: *(off stage)* The things I whispered in your ear!

YACINE: *(off stage)* Let's go over to the fountain and listen to the water.

They enter.

SAHIRA: The fountain is still there, but there's not a drop of water. Water is scarce here, scarcer than radium! *(She sits.)* It was at this very bench that I came to bid farewell to the city before going into hiding at the eagle's nest.

YACINE: What made you leave Algiers?

SAHIRA: I no longer felt comfortable in this violent city. Too many murders, too many deaths too soon forgotten, too many living who had learned to live with their cowardice, their indifference, their selfishness. And in addition, I was having problems with money.

YACINE: You didn't go to see the leaders, people in charge who could have helped you?

SAHIRA: What leaders, what people in charge? You had to make a thousand and one devious maneuvers just to get one of their flunkies to give you an appointment. Didn't you read the newspapers while you were out of the country?

YACINE: Yes, I did. Abroad, Algeria's image was excellent. Our leaders were regarded as statesmen, with a sense of history.

SAHIRA: A sense of history—them! My poor darling! The only sense they had was a sense of occasion... and a sense for business! Do you remember Chibane, the political commissar?

YACINE: Of course. He oozed vanity like mist off a sweating donkey.

SAHIRA: You remember Yousef, who supplied us with weapons?

YACINE: The Condottiere! He dreamed of being a legendary hero!

SAHIRA: Both Chibane and the Condottiere went into business. Today, they're immensely rich.

YACINE: And Sassi, the one you saved from certain death?

SAHIRA: Sassi? He's a high party official. He was appointed ambassador several times, I don't remember where.

YACINE: If I understand correctly, there was no one left to love this country and serve it.

SAHIRA: Oh no, there were many people who loved it and wanted to serve it. But they were all singled out, given labels and then methodically, systematically shunted aside and excluded from the community. You were told: it was the Party-State.

YACINE: Who would have thought that the NLF, the vehicle of a people's liberation, would over the years turn into an instrument of coercion, a springboard for scoundrels?

SAHIRA: How did you return? Plane or ship?

YACINE: By ship. Just to admire the coastline.

SAHIRA: And how did it look that day?

YACINE: Fascinating, at first glance...

SAHIRA: And then, as you came nearer, all those houses piled up like dominoes, that dazzling light!

YACINE: The whole scene seems to pierce to your very heart. How beautiful they are, all those open dwellings...

SAHIRA: Which seem like stairs, terrace upon terrace, descending step by step...

YACINE: Through the sounds of the city, to the sea!

SAHIRA: What struck you as you disembarked?

YACINE: *(after a brief pause)* Nothing.

SAHIRA: What are you hiding from me? *(A pause.)* You saw the hordes of beggars, is that it?

YACINE: I saw only one.

SAHIRA: Only one?

YACINE: Yes, but he resembled a dog. He was scrawny, his eyes were frightened, like those of a beaten dog. So much like a dog that I thought: it's a dog standing there on its hind legs, trying to look like a man.

SAHIRA: And you felt that that dog had appeared like a kind

of oracle to tell you that the city was filled with packs of beggar dogs?

YACINE: Yes. That was the impression I had. *(The old woman enters slowly.)*

SAHIRA: See what thirty years of NLF-State Party rule have done to our people. *(A pause, then suddenly)* Look, over there, that old woman who's just sat down, she's one of them! *(Yacine goes over to the beggar.)*

YACINE: Good day, grandmother.

THE OLD WOMAN: You wished me good day?

YACINE: I said good day.

THE OLD WOMAN: *(rising to leave)* I understand. I'll go beg somewhere else.

YACINE: Why are you leaving, grandmother?

THE OLD WOMAN: You don't have to explain. I understand...

YACINE: But I don't!

THE OLD WOMAN: Listen, my boy, the police are the only ones who pick up beggars and say "good day." And the beggar who wants to stay in one piece doesn't wait for them to say it twice.

SAHIRA: *(laughing)* He's not after beggars, grandmother! *(Yacine reaches into his pocket, draws out a bill and hands it to the beggar woman.)*

THE OLD WOMAN: *(in astonishment)* My boy, there's some mistake!

YACINE: No, I know what I've given you.

THE OLD WOMAN: It's too much. Usually... *(She falls silent.)*

SAHIRA: Go on! Usually?...

THE OLD WOMAN: I can't say anything in the presence of a Muslim sister...

SAHIRA: But I'm not a Muslim sister!

THE OLD WOMAN: So why the veil over your face?

SAHIRA: It's cool. My throat is sensitive. So... "usually...?"

THE OLD WOMAN: *(mockingly)* Sensitive throat, is it? Well, I'm sensitive too, I've got a sensitive mouth. And these flowers too, they've got sensitive ears!

YACINE: What do you mean by "ears?"

SAHIRA: She's talking about the ears of informers.

THE OLD WOMAN: *(returning the money to Yacine)* Here, take back your money!

YACINE: You've nothing to fear from me!

THE OLD WOMAN: I've everything to fear from a gentleman who says good day to me and hands me a big bill! I've been holding my hand out for more than twenty years, rain or shine, and I've never seen anything like that! Never!

YACINE: But people do give you something, don't they?

THE OLD WOMAN: Sometimes, but mostly the crowd just

passes by, like a river rushing to the sea. When God touches a few good people, they will toss me a coin, without getting near me. Do you know what total indifference is like?

SAHIRA: Yes, it's like being blind and lost in the desert.

THE OLD WOMAN: And now someone hands me in a second what it would take me a whole year to collect! And you want me to think that's normal? Go on... Leave me alone!

YACINE: Grandmother. I am the child of the dawn!

SAHIRA: Open your heart to him, he's come to change things!

THE OLD WOMAN: Child of the dawn? In my day we used to say love child.

SAHIRA: It's the same thing, grandmother. He was born on the first day of independence!

THE OLD WOMAN: *(after having given them a hard look)* The first day of independence, is it?

YACINE: Yes, the first day of independence.

THE OLD WOMAN: *(suddenly)* Be careful! Don't push me too far! Sometimes I get carried away!

YACINE: Forgive us, if we've offended you.

THE OLD WOMAN: You said a word I don't like to hear: independence! It makes me furious! Independence! Do you know where I live? In a flea bag, in a shack built on the bare ground. We live ten to a room! The house is falling apart, there's no water, no electricity!

YACINE: There are ten of you in... in that...

THE OLD WOMAN:... in that hell, that's the word you're looking for. You can imagine what a snake pit it is, ten people
crowded together in the same room? Children... there are
children everywhere! All we've ever been able to produce
are mobs of kids!

SAHIRA: They're your children?

THE OLD WOMAN: They belong to my two daughters, I've
disowned both of them. And the second with a squalling brat.
Sometimes you've got to stuff a rag in his mouth when he
yells too much, so that the old man, my crippled husband,
can recite his Koran!

YACINE: Calm yourself, grandmother.

THE OLD WOMAN: Let me tell you something. It wasn't
worth fighting for seven years just to end up like this!

SAHIRA: But grandmother, there was a revolution!

THE OLD WOMAN: What revolution? Revolution my ass! Who
were the people things changed for in this country? Who got
themselves appointed High Chancellor of the Order of Merit,
Vice-Chancellor of the Order of Dignity! Have you heard about
those great titles they thought up especially for party members?

YACINE: Titles, grandmother! You're out of your mind!

THE OLD WOMAN: Out of my mind, am I? Out of my mind?
They called it a people's revolution! Ha! Was it worth it, all
that celebrating, all those hymns of victory, all those phal-
lic dances, only to end up with them getting titles like
Padishah, Prince, Highness!

YACINE: *(to Sahira)* Is it true, what she's saying?

SAHIRA: Yes. They've created a whole aristocracy.

YACINE: *(outraged)* Titles of nobility!

THE OLD WOMAN: But just between us, the only thing high-class about them are their tailors—not their hearts, and not their souls! Despite their high-faluting titles, they are bums, and as ridiculous as some poor idiot straddling his donkey! And that's my last word, good luck to you!

> *She exits rapidly as two men enter talking, in the midst of a conversation already begun.*

SAHIRA: *(leading Yacine away)* Come on, we might as well take a look at our fountain.

> *They exit. The two men go to the bench. Each of them is holding a manuscript.*

CÉSAR: Here, this will be a quiet place to rehearse.

ANTARÈS: Which scene shall we do?

CÉSAR: The scene where Antarès, the butler, comes to inform César, his master, of the gossip about him at court.

ANTARÈS: Couldn't you could have given my character some other name than Antarès? I don't feel right about that name!

CÉSAR: Mine suits me fine!

ANTARÈS: Yes, but yours is César! And César, that sounds imperial, while mine... Antarès...

CÉSAR: Antarès, that's the name of an immense star!

ANTARÈS: Exactly! And when you're little, like me, a name like that can give you a complex!

CÉSAR: That's enough! Let's rehearse! *(After a brief pause, he assumes his role.)* So, Antarès, what do they say of me at court?

ANTARÈS: They say, Sire, that you are fond of power.

CÉSAR: I am fond of it, yes, because I achieved it through a harsh struggle against predatory colonialism! France itself recognizes that it was an epic battle!

ANTARÈS: *(stepping out of character)* What if we used "Mahabharata" instead of epic?

CÉSAR: *(also stepping out of character)* What was that word?

ANTARÈS: Mahabharata.

CÉSAR: What's that supposed to mean?

ANTARÈS: What! You mean you don't know?

CÉSAR: No. And that's kind of insulting, because after all I'm the playwright, I'm supposed to be the educated one, you're just an everyday second-rate actor!

ANTARÈS: Forgive me, I've offended you! But Mahabharata is a fairly familiar term...

CÉSAR: *(scathingly)* And what is this "mabarata" supposed to mean?

ANTARÈS: No: it's Mahabharata.

CÉSAR: Marabata.

ANTARÈS: Ma-ha-bha-ra-ta!

CÉSAR: *(sharply)* Which means? Shit!

ANTARÈS: Mahabharata, it's the name of the great epic poem of India!

CÉSAR: *(regaining control of the situation)* If you don't mind, we're rehearsing my play! Let's start again! *(In character)* They say I'm fond of power...and that's it?

ANTARÈS: Ah! Oh yes, Sire. They do admire your eloquence!

CÉSAR: And God knows, I am a very fountain of patriotic speeches!

ANTARÈS: *(out of character)* May I? The character of César, you know, I think that the farther along in the play you go, the more he starts to turn into a high-flown speechifier instead of sounding like a real politician.

CÉSAR: He's a character who employs allegory as naturally as you blow your nose!

ANTARÈS: And metaphor like we piss, you'll pardon the expression, and hyperbole like sitting on the john! Don't you think it's a little bit exaggerated?

CÉSAR: You're going to end up by annoying me so much that I'll be forced to take away your part.

ANTARÈS: Oh, I beg your pardon! Forget I said anything. Let's go on with it.

CÉSAR: I'm amused by the way you give in the minute I get angry. You have no dignity at all, my poor friend.

ANTARÈS: Actually, I do have a little, but it's been all flattened out, like one of those fish. I just take whatever's handed out to me, reprimands, insults...

CÉSAR: Do you know why I don't take away your part? It's because in real life you're just as much of a coward and just as spineless as your character. That's true, isn't it?

ANTARÈS: Yes, it's true. I was born tired. Work bores me. You mistreat me, you humiliate me all the time, but you do provide me with a prebend, and that's the important thing!

CÉSAR: And what's that word supposed to mean: prebend?

ANTARÈS: It means a daily food allowance.

CÉSAR: *(with contempt)* You mean like your dog food?

ANTARÈS: *(after looking at him for a moment)* You know, sometimes I hate myself for being such a coward, for being so spineless, only the thing is: I feel that I'm nothing, nil. And so you have to yell at me, even give me a kick in the behind, so that I feel I'm alive. I'm one of those people who can't say: I think, therefore I am. What I say is, my ass is sore, therefore I must exist!

CÉSAR: *(with an imperious gesture)* That will do! Enough! Back to the play! And no more interruptions!

ANTARÈS: There's just one thing I'd like you to clear up for me: why is your character, César, so fond of power?

CÉSAR: *(brandishing the manuscript)* It is there in the text, in black and white! *(Reading)* I am fond of power because if I have power I don't need drugs to get high, I don't need food to stay alive, I can experience a happiness that's beyond reality! Having power is like feeling weightless without having to be an astronaut!

ANTARÈS: There you are! I get it!

CÉSAR: No, you don't get it at all! *(He searches through the manuscript.)* We'll go back to the preceding scene, page 14.

Yacine and Sahira reenter.

ANTARÈS: *(looks for the place and finds it)* Now, let's see. *(Assuming his role)* Sire, they say that of late the people have been complaining!

CÉSAR: *(acting)* The people complain a lot, but out of habit, not out of conviction. They like making the rich feel guilty!

ANTARÈS: But this time, Sire, the people are serious!

CÉSAR: What are they complaining about? They've been given a flag, ministers, ambassadors, bank presidents, chancellors, constables! We can't do everything all at once!

ANTARÈS: That's just it! The people in all these high positions we've created are getting rich far too quickly!

CÉSAR: The people are stupid! We've given them the greatest kind of wealth: we've given them mosques, we've given them religious schools. They've got to be realistic!

ANTARÈS: But what they've been given hasn't worked. There are too many poor people today, too many beggars!

CÉSAR: So much the better! That way, there will be fewer delinquents!

ANTARÈS: Yes, but the people are hungry! And because they have to beg all the time, they're no longer strong enough to stand!

CÉSAR: You can beg sitting down. Why don't they do it that way? You're right to speak to me about it. I'm going to suggest giving the beggars free folding chairs. That would be an excellent public-relations move for the NLF.

ANTARÈS: The Holy Book says that God the Almighty loves the poor. In another world, they will be richer than kings, richer than the Gulf sheiks!

CÉSAR: If that's the case, I'll suggest that the folding chairs be leased, not given away.

> *During this scene, Yacine and Sahira first exchange puzzled looks and then find themselves having a hard time controlling themselves. Finally, they cannot contain themselves any longer. Yacine breaks in.*

YACINE: *(interrupting)* This is shocking! Absolutely shocking!

SAHIRA: You're disgusting, totally disgusting!

YACINE: The November uprising, does that mean nothing to you?

CÉSAR: What's got into you all of a sudden, sir?

YACINE: I'm one of those who fought in the shadows. I bore arms, I was in many battles!

SAHIRA: He held his head high, he was full of pride!

YACINE: We both lived through harsh days and nights in those war years. Nights hiking through harsh terrain, in wind and rain, days beneath the burning sun. The only thing that kept us going was honor.

SAHIRA: We are still mourning the dead, there are still wounds that have not healed!

CÉSAR: But what's got into both of you? Do you think I don't know there was a first of November, a revolution?

ANTARÈS: Yes sir, we both know that. We even went to the celebration for the declaration of independence!

YACINE: So then, how can you say such terrible things about the people?

CÉSAR: We're just as patriotic as you are, sir! But we're rehearsing a play, one of which it is my honor to inform you that I myself am the author!

ANTARÈS: That's it! It's a play.

YACINE: You're rehearsing a play in a park?

ANTARÈS: This play, it takes place in a park, so it's only fitting. He's a realistic playwright, sir.

CÉSAR: *(haughtily)* More than that, sir. I'm a committed playwright! I write about my own time, I see the evils inflicting our society, and I denounce them! Yes sir, I, personally, am denouncing!

YACINE: Pardon me, but I thought...

SAHIRA: That's all to your credit.

YACINE: I congratulate you! It is very courageous of you to defend the people!

CÉSAR: Who has said anything about defending the people? Haven't you understood the symbolism of my play? I'm denouncing the poor! They've become a plague, they multiply by leaps and bounds! And what's worse, they're the majority of the fundamentalist faction!

SAHIRA: *(to Yacine)* Do you see why I left the city, Yacine?

YACINE: Vanity and contempt! *(Suddenly raising his voice)* Go away!

ANTARÈS: Just hold it there, sir! Not on that note! I should warn you: this gentleman is a writer who has party approval. He has been given an honorary degree! And he's an officer in the National Order of Merit. What's more, he's also the nephew of Secretary Sidna, better known as the whale. You don't know him?

YACINE: *(dryly)* No.

CÉSAR: But he was formerly in the underground. Now, God be praised, he's turned his attention to business!

SAHIRA: He's told you to go away!

CÉSAR: Let's go, Antarès, he's one of those pure heroes, and as I said in one of my earlier plays, heroes are only convincing in war time; in everyday life, they're worthless! I'm sure that if I asked him to give you a kick in the behind, he wouldn't have the courage to do it.

SUCH GREAT HOPE

ANTARÈS: Do you think so?

CÉSAR: I'll bet you lunch!

ANTARÈS: *(intrigued)* Lunch?... *(César nods in agreement.)* In that case, let me give it a try. *(He stands in front of Yacine and presents his rear end.)* I'm a little short of funds today. Come on, you'd be helping me out. *(Yacine does not respond.)* Come on, do us a favor. *(Yacine remains unmoved. Disgustedly, Antarès turns on him.)* You're beneath contempt! I have no respect for you!

YACINE: *(in a rage, shouting)* Go away!

> *César and Antarès exit quickly; at the same time, the old beggar woman reenters, running.*

THE OLD WOMAN: God be praised, you're still here! There are two bearded men looking for you!

YACINE: For us?

THE OLD WOMAN: *(to Yacine)* No, for you!

YACINE: What do they want me for?

THE OLD WOMAN: When bearded men are looking for you it's as good as having the Devil himself after you, you just pick up your feet and start running. You'd better be off!

SAHIRA: She's right. Come on, let's go!

YACINE: I want to know what they want me for.

THE OLD WOMAN: If I were you, I wouldn't ask them!

YACINE: I want to see them!

SAHIRA: Wherever they go, blood is shed.

THE OLD WOMAN: Listen to her! Leave!

YACINE: I'm not going to run away!

SAHIRA: Yacine!

THE OLD WOMAN: They strike like lightning, and they're full of hate!

SAHIRA: Do you want to get yourself killed?

YACINE: Why would they kill me?

THE OLD WOMAN: Because they're vengeful and bitter, and they enjoy killing. And afterwards, they like to bellow curses over the bodies of the dead!

YACINE: I'm not running away!

SAHIRA: *(pleadingly)* My love, I told you: they murder poets, they strangle professors...

THE OLD WOMAN: *(breaking in)* They even strung up a police-man!

SAHIRA: Remember what they did to me, Yacine!

YACINE: Reason enough to make them account for it!

SAHIRA: *(trying to pull him away)* Come on, Yacine! They killed President Boudiaf!

THE OLD WOMAN: *(sharply)* No, my child, the President, that wasn't them.

SAHIRA: What do you mean, not them?

THE OLD WOMAN: The President, that was a whole network of interests, and us!

YACINE: What do you mean by that?

THE OLD WOMAN: A mixture of money, ambition, the will to power... He was murdered by people who wanted power because they were afraid that they'd never get any. And then there was us, because we didn't protect him by uniting behind him!

SAHIRA: You're wrong, grandmother. He was killed by the Islamic extremists!

THE OLD WOMAN: No, my child, I can assure you...

SAHIRA: How can you be so sure?

THE OLD WOMAN: It's only common sense. The beards kill people from behind, they take them by surprise, and then they cut and run.

SAHIRA: And that doesn't convince you?

THE OLD WOMAN: Killing like that, it's a kind of subtraction, and the beards are good at subtraction! But killing the President of the Republic, come on, to do that you need to know your algebra and your plane geometry, you know what I'm saying!

YACINE: *(amused)* Old lady, do you even know what algebra and plane geometry are?

THE OLD WOMAN: I found out when President Boudiaf was done in. My nephew, he's in high school, he explained it to me. The sad thing is, he won't be able to continue with his studies.

YACINE: Why not?

THE OLD WOMAN: That's the way it is here. Poor children start in with their studies, but they never get to finish them. Only the children of high officials are able to continue with theirs in the universities abroad.

YACINE: *(to Sahira)* Is she telling the truth?

SAHIRA: Yes, my love, it's quite true. The children of the nomenklatura are taught as though they'd been born in an age of high technology and space travel, and the children of the poor are plunged into the Koran and endless evocations of the great Arab past!

THE OLD WOMAN: That's how they've turned the young people into a generation of old men. *(Abruptly)* You know what else he told me, my young nephew? When history adds up the bill, all it will remember is Boudiaf's name, because it was his father—his country—and his mother—the revolution—that killed him.

SAHIRA: Probably because he was Algeria's last hope.

THE OLD WOMAN: The people don't call him Boudiaf, they call him Ramses the Great!

SAHIRA: While he was alive, he was unjustly rejected and shunted aside. Everyone hated him because he didn't share their vices and because he didn't give a damn for honors and sinecures.

THE OLD MAN: *(to Yacine)* Now, get going. I'm only a poor

woman who's had a hard life. My suffering has been so great that it seems to me it's older than I am. Maybe that's why I can sense things. I have a feeling that you're asking for trouble, so I'm begging you, go!

YACINE: You're a good woman. *(He digs in his pockets, takes out some money and puts it in her hands.)* Here, take this, take all of it, I hope it will give you what you wish for.

THE OLD WOMAN: Surely not!

YACINE: Do you want more?

THE OLD WOMAN: If you gave me all the gold in the world, it wouldn't be enough for what I wish for! And yet, I've only one wish.

YACINE: And what might that be?

THE OLD WOMAN: I wish that they'd sit in judgment on the ones responsible for the troubles we've had since independence. Now go, while there's still time.

YACINE: I won't run away.

SAHIRA: Yacine, look what they've done to me! My ugliness should be enough for you...

YACINE: Sahira, you are not ugly! You are beautiful, with the beauty of the sun as it rises above the horizon at dawn! You are the unjust wound to which we must pay homage.

THE OLD WOMAN: *(sharply)* Too late... there they are! Forgive me for running off, but there are people who depend on me... and believe me, it's hard being depended on, when you're poor!

She exits quickly while the two bearded men, who entered as she spoke, advance towards Yacine.

FIRST BEARDED MAN: We are looking for the one who calls himself the child of the dawn.

YACINE: What do you want of him?

SECOND BEARDED MAN: Are you he?

YACINE: I repeat: what do you want of him?

FIRST BEARDED MAN: They say he is an infidel.

YACINE: What do you mean by "infidel?"

SECOND BEARDED MAN: A pariah who does not observe the five commandments of Islam.

YACINE: I observe them.

FIRST BEARDED MAN: It's not enough to make your five daily prayers, to give alms only to the faithful...

YACINE: *(interrupting)* Why that restriction?

FIRST BEARDED MAN: Alms to the faithful only, because all infidels are to be put to the sword!

SECOND BEARDED MAN: And, therefore, scrupulous observance of the five commandments of Islam is not enough! *(A thought strikes him, and he suddenly turns to the First Bearded Man.)* Recite them! Let's see if you still leave one out, like you did the last time!

FIRST BEARDED MAN: *(taken by surprise)* You really want me to?

SECOND BEARDED MAN: *(in a commanding voice)* Recite them!

FIRST BEARDED MAN: Well... well... These are the five commandments: the profession of faith, the five daily prayers, Ramadan, the pilgrimage to Mecca... *(He stops, nearly at the end of his tether)* And... and...

SECOND BEARDED MAN: *(triumphantly)* See! You still forget one of them!

FIRST BEARDED MAN: *(trying to justify himself)* But not always the same one!

SECOND BEARDED MAN: *(almost paternally)* That doesn't matter! You always forget one. *(Suddenly raising his voice, in a scolding tone)* One of these days...

FIRST BEARDED MAN: *(whining)* It's not my fault if I have lapses of memory.

SECOND BEARDED MAN: *(in a conciliatory tone)* We'll forget about it for this time. *(Scolding again)* The next memory lapse, I'll get you! The fifth one you forgot is the Zakat! The obligatory tax!

FIRST BEARDED MAN: I thought I'd said that one.

SECOND BEARDED MAN: *(turning to Yacine)* As we were saying, scrupulous observance of the five commandments is not enough. You have to take a vow against pleasure, love, joy. Only then will you be allowed to enter Paradise!

YACINE: You'll forgive me, but your Paradise is way out of my range.

SECOND BEARDED MAN: *(to the First)* What does he mean by that?

FIRST BEARDED MAN: He means that he thinks it's too expensive.

SECOND BEARDED MAN: *(outraged)* Are you sure that that's what he means?

FIRST BEARDED MAN: Ask him.

SECOND BEARDED MAN: *(still addressing the First)* He probably doesn't know that we kill unbelievers, that we take the lives of heretics, that we slit the throats of skeptics?

FIRST BEARDED MAN: Why are we wasting time arguing with each other? Usually we ask them the question, and if they hesitate at all, we send them to Hell!

SECOND BEARDED MAN: *(to Yacine)* Learn, Stranger, that the highest happiness of being welcomed by God into Paradise is something that must be earned. Today, we will be generous, because we find you in the company of a Muslim sister.

SAHIRA: I'm not a Muslim sister!

FIRST BEARDED MAN: Don't take that tone, sister. You are addressing a future Emir of the Islamic Republic!

SAHIRA: Is that so? The Islamic Republic will really be something, with you two!

SECOND BEARDED MAN: Don't speak foolishly! You don't know what the Islamic Republic is!

SAHIRA: You want to turn Algeria into a little Iranian hamlet? Or a trading post for Saudi Arabia?

SECOND BEARDED MAN: Sister, you are mistaken. Once we've built our Islamic Republic, Iran and Saudi Arabia will be *our* colonies!

YACINE: *(lifting Sahira's veil)* Look! Your supporters are the ones who burned her!

FIRST BEARDED MAN: If she was burned, she must have deserved it! Our laws are the most just and humane in all the world!

SECOND BEARDED MAN: That's right, remind him of them while you're at it. What do we do with thieves?

FIRST BEARDED MAN: *(delighted to answer)* Cut off their hand.

SECOND BEARDED MAN: What do we do with liars?

FIRST BEARDED MAN: Rip out their tongues.

SECOND BEARDED MAN: With a woman taken in adultery?

FIRST BEARDED MAN: Stone her!

SECOND BEARDED MAN: Those who disparage the faith?

FIRST BEARDED MAN: Public beheading by the sword!

SECOND BEARDED MAN: Bravo! Bravo! You didn't forget anything that time!

FIRST BEARDED MAN: What do we do with a man who is unfaithful to his wife?

SECOND BEARDED MAN: *(provocatively)* What do we do to an adulterous husband?

FIRST BEARDED MAN: He gets killed too?

SECOND BEARDED MAN: No, you idiot! He is told to disavow his wife and take another one, so long as he continues to despise the delights and pleasures of the flesh.

FIRST BEARDED MAN: We stand here talking and talking, but he's still alive!

SECOND BEARDED MAN: *(recognizing the obvious)* By God, he is! *(to Yacine, curtly)* I must tell you...

YACINE: *(interrupting him)* You've nothing more to tell me! You and your friend, you live on too high a level for me! Off with you!

SECOND BEARDED MAN: *(to the First)* What does he mean by that?

FIRST BEARDED MAN: He means that we should go away.

SECOND BEARDED MAN: He obviously doesn't know that we hate those who do not side with us.

FIRST BEARDED MAN: Obviously. Tell him.

SECOND BEARDED MAN: *(to Yacine)* We are willing to engage in any kind of slaughter, any butchery, any destruction, to wipe out the abomination of poetry, the abomination of science, the abomination of any alliance between a true believer and an infidel!

YACINE: In short, the hand that picks a rose...

SAHIRA: *(continuing, going along with him)* The fruit a mouth might savor...

YACINE: A kiss that lingers on the lips like a bee on a flower...

SAHIRA: The gentle tenderness of tears...

YACINE: The full harmony of two bodies joined in the same delight...

SAHIRA: All things in life that are a gift from God...

YACINE: ... that instill happiness, that give strength and courage...

SAHIRA: All those things that dazzle and enchant us, every wonder...

YACINE: The land of my village and all my neighbors who dwell there...

SAHIRA: And you are asking us to deny all those things?

SECOND BEARDED MAN: *(flustered by their flow of words, then suddenly shouting)* Watch out! *(A pause. Then, in a milder tone, to the First Bearded Man)* I didn't get everything they were trying to say...

FIRST BEARDED MAN: *(stammering)* I... I... I've forgotten almost all of it...

SECOND BEARDED MAN: *(loudly)* Don't make me angry! You'd better remember at least one sentence!

FIRST BEARDED MAN: *(in a panic)* He said: the land is my village and the man... the men in it are my neighbors...

SECOND BEARDED MAN: All the men?

FIRST BEARDED MAN: All the men.

SECOND BEARDED MAN: *(still to the First)* Including infidels?

FIRST BEARDED MAN: *(addressing Yacine)* You weren't precise. Including infidels?

YACINE: All men, East, West, North and South!

SECOND BEARDED MAN: In other words, you are not a good Muslim!

YACINE: *(worked up)* Listen, you two! I am a Muslim, but I hate being forced to be more of a Muslim than my conscience dictates! I hate being made into a Muslim that follows orders like a soldier. *(Shouting)* Go away!

SECOND BEARDED MAN: *(to the First)* No doubt about it, he's an atheist! *(Giving an order)* Cut him down like a dog!

> *The First Bearded Man takes a revolver from his pocket, caresses it delicately and then aims it at Yacine. Sahira, in a spontaneous movement, shields him with her body.*

SAHIRA: No! Can't you see? I'm the fallen sister. The proof is in my face!

> *The Old Woman runs in.*

THE OLD WOMAN: *(to the Bearded Men, as she enters)* Brothers, save yourselves! The Police! The Police are coming!

FIRST BEARDED MAN: *(hastily returning his gun to his pocket)* God bless you, Old Woman, for your zeal and dedication!

SECOND BEARDED MAN: We will pray for you, Old Woman. *(To Yacine, threateningly)* We'll find you, even should you hide in your mother's womb! We'll find you!

Both run off.

THE OLD WOMAN: *(triumphantly, and unexpectedly)* You got a cigarette?

YACINE: Why? Do you smoke?

THE OLD WOMAN: Not me! I only want to pretend. I allow myself that luxury to prove to myself that I'm free to do anything that does not offend God. *(Mischievously)* And because I managed to pull it off!

SAHIRA: Pull what off?

THE OLD WOMAN: The police trick! It always works like gangbusters!

YACINE: The police... it wasn't true?

THE OLD WOMAN: Of course it's not true! I was watching what was going on from over there, along with a lot of others, as a matter of fact. I was hoping that someone a little better dressed than me would come to bail you out, but they all just stood there with their mouths hanging open. Then I began to be afraid for you, so I jumped in...

YACINE: *(offering her a cigarette)* You want a light?

THE OLD WOMAN: Oh, no. Just to hold it between my fingers and know I can smoke it if I feel like it. Now, my children, off with you, and quickly! You'd better leave the country!

YACINE: We can't do that, grandmother.

THE OLD WOMAN: Why?

SAHIRA: We've given ourselves one last chance. We can't leave everything hanging.

THE OLD WOMAN: A chance to do what?

YACINE: I told you: I am child of the dawn, and I want to change things.

THE OLD WOMAN: *(flabbergasted)* You want to change things? Are you crazy? Ramses the Great couldn't do that, even with the revolution behind him, and YOU want to change them... you?

YACINE: I want at least to try.

THE OLD WOMAN: No one will do it, not you, not anyone. Never! Unless... Yes, there is one thing you might be able to do: Go tell those who are really governing us that the people, all the people, the real people all over the country, will never follow them if they do not put on trial the men responsible for all the troubles we have had since independence!

SAHIRA: You've got trials on the brain, grandmother!

THE OLD WOMAN: The people have trials on the brain. But I'm talking about real trials. Not sham trials, not speeches! About legitimate judges! *(She assumes the solemn stance of a prosecutor, but continues to speak simply.)* You had a population hungry for dignity, peace and brotherhood! Why did you turn them into dogs? This land was rich when it became independent, why did you turn it into a nation of the disabled? Do you see where your depravity, your corruption, and above all your contempt, have led us?

YACINE: Go on!

THE OLD WOMAN: *(with restrained emotion)* Before independence, I was a cleaning lady for the European settlers. It wasn't perfect, but they never treated me disrespectfully. *(A pause.)* Losing that job put me on the streets. I didn't want to beg. I looked around for work, and finally I found a job with a woman who was one of the new ruling class, married to some party official. *(Pause.)* You should have seen HIM: he looked like a bug, and vain to boot! He thought he was God the Father! He'd only eat veal or leg of lamb, he only drank imported wine, French, Italian... I began to think his saliva was honey and that he shat precious stones when he sat on the john, I even thought his wife was probably in awe of his great golden cock... and then one day... that golden cock got one of my daughters pregnant, she was only in her teens, pretty as a picture. *(Pause.)* I went to see him to get him to give me what he owed me. He had his servants throw me out! They beat me and spit on me! *(Pause.)* Believe me, you mustn't expect anything from this country!

> *The two Bearded Men return silently. The First Bearded Man draws his revolver. He approaches the Old Woman.*

FIRST BEARDED MAN: *(shouting)* You damned beggar, you lied to us! You'll burn in hell in some damned witch's pot!

> *He fires several shots at the Old Woman, who falls to the ground, while the two Bearded Men run off. Sahira and Yacine are struck dumb. Sahira bends over the Old Woman and then gently closes her eyes with her hand.*

SAHIRA: She's dead. And so is our last chance, Yacine.

BLACKOUT

SCENE FIVE

Return to the eagle's nest. It is early morning. Sahira, Wisdom and Yacine are on stage. There is a fairly long pause.

YACINE: *(abruptly)* What now, old man?

WISDOM: I can understand your being upset by the old woman's death. But it's hard for me to enlighten you. *(A pause, then he turns to Sahira.)* What does Sahira think about it?

YACINE: Sahira is brooding.

SAHIRA: I'm not brooding. I'm boiling! And you know why!

YACINE: *(turning back to Wisdom)* What do you advise me to do?

WISDOM: I'm afraid we're not going to be able to avoid a civil war.

YACINE: Do you think that our army is divided too?

WISDOM: I don't think so. The army could restore order in the country, but it can't bring the factions together. Indeed, what could reconcile the jackal with the wolf?

YACINE: But come on, old man! There are some democratic parties in the country!

WISDOM: Democratic parties so-called, yes, but I doubt there are men who think democratically.

YACINE: Why?

WISDOM: Because that's an endemic problem. The tribal spirit is deeply rooted in us. The notion of democracy is foreign to us. Furthermore, we're emerging from thirty years of one-party, NLF rule, of rule by its hierarchy who had not only hoped that they would retain power for life but that they would also be able to hand it on to their descendants.

SAHIRA: Thank you, Wisdom!

YACINE: Why do you thank him?

SAHIRA: Because he saves me from having to say what I think!

WISDOM: *(thoughtfully)* Democracy... We should have thought of it right after independence. But the people preferred to put their trust in the NLF that had just freed them. That was their big mistake.

YACINE: And so because the people made a mistake they're going to have to pay for it till the end of time?

WISDOM: *(to Sahira)* What do you think about it, sincerely?

SAHIRA: I've already given him my advice, Wisdom. I've told him that from now on, neither of us has any right to speak.

WISDOM: Why?

SAHIRA: Because the day of the assassins has come. From now on, they and they alone will speak! The corpses are piling up: after the police, the soldiers, the military, now they're shooting down doctors, poets, journalists, they're cutting the throats of psychiatrists, professors, sociologists...

YACINE: *(breaking in)* There's something about those murders that I don't understand. How can our people go on supporting the killers?

WISDOM: When the people supported them in the past, the Islamists hadn't yet killed anyone. They supported them because they were denouncing the depravity and corruption of the State Party and promising to punish all the NLF leaders who were responsible.

YACINE: But I notice that the people that are being murdered today had no connection to the NLF, that some of them were even violently against it!

WISDOM: *(with a change of tone)* It's time for me to be at my prayers.

YACINE: First, explain to me why the Islamists aren't murdering their former enemies but are concentrating instead on men who are in no way responsible for the nation's collapse?

WISDOM: Because the Islamists are the children of the NLF. A child doesn't kill its father, even if he secretly hates him. Sooner or later they will all be back: the Devil giveth, and the Devil taketh away! *(He turns to leave.)*

YACINE: You're going, and you don't leave me one word of comfort!

WISDOM: What can I tell the child of the dawn? You are the one who feels, the one who is in harmony—hard to maintain these days, but harmony nonetheless—with your country. If you think that your desire to do something more for it is deep enough and in line with your innermost self, then do it! If you aren't sure, then don't. May you fare well! *(Exits.)*

YACINE: Help me, Sahira!

SAHIRA: You're not a good loser, my love.

YACINE: Why do you say that?

SAHIRA: We were given one chance, not two. We lost it with the old woman, but you persist in wanting to *do* something!

YACINE: It's our country, Sahira! Its history is entrusted to us, we are responsible even for the lives of those who lived here centuries ago, for those who live here today. Whatever we say, whatever we do, we are an extension of them, we do not have the right to be indifferent!

SAHIRA: Well, I'm tired of dragging this country and its never-ending tragedy behind me. I'm fed up with its crushing me, breaking me, eviscerating me. I'm fed up with the poor crawling like maggots in the dirt, with the rich bloated up like wineskins, with the so-called blessings of the NLF and with all its lethal and epileptic offspring!

YACINE: *(taking her into his arms)* Calm down! Please?

SAHIRA: *(beseechingly)* Yacine, I want out of this nightmare.

YACINE: How beautiful you must have been in the midst of all your candles! My strange little Sahira! Let yourself go a little, relax.

SAHIRA: *(kissing him)* There! I'm calm now. I can talk to you without getting upset. Yacine, it's over. The evil can't be undone. It's been over ever since the mobs emerged from God knows where, with all their followers, and began to bleed the country systematically!

YACINE: And yet, Sahira, our dawn was miraculously beautiful, and with one fell swoop it wiped out a century of justice denied!

SAHIRA: And what if we didn't really earn it? What if we only stole our freedom?

YACINE: How can you say that, you of all people? You lived in the eagle's nest with all our comrades. You witnessed their sufferings, their fatigue, their pains, all borne with pride. Of all the wounded men you cared for, was there one who complained, one who regretted having fought? We were all ready, sometimes against all reason, to shout into the wind, to fight against the storm, to shout that it was honorable to die, even with all our lives before us, so that our country could be reborn.

SAHIRA: What just country did you want?

YACINE: You know very well what country we wanted!

SAHIRA: I want you to tell me again.

YACINE: We dreamed of a country faithful to itself, living in brotherhood with the rest of the world...

SAHIRA: And what else? *(A pause.)* You don't dare say it? I'll say it for you: It is honorable to die when your death can reconcile the heart of the man who has with the heart of the man who has not!

YACINE: Why do you remind me of that?

SAHIRA: So that you will understand that you fought your revolution as a poet, and that others did so with a passion to avenge themselves for a hundred and thirty years of being kept in the dark, held down, poor. And what did they make of your starry revolution and your dream of tree-planted hilltops?

YACINE: Don't mock me!

SAHIRA: So long as you cannot face these facts, you will be unable to put it behind you! The resolution they were waging was not the same as yours. For thirty years now, they've been feeding the people with honor, with glory, with martyrdom! They've kept drumming it into them: You're Arabs, be Arabs! You're Muslims, be Muslims! *(Suddenly changing tone)* Look! Even now, the house is on fire and they're still reciting the prayer book and telling them they must believe in God and in the Arab nation... and you're still saying, "The earth is my village!" You know it's true, Yacine.

YACINE: I thought I'd pulled you out of that swamp of hatred you were bogged down in, and I see, I sense that again...

SAHIRA: You know, Yacine, when hatred seizes you it pierces your flesh, it alters the blood, the veins, the heart, it gives you a new, tougher skin. It invades you, like maggots invade the bodies of wild beasts.

YACINE: I have to decide. Your hatred doesn't help me. It blinds you and keeps you from being lucid. *(He draws away and gazes towards the horizon.)*

SAHIRA: Look at the sky all you like! It's empty!

YACINE: Have you lost faith as well?

SAHIRA: The sky is empty, or if it isn't it's guilty of having selected murderers to deliver its message!

YACINE: My Seagull! Control yourself!

SAHIRA: *(shouting)* I tell you again, I've had my share! Thirty years of miserable life. Thirty years of miserable death, thirty years of miserable hope and for what... Look at your Seagull's faced burned with acid by the monsters created by the NLF!

(Yacine takes her in his arms. After a short pause, Sahira continues in a determined voice.) Yacine, you've got to leave. You must go, leave the country.

YACINE: Leave the country?

SAHIRA: You've nothing more to do here!

YACINE: I am the poet-intermediary of my people!

SAHIRA: Haven't you understood, or don't you want to? *(Changing tone)* Do you remember what you told me, thirty years ago, when you went away, your last words?

YACINE: No, I don't remember.

SAHIRA: You will. You told me: I have to leave, because I must bear witness for a proud, generous Algeria, a tolerant Algeria open to the world...

YACINE: Yes, probably...

SAHIRA: Well, today Algeria is neither proud nor generous nor tolerant, and it is open only to the Arab and Islamic world. *(Forestalling his reply)* Wait! I haven't finished! You also said: I have an appointment with my century, a meeting with mankind. I must not miss this rendez-vous with the world. Well, Algeria belongs to the Islamic Republic, or at least to those factions greedy for power and openly tearing each other apart.

YACINE: I must do something, I feel it. This despair, this anger, this hatred seething under the sun, demands it of me. I am responsible and accountable for what will or will not happen here tomorrow.

SAHIRA: So go! I absolve you of any future regret! Go and bear witness to those who can still be happy, those who believe that man needs man as the flower needs the bee, as the furrow needs grain. They are the ones you should be telling: Never despair, or if at times the night seems long and you are at the end of your strength, you must know that there is always new hope, unimaginable hope, hope that can suddenly transfigure you...

YACINE: *(finishing her speech)* ... ready, when great trials bring doubt, to cast the seed into the wind where a gust can carry it to the ends of the world. Those are my words you're repeating to me. I didn't know you had such a good memory.

SAHIRA: I fervently accepted everything that came from you, I kept it devoutly, because for me, Yacine, you are the first, the unique love, the love you know at once will never never come again. Kiss me. *(They kiss. A pause. Suddenly, she breaks away and speaks with violence.)* It's exciting, isn't it, to kiss a heretic whose face has been marked with the seal of wickedness!

YACINE: Sahira, why do you say that?

SAHIRA: *(cynically)* The acid trickled all down my body. You'll see when I undress, when I stand naked...

YACINE: *(interrupting her, distressed and sorrowful)* Please, don't use that tone.

SAHIRA: *(launched, in the same voice)* ... When I stand naked you'll see more burn scars than beauty spots! *(She begins to laugh.)* Or maybe you'll think that the marks you see are rubies!

YACINE: Don't talk like that, not with that voice!

SAHIRA: And why not, my darling?

YACINE: That's a word you've never used.

SAHIRA: Because it's one you hate. Now, I don't care whether you hate it or not!

YACINE: What has come over you all of a sudden?

SAHIRA: I've just realized, as you were kissing me, that I hate you as well!

YACINE: Sahira!

SAHIRA: *(unable to stop)* I hate you like I hate this country, like I hate this people, like I hate their Arab-Islamic vocation, their Arabness, their Arabism, their Arabicity, their Arabitude... Go! Go away! Go!

YACINE: Sahira!

SAHIRA: Go!

YACINE: *(after a pause)* So I will return empty handed from this pilgrimage? All I will have seen is the flaming vanity of the NLF big shots? The horrible poverty of a disoriented people? The killer insanity of Khomeini's green army? I could have borne the memories of shame, the memories of corruption, of the Ayatollah's madness, but I cannot bear the memory of your eyes blazing with hatred! *(A pause.)* You're going to let me leave without a word? Or will I go with only the cold words of some star world... *(A pause.)*

SAHIRA: *(in a gentler voice)* Go away from here, leave this country as soon as you can. Take the first plane. You mustn't become soiled, not you! Knowing you have managed to remain yourself, the warrior with the silken hands, the prodigal child of the dawn, will help me to live on. This time, I'm begging you: Save yourself and save me in your memory, as I was once, your Seagull.

BLACKOUT

SCENE SIX

Back in the hospital room. The nurse is seated by Yacine's bed. The doctor enters carrying X-rays.

DOCTOR: Well?

NURSE: He's been delirious. I catch a phrase here and there. He spoke of an eagle's nest, a park, a seagull...

DOCTOR: I've just got the X-ray results. They aren't very good.

NURSE: What do you mean?

DOCTOR: Kidney failure combined with heart failure. He's a goner.

NURSE: *(sadly)* Goner? *(Abruptly)* Doctor, he moved his lips. He's probably going to ramble on some more...

DOCTOR: *(showing her the X-rays)* See where the two bullets are lodged. There, especially, that's a hard one...

NURSE: But doctor, the man's a poet.

DOCTOR: I know he's a poet.

NURSE: It's a tragedy for the country!

DOCTOR: *(with a shrug)* The country ignored him while he was alive, you can imagine after he's dead! It's a sad thing for that woman who's waiting.

NURSE: She's back?

DOCTOR: She never left. She's been waiting since a while ago.

NURSE: Did you tell her he was done for?

DOCTOR: I didn't dare. I feel sorry for her, with her poor burned face, it looks like it must have been acid.

NURSE: But she's got to be told.

DOCTOR: You do it. It will be easier, woman to woman. You'll be better at finding the right words than I would be.

NURSE: You're right, I'll go.

The nurse exits.

YACINE: *(offstage voice)* Seagull, I left, as you wanted. I wrote you from Paris, which felt like being at the edge of the world. No sooner had I arrived there then I was sorry I'd left you. But your memory stays with me, it's tugging at me right now. I was wrong, I should have stayed there with you. Loving a woman, a country, means you agree to live with them through all the long exile, all the great suffering they experience. If I stay away from you, I'll be living a life of fear and shame. I fear for the civil war that is coming and I'm ashamed of having run away at the very moment you needed me most. I'm going to stay here just long enough to gather my thoughts, and then I'll be back. We'll do something wonderful together. We'll go street to street, door to door, town to town, telling our people exactly what has happened. We'll tell them the truth straight out, in plain language. Big words have already caused too much pain. We'll tell them: Your uprising was just, your independence was real. But the freedom-fighting NLF is dead, it died on the day it took power. What took over was a counterfeit and fake NLF, one that shamelessly went to bed with the revolution. Between them, they produced a bastard child. But you, my people, you did not know that, you thought that it was a legitimate son. You had your reasons, and history will not hold it against you. We'll tell them: This time, beware that your innocence and trust do not again fall into the trap that the father is already setting to ensure that his son will come into his inheritance. The father and son are one and the same. They're both sensation mongers, smooth talkers avid for power. With the father, you had a vain, contemptuous, corrupt nomenklatura. With the son, you will have the pitiless theocracy of the Ayatollahs, equally vain, equally depraved. The father brought you ruin. The son will bring calamity. The father severed you from the world. The son will cut you off from mankind. The father lynched the dawn, the son will consume your future in fire, along with any chance of your becoming a part of the world at large. We'll tell them: You must get hold of yourselves! You must take control of your fate, you must assume responsibility for your country. Act with brotherhood toward each other, but drive away both father and son, send them back to the devil, for from there they came! If you don't, and if you don't do it now, then Algeria will sink into the darkness, like a ship sinking on the high seas, deep under the waters. And your uprising will have been for nothing! Your independence will have been for nothing! You will go back to being what you were before, the pariah of nations, and—know this, my people—if that should happen, then you will have no excuse in the eyes of history.

The nurse reenters.

DOCTOR: He began rambling after you left.

NURSE: What did he say?

DOCTOR: I couldn't catch everything. Did you tell the woman? *(The nurse does not reply.)* The look on your face! What's happened?

NURSE: Doctor, I didn't dare tell her.

DOCTOR: Why?

NURSE: I have the feeling she won't survive his death. And then... She's so full of hope. *(With a change of tone)* What was he going on about?

DOCTOR: The only words I could catch were: No excuse in the eyes of history.

∾

Wajdi Mouawad

Wedding Day at the Cro-Magnons'

Translated from the French by
Shelley Tepperman

UBU REPERTORY THEATER PUBLICATIONS
NEW YORK

Wajdi Mouawad, born in 1968, has made an indelible mark on the Quebec theater community as an actor, director and author of five startling plays, including *Willy Protagoras enfermé dans les toilettes (Willy Protagoras Locked in the Bathroom)* and *Les Mains d'Edwidge au moment de la naissance (Edwidge's Hands at the Moment of Birth)*. His is a totally original voice, spanning the cultural gaps that can exist between his native Lebanon, North America, Quebec and Europe. He has directed productions for Montreal's Théâtre O Parleur, Belgium's Théâtre de Poche and the National Theatre School of Canada, including his own adaptations of Louis-Ferdinand Céline's *Voyage au bout de la nuit (Journey to the End of the Night)* and Jules Verne's *Around the World in Eighty Days*. Wajdi has also performed his own dramatic works on Radio Canada FM and has starred in his one-man play *Alphonse,* which toured France after its successful Montreal run.

Shelley Tepperman is a translator and dramaturg with a special interest in Quebecois and Latin American theater. She has translated thirteen plays from Quebec, most of them by playwrights of "la relève"—the "new guard." Two of these, Yvan Bienvenue's *In Vitro* and Dominic Champagne's *Playing Bare,* have been short-listed for the Governor General's award in translation. Other recent translations include two Mexican plays and several contemporary Italian short stories, two of which she recently dramatized for the Canadian Broadcasting Corporation's radio network.

Wedding Day at the Cro-Magnons' had its English-language premiere, in Shelley Tepperman's translation, at the National Arts Centre Atelier in Ottawa, Canada, on April 10, 1996. After a ten-day run the production transferred to Theatre Passe Muraille in Toronto where it ran from May 7 to June 2, 1996.

Director	**Banuta Rubess**
Assistant Director	**Vikki Anderson**
Set and Costume Designer	**Sue LePage**
Lighting Designer	**Bonnie Beecher**
Music and Sound Design	**Marc Desormeaux**

CAST

Nazha	**Beverly Wolfe**
Neel	**Alon Nashman**
Nelly	**Arsinée Khanjian**
Souhayla	**Diana Fajrajsl**
Neyif	**Earl Patsko**
Gentleman/Sheep	**Robert Kennedy**

Produced by the **National Arts Centre Atelier**
Gil Osborne, *Artistic Associate, English Theatre*
Andis Celms, *Producer, English Theatre*
Susan Serran, *Artistic Producer, Theatre Passe Muraille*

WEDDING DAY AT THE CRO-MAGNONS':
FROM PAGE TO STAGE

The translation of *Journée de noces chez les Cro-Magnons (Wedding Day at the Cro-Magnons')* was originally commissioned as part of the February 1994 edition of INTERACT, the Factory Theatre's festival of recent Quebec plays in translation. Jackie Maxwell, then Artistic Director of Toronto's Factory Theatre, dramaturged the first version of the translation and staged the first public reading of the play.

In the fall of 1994, Theatre Passe-Muraille and the National Arts Centre Atelier became committed to further developing the play in English. Under the guidance of director/dramaturg Banuta Rubess, the author and translator continued re-writing and polishing, and the new material was tested and refined through workshops held in March 1995 and January 1996.

Along the way, there were various public readings of the play: at the Quebec Roundup at Edmonton's Northern Light Theatre directed by Don Kugler; at Pink Ink and Ruby Slippers' Acts of Passion translation series in Vancouver, directed by Katrina Dunn; and at the NAC Atelier's Page to Stage Festival of New Work, directed by Michael Devine. In July 1995, the author and translator spent two weeks in residence at the Carnegie-Mellon Showcase of New Plays in Pittsburgh, where a version of the play was presented in three staged readings directed by Michael Montell. All of these provided valuable opportunities to hear the work read by different actors in different settings.

The author and translator would like to thank Gil Osborne, Andis Celms, Banuta Rubess, Garry Bowers, Linda Gaboriau, Frank Gagliano, Susan Serran, Paul Lefebvre, and all the artists who participated at the various stages of development.

Their feedback, generosity of spirit, and belief in the play and the translation have improved and enriched it. Special thanks to the Writing and Publication Section of the Canada Council for their continued translation funding.

An important note: The version of the play published here is the fruit of the collaboration with Banuta Rubess and was developed and edited specifically for the 1996 Theatre Passe-Muraille/National Arts Centre co-production. A translation of the original version is published in *New Quebec Voices*, Scirocco Drama, Montreal, 1997.

SHELLEY TEPPERMAN
1997

For Shelley Tepperman
For Paul Lefebvre
With all my friendship

I would like us all to lay down our arms,
because I carry my only weapon openly
while others conceal the weapons they have.

THOMAS SANKARA
President of Burkina Faso
Assassinated on October 15, 1987

In the battle between you and the world,
protect the world.

FRANZ KAFKA

CHARACTERS

NEYIF, *the father,* sixty-five years old
NAZHA, *the mother,* fifty-five years old
NELLY, *the daughter,* thirty years old
NEEL, *the younger son,* seventeen years old
SOUHAYLA, *the neighbor,* thirty-four years old
THE GENTLEMAN, *a foreigner,* thirty-three years old

PRONUNCIATION OF CHARACTERS' NAMES

NEYIF: rhymes with "hey, thief." Accent on the second syllable.
NAZHA: Naz' ha. Both syllables rhyme with "what." The "h" is aspi-
   rated.
NEEL: rhymes with "heel." Should not be elongated to two full syllables.
SOUHAYLA: Sou hay' la. "Sou" rhymes with "soup." "Hay" rhymes
   with "fry." "La" rhymes with the musical note.

ACT 1

A middle-class apartment, visibly damaged by bombing. Morning.

NAZHA: That's not how it's gonna start this time!

NEEL: It always starts the same way, mama!

NAZHA: Shit!

NEEL: How else do you want it to start, if not the same way?!

NAZHA: What is this garbage?!

NEEL: Always, always, always the same way!

NAZHA: Who chose the lettuce—you or the Armenian?!

NEEL: Mama!

NAZHA: Was it you or that monkey turd who chose this lettuce, Neel?!

NEEL: It was him!

NAZHA: Would you look at this! Stick your nose in it!

NEEL: Mama!

NAZHA: Stick your nose in it!

NEEL: Don't get so UPSET!

NAZHA: And now explain to me how on earth, I mean, *what brilliant technique* am I supposed to use to turn shit like this into food!

NEEL: All right! Don't get so upset about the fucking lettuce! I'll just get some more!

NAZHA: What are you doing?!

NEEL: I'll go to the Greek's this time!

NAZHA: Oh, that's brilliant. My son is an ass. I have an ass for a son!

NEEL: And if I don't find any lettuce at the Greek's, I'll steal some from the sheikh's garden!

NAZHA: Where the goddam fucking hell do you think you're going?!

NEEL: To the Greek's to get your goddamn fuckin' lettuces!

NAZHA: That's right. Great. And afterwards, I'll simply have to drag our neighbours to your funeral! Just imagine the looks on their faces... Don't you dare leave this house!

NEEL: It's pretty stupid to do this on a day they're bombing!

NAZHA: How could we have known? We couldn't have guessed! What do you want... You can't predict idiocy like you can predict the weather!

NEEL: Speaking of the weather, it isn't exactly rosy; over there, the sky is frowning at us; soon it'll be all black!

NAZHA: Fine. Your sister's dress will look all the more white!

NEEL: My sister's dress is still at the dressmaker's!

NAZHA: He's going to bring it over before noon.

NEEL: Let's hope he doesn't get blown up on the way!

NAZHA: *(returning to her lettuce)* He wiped himself with it!

NEEL: Sunshine all day, they said. Don't make me laugh!

NAZHA: He wipes his ass with his lettuces, that disgusting slob! Don't ever go back to the Armenian's, do you hear me?!

NEEL: We'll never go back to the Armenian's.

NAZHA: He sells lettuce that smells like fish.

NEEL: What do you have against fish?

NAZHA: Bring me a bag and throw out this crap. We aren't having salad.

NEEL: No salad.

NAZHA: Right, no salad. No salad. You don't need salad for a meal, my boy. Come to think of it, it's even better not to have salad at all.

NEEL: I told you it'll always start the same way. Always, always, always.

NAZHA: You think so? No! No! If there isn't any salad, we'll make potatoes. I know, we'll fry them! Yes, that's it. We'll make fried potatoes! Go get me the cloth bag under the kitchen sink, I think I still have some good old potatoes left. Hell's bells! No one's gonna tell me there won't be a wedding feast the day of my daughter's wedding. We'll make potatoes.

NEEL: These potatoes of yours are rotten, mama!

NAZHA: Well, even more reason! We have to finish them off. We can't let ourselves throw out food when there are men fighting just a hundred yards away. No, we're going to fry those potatoes.

NEEL: If the potatoes are fryable, we'll sure as hell fry them.

NAZHA: Come on. Don't dawdle, we still have to skin them.

NEEL: If the potatoes are skinnable, we'll sure as hell skin them.

NAZHA: Fuckin' shit! With all this I still haven't finished.

NELLY: *(off)* When are we going to Berdawnay? Next Friday?

NAZHA: Not again!

NEEL: That makes three times in two hours.

NELLY: *(off)* When are we going to Berdawnay?

NEEL: Next Friday!

NAZHA: She must have fallen asleep under the sink again. Go and get her.

NEEL: And Walter?

NAZHA: Walter didn't sleep at home last night.

NEEL: Again?

NAZHA: As usual.

NEEL: But he promised he'd come and play with me.

Souhayla knocks and enters carrying several delicious-looking plates of food. In the distance, light bombing is heard.

SOUHAYLA: Finally!

NAZHA: Souhayla!

NEEL: He promised me!

SOUHAYLA: I came to give you a little hand!

NAZHA: You're such a darling, Souhayla!

NELLY: *(off)* When are we going to Berdawnay?

Souhayla puts the dishes down.

NEEL: Next Friday! He promised he'd come and play with me.

NAZHA: But you shouldn't have! No really, you shouldn't have. It's too much! It's really too much! Ya aybeyshoom! Really, ya aybeyshoom! But why did you go to so much trouble! My goodness!

SOUHAYLA: The women and I decided to make you these few little dishes.

NELLY: *(off)* Next Friday?

NEEL: Next Friday.

SOUHAYLA: They're all going to come, you know.

NAZHA: They're all going to come?

SOUHAYLA: All of them! With their husbands and daughters.

NELLY: *(off)* Next Friday?

NEEL: He promised me!

NAZHA: Stop it Neel!

NEEL: Yes, but he promised me!

NAZHA: He promised, he promised... He always promises.

NELLY: *(off)* Next Friday?

NAZHA: And go check on your sister! Excuse me, my dear Souhayla! This is all so embarrassing. My God! Fassoulia! And Tabbouleh! Go and see your sister, Neel. And a plate of keshk—and kibbeh, of course. Oh, don't they smell delicious! What an aroma!

SOUHAYLA: The neighbours are very happy for your daughter! They all told me! They're going to wear their prettiest dresses.

NAZHA: It's going to be an incredible party. The bombs will freeze in the sky!

NEEL: But the rain sure won't!

NAZHA: Ya aybeyshoom! All the work *I* was supposed to do. Really, it's too much. It's much too much!

NEEL: I guess I'll go get the bag of potatoes.

NAZHA: *(to Neel)* Make the coffee while you're in there! What a delicious smell!

Neel has left.

SOUHAYLA: Is he all right? He seems a bit nervous these days.

NAZHA: Oh! The poor thing. Maybe one day things will sort themselves out in that poor head of his. I don't know... We can only hope...

SOUHAYLA: It can't be very easy for you!

NAZHA: Don't ask! We just can't send him to school. The situation is too volatile!

SOUHAYLA: All of us women understand your plight. We all talk about it!

NAZHA: I know. He should never have been born!

NELLY: *(off)* Next Friday we're going to Berdawnay?

NEEL: *(off)* That's right. Next Friday we're going to Berdawnay.

NAZHA: My dear, he can only bear the sound of the bombing when he's inside the house!

SOUHAYLA: Unbelievable! He's really that sensitive?

NELLY: *(off)* Are we going to eat kneffay?

NEEL: *(off)* Are you kidding? We're gonna stuff our faces with it!

NAZHA: His father and I don't know how to help him get used to the bombing. Maybe he'll learn to enjoy it!

SOUHAYLA: Poor boy! Poor Neel.

NEEL: *(off)* Mama! Your potatoes stink! They reek!

NAZHA: We don't have any choice, Neel. If you want you can come and peel them here!

NELLY: *(off)* When are we going to Berdawnay to eat kneffay?

NEEL: *(off)* Next Friday.

NELLY: *(off)* Next Friday we're going to Berdawnay to eat kneffay?

NEEL: *(off)* Yes!

NELLY: *(off)* Next Friday?

NEEL: *(off)* Next Friday.

NELLY: *(off)* When are we going to Berdawnay?

NEEL: *(off)* Next Friday!

NELLY: *(off)* Next Friday we're going to Berdawnay to eat kneffay?

NEEL: *(off)* Yes!

NELLY: *(off)* When are we going to Berdawnay to eat kneffay? Next Friday?

NEEL: *(off, yelling)* Yeeessssss!

NAZHA: Oh, but the fiancé, my dear Souhayla, just you wait... the fiancé! The fiancé, Souhayla... he's the kind of... he's so... Ah! He's a man full of... charm, yes! Charm, my dear! Charm!

NEEL: *(entering with a pot of Turkish coffee)* I'm fed up! I'm fed up! I am completely fed up!!!

NAZHA: Stop whining, Neel.

NEEL: She doesn't want to wake up!

NAZHA: Be careful, Neel! Darling, you're spilling coffee every-where! Here you go, my dear Souhayla.

SOUHAYLA: So... the fiancé?

NAZHA: He's so charming, my dear, he's unbelievably charm-ing. Did you know he bought a car for the occasion?

SOUHAYLA: A car!

NAZHA: Ah, yes, my dear! A car! From Europe! That's right!

NELLY: *(off)* What's new?

NEEL: Everything's old.

NELLY: *(off)* What's new?

NEEL: Everything's old.

NELLY: *(off)* Everything's old?

NEEL: Everything's old!

NELLY: *(off)* When are we going to Berdawnay to eat kneffay?

NEEL: Next Friday!

NAZHA: A beautiful car, yes! What do you think? We weren't going to give our little girl away to just anyone!

SOUHAYLA: With the war it isn't easy to find somebody suitable in this country.

NAZHA: Ah yes! We said—her father and I—that since in a situation like ours it's been impossible to give our children a decent education, we might as well give them, yes give them away, to someone who's had the time, that's it, the *time*! Who's had the time to go to school, to study, to *become* somebody!

SOUHAYLA: That's right. That's exactly it! To become somebody. To *be* somebody.

NAZHA: What do you want, in this country, nobody is a somebody anymore!

SOUHAYLA: What it comes down to is that there's simply no one left in this country!

NELLY: *(off)* Next Friday we're going to Berdawnay?

NEEL: Goddam fuckin' shit!

NAZHA: Neel!

NEEL: I'd like to fall asleep all of a sudden, all over the place too!

NAZHA: Stop it!

NEEL: And your potatoes are not peelable!

NAZHA: Stop yelling, do you mind!

NEEL: They're NOT PEELABLE!

NAZHA: *(placating)* Yes they are, they are, sweetie, they are.

NEEL: The minute I get a grip so I can peel them, they fall apart in my hands!

NAZHA: You're squeezing them too hard!

NEEL: I'm hardly touching them!

NAZHA: Here! Look! You have to hold them gently! Go on! We'll tell everyone *you're* the one who peeled them!

SOUHAYLA: You're making potatoes for your daughter's wedding?

> *Nazha and Neel speak the following two portions of dialogue simultaneously.*

NAZHA: They're to go with the mutton! To go with the leg. The leg of mutton.
NEEL: Between potatoes and lettuce that smells like fish, *I* wouldn't have had to think twice...

NAZHA: We have a leg of mutton. And to go with the leg of mutton, we're going to fry some potatoes.
NEEL: *I'd* have gone for the fish! At least the fish was fresh!

SOUHAYLA: Well, *I* brought you a little something! Now it's nothing much...

NAZHA: What is it?

SOUHAYLA: Open it up and look!

NAZHA: You shouldn't have! You really shouldn't have! Souhayla! Ya aybeyshoom! Really! Ya aybeyshoom! Ooooh! Beyleywa! You must be insane! This is far too extravagant!

SOUHAYLA: For a wedding, my dear Nazha, nothing's too extravagant!

NEEL: Barfable shitty potato mush!

NAZHA: Neel! You're starting to get on my nerves! I'd like to drink my coffee in peace.

NEEL: I'm fed up to my ass! I'm a little boy in the prime of my youth and my role doesn't consist of peeling unpeelable potatoes! I should be playing outside with my friends! I want to go play outside with my friends!

NAZHA: You can't! There are too many snipers.

NEEL: Where's Walter? Where is he?

A violent explosion, fairly close by.

SOUHAYLA: My God, what a storm! Nature's certainly very powerful!

NEEL: That's not a storm! That was a 255 that just exploded in the south quarter.

NAZHA: If only it were a storm! It might calm everybody down!

NEEL: I'm sick to death of these potatoes that smell like war. They're giving me a pain in the balls. I can't peel them. They're all soft and they're falling apart in my hands. Enough is enough! I'm sick of this!

NAZHA: All right! All right! Stop yelling!

NEEL: I'm sick to death of this dump! I'm sick to death of

this wedding! It gives me a pain in the balls, do you hear?! A pain in the gonads! One more putrid potato and they're gonna burst!

NAZHA: That's enough! I said that's enough! Stop peeling the potatoes! You're right, they're not peelable!

NEEL: They're rotten!

NAZHA: You're right, the potatoes are rotten! And they fall apart in your hands!

NEEL: Fucking right!

NAZHA: That's enough! We'll make *mashed* potatoes! We'll serve them *mashed*! Go and put them in the mixmaster!

SOUHAYLA: Is there something *I* can do?

NAZHA: Oh no, my dear Souhayla! Ya aybeyshoom! You're here to brighten up my morning by having a little coffee with me! Anyway, there's really nothing I can do until Neyif gets back from the slaughterhouse. He's gone to get the mutton.

SOUHAYLA: But surely there are other things to be done...

NEEL: Tickle my bum.

SOUHAYLA: What can I help you prepare?

NEEL: Tickle my hair.

NAZHA: Well, I have to scoop out the battenjen and the coussa. Maybe I still have some eggs...

NEEL: Tickle my legs.

SOUHAYLA: Well then! Let's get to work on the coussa and the battenjen. Do you have a dishtowel?

NEEL: Tickle my bowel.

NAZHA: Neel!

NEEL: You can't even have fun around here anymore!

NAZHA: *(to Neel)* Go get me the paper bag on the kitchen counter!

NEEL: When I think that right now, in America, black men 10 feet tall are playing basketball...!

Neel exits.

SOUHAYLA: Don't get upset, my dear. His brother's absence must be upsetting for him. You have to understand him!

NAZHA: I understand him! I understand him! It's just that I'm starting to lose my fucking patience!

NELLY: *(off)* Mama.

NAZHA: *(to Souhayla)* She's awake! *(To Nelly)* Yes darling?

NELLY: *(off)* Is my dress here yet?

NAZHA: Not yet sweetheart. The fiancé, Souhayla, he's... he's very.... virile!

SOUHAYLA: Ahhhh!

NAZHA: He's tall, he's strong, he's noble, he's handsome!

SOUHAYLA: Ohhhh!

NAZHA: And people say he's very smart! Yes! Cultured! That he's rich, and that he can walk right into a career in a skyscraper!

Neel enters with several eggplants and zucchini.

NEEL: Here's the coussa and the battenjen. Now *I* get to mix-master the potatoes.

NELLY: *(off)* Mama.

NAZHA: Yes darling?

NELLY: *(off)* Who's there?

NAZHA: Souhayla.

NELLY: *(off)* Hello Souhayla.

SOUHAYLA: Oh! Nelly! I'm so happy! I'm so happy! I am so happy!

NEEL: There you go: she's very happy and we're absolutely thrilled for her.

A very violent clap of thunder.

SOUHAYLA: Oh my God! What on earth is that!

NEEL: It's the storm, calm down! Calm down!

NAZHA: It was awfully close!

SOUHAYLA: You're sure it was only the storm?

NEEL: *I* can tell the difference between the storm and a 255 or even a 590!

NELLY: *(off)* When are we going to Berdawnay?

NEEL: Next Friday.

NAZHA: She's fallen asleep again.

NEEL: It can only start the same way, I'm telling you!

> *Nazha places her coffee cup upside down on the table. Souhayla follows suit.*

NAZHA: Let's start scooping, my dear, let's start scooping, that's all we have left to do!

SOUHAYLA: We have to hurry, the morning's almost over! What time is the fiancé arriving?

NAZHA: At 4:00, like all fiancés.

NELLY: *(off)* We're going to eat kneffay?

NEEL: *(to Nelly)* We're going to eat kneffay. *(To Nazha)* It's starting to rain, see, it really was the storm!

SOUHAYLA: The battenjen is lovely!

NAZHA: Isn't it!

SOUHAYLA: Is it from the Armenian's?

NAZHA: No my dear! It's from the Greek's—at least HE watches where he puts HIS vegetables!

SOUHAYLA: People say the Armenian is vulgar—

NAZHA: He is vulgar, my dear, he is! And his dog! That mag-got-ridden mutt! Good God. Always prancing all over the store. All you can see is a swarm of flies around a rotting car-cass! That dog makes me want to puke! There is nothing more repulsive than that drooling shit-encrusted fleabag!

Neel turns on the mixmaster. The noise is monstrous.

NAZHA and SOUHAYLA: Ahhh! What on earth is that?

NEEL: The mixmaster!

SOUHAYLA: It's the mixmaster!

NAZHA: Neel!

SOUHAYLA: He can't hear you!

NEEL: Mama...

NAZHA: What?

SOUHAYLA: What?

NAZHA: I said: What did you say?

SOUHAYLA: I said he can't hear you!

NEEL: Mama! Mama! I can't make it stop!

NAZHA: I'll go unplug it.

SOUHAYLA: What?

NEEL: I don't know how to stop it, I don't know how to stop it, I don't know—

Nazha unplugs the mixmaster.

NAZHA: Finally! What a relief!

SOUHAYLA: Ah! Silence at last!

NEEL: Ah! Don't yell at me, mama! I—I—I don't know what I'd do if you yelled at me, mama! Maybe throw myself against the wall, or even—out the window! Yes, out the window if you yell at me, mama!

NAZHA: But...!

NEEL: Mama! I love you! You're dead!? Already! This goddamned war! Mama! Help! My mother is dead and it isn't a dream!

NAZHA: Neel, sweetheart! My baby! Don't be silly! It's not your fault if the mixmaster doesn't work! And why did you say I'm dead, you fool!

NEEL: Where's Walter who still isn't here?

NAZHA: Why did you say I was dead?

NEEL: And where's Papa?

NAZHA: Papa will be here soon! You know what your father's like, he hates getting wet! So he must be staying dry somewhere!

NEEL: With the leg of mutton?

NAZHA: Yes! Yes darling! With the leg of mutton!

NEEL: And he'll be here soon?

NAZHA: Yes. Soon. All right! Now, we have work to do!

SOUHAYLA: The battenjen, and the coussa! Because, after all, it's a special day today! You really have to do this in style! It isn't every day you marry off your only daughter!

NAZHA: Not it's not! Not every day... it isn't every day you marry off your only daughter!

SOUHAYLA: What is our Sleeping Beauty doing?

NEEL: She's taking a bath!

SOUHAYLA: Does she still drop off to sleep as often?

NAZHA: Still!

SOUHAYLA: Poor Nelly! This slumber that descends on her without warning, wherever she happens to be!

NAZHA: In a war-torn country narcolepsy is a gift from God!

NEEL: You can say that again!

NAZHA: Oh! The potatoes! Go get the wooden pounder and mash them by hand.

NEEL: *(exiting)* This is really gross!

NAZHA: The grounds must be ready by now! Let's see what they were hiding!

SOUHAYLA: Nazha! We don't have time to waste on silly games.

NAZHA: We have time! We have time!

NEEL: *(returning, humming)* Sleeping Beauty, lily white, tiptoed through the piercing night!

> *Nazha looks closely at the cup of coffee, turning it. She studies it in an unsettling silence. Souhayla is on pins and needles.*

NAZHA: I see a man!... A young man. Young and strong.

SOUHAYLA: The same one as last time??

NAZHA: I think so...! Yes, there he is—the same one as last time. He's waiting. Standing by a gate. He seems to be waiting for something, I don't know what.

NEEL: He's waiting for death. Any man waiting in this country, especially if he's young and strong, won't stay alive very long.

NAZHA: Beside him is a rooster! A white rooster crowing into the sunset. A white rooster invoking the night who doesn't seem to notice the young man who doesn't move an inch!

NEEL: With the size of a coffee cup, it's not like there's anywhere he could *go!*

SOUHAYLA: This young man... what does he look like?

NAZHA: Long black hair... and strong, he's very strong! He's wearing tight pants, and his shirt is unbuttoned to the navel. He's waiting!

NEEL: One day you'll read potatoes and you'll see my face, I swear it...

> *Neel exits with the dish of potatoes.*

NAZHA: You don't know anyone young and strong with long black hair who wears tight pants??

SOUHAYLA: Yes, my father! But he isn't young and he never wears tight pants, he says they give him a rash.

NAZHA: What can I tell you? Mark my words, my dear Souhayla, you'll be married before Christmas.

SOUHAYLA: Before Christmas?

NAZHA: Before Christmas!

SOUHAYLA: From your mouth to God's ear. *(A beat.)* Actually, it's too cold before Christmas.

NELLY: *(off)* Next Friday we're going to Berdawnay?

NEEL: *(off)* Yes.

SOUHAYLA: I'd rather wait until May.

NAZHA: Let's get started on the hummous. Neel! Go get the hummous! Oh my God! The mutton! Neyif isn't back yet! With snipers all over the place! Let's hope nothing's happened to him! *(To Neel)* Get a plate for the beyleywa too. Those vultures are everywhere!

NELLY: *(off, a horrified shriek)* Mama!

SOUHAYLA: My God! What's the matter with Nelly?

NAZHA: She must be dreaming and calling me in her sleep!

NEEL: *(off)* Mama! Nelly just fell down all naked under the sink!

SOUHAYLA: Oh my God!

NELLY: *(off)* Mama!

NAZHA: She must be having a nightmare!

Nazha exits, Neel enters.

NEEL: Poor mama! It's amazing she's still so lucid!

SOUHAYLA: Now, now Neel! That isn't very nice!

NEEL: So tell me, Souhayla, what are you doing here today? What on earth compels you to want to witness this pathetic farce?!

SOUHAYLA: What farce Neel?

NEEL: How can you be so dense?!

SOUHAYLA: You're really in sad shape today! Yes, very sad! In fact, you're very unpleasant. You're in one of those moods that upset your mother. Why are you so hateful?

NEEL: When Walter's away, my mind starts to vegetate. Don't hold it against me.

SOUHAYLA: People are saying he's fallen in battle.

NEEL: People say lots of things.

SOUHAYLA: Did he really sleep here last night?

Several bombs in the distance, fairly close together.

NEEL: You love him!

SOUHAYLA: I like him!

NEEL: It's really unbelievable!

SOUHAYLA: What's unbelievable?

Several bombs in the distance, fairly close together.

NEEL: Being that jealous! You're jealous, Souhayla.

SOUHAYLA: What am I jealous of?

NEEL: Of Nelly. You're jealous because she's getting married while you, poor Souhayla, you're fat and you're ugly. No one will ever want you.

SOUHAYLA: You're wicked!

NEEL: Poor Souhayla! You were born in the wrong century! You aren't very pretty and these days people can't be forced to marry just anyone!

SOUHAYLA: Ne... Neel.

NEEL: To have any hope of getting married, you'd have to have been born into one of those rich families in the middle ages where looks were never an issue; but it's not just that you're not pretty, you...

NAZHA: *(entering and interrupting)* She'll be as radiant as the sun!

SOUHAYLA: I want you to know, Neel, that what you just said was very hurtful and—

NAZHA: Someone's coming up the stairs!

NEEL: It's my father with the mutton!

NAZHA: What a racket!

Neyif enters, but he stays in the doorway.

NEYIF: A knife! Quick! A dagger! A big one! The kind you find on murderers. The kind that really slices! A knife, I said! A knife, so I can finish it off once and for all! Godammned fucking cocksucking cuntlicking shit! Nazha! I told you to bring me a big knife!

NAZHA: Come in! Come inside! We'll see about the knife later. Come inside for now!

NEYIF: Stop arguing! The sheep is still alive, I had to leave the butcher's like a bat out of hell... They bombed the shit out of it!

Neyif is visibly fighting with a sheep who is determined to get into the apartment.

NEYIF: Would you bring me a knife so I can finish him off, so I can Julius Caesar him for you *(The sheep bleats.)*—THE BIG KNIFE.

NEEL: You're going to slit its throat?

NEYIF: No, I'm going to cut its toenails! Hurry up and stop arguing!

A sharp whistle. Bombs start falling again very close by.

NEEL: A D.C. 470 with a flammable head, those are vicious! Take cover!

Violent explosion.

NEYIF: Stupid sheep! It's biting my ankles!

NAZHA: Well, knock it out!

NEEL: Papa!

NEYIF: What do you want me to knock it out with?

NAZHA: With the hammer! Neel, go get the hammer!

NEYIF: Never mind the hammer, just bring me a knife.

SOUHAYLA: Where's your knife! I'll go get it...

NEYIF: In the second drawer in the kitchen cabinet!

The sheep bleats.

NEYIF: Shut up!

NAZHA: Just knock it out for fuck's sake. It'll be cleaner that way!

NEEL: You aren't going to slit its throat right on the landing!

A violent explosion.

NEYIF: Can you come and take over for a minute!

NEEL: Give me the sheep!

NAZHA: Don't let it get inside! If it shits on the carpet I'm gonna slit *your* throat.

NEEL: You have to be gentle with it!

SOUHAYLA: I couldn't find the knife but you could try these sewing scissors.

NEYIF: They're not very sharp, but they'll do the job.

A violent explosion.

NEYIF: Come on!

NEEL: You aren't going to cut the sheep's throat, papa!

NEYIF: Don't get sentimental! We have to kill it or there won't be any wedding meal! Come here my little lamb chop!

SOUHAYLA: Isn't it getting a bit dangerous to stay up here?

NAZHA: Watch the carpet!

The sheep bleats.

NEEL: You're starting to get it upset again!

NAZHA: Give him back the sheep, Neel.

NEYIF: Give me back the sheep!

NEEL: No!

A violent explosion.

SOUHAYLA: Come here, Neel honey! You shouldn't see this.

NEYIF: All right! A man's gotta do what a man's gotta do.

NAZHA: Watch the carpet!

NEEL: Nelly! Nelly!

A violent explosion.

SOUHAYLA: The bombing is getting close again! We have to shut the windows!

NEYIF: Now! How are you supposed to cut a sheep's throat?

NEEL: Nelly! Nelly! He's going to slaughter the sheep! Wake up, Nelly! He's going to slit its throat! His knife is already in the air!

NEYIF: Shit! This is disgusting!

Agonized cries from the sheep. A violent explosion.

NEYIF: Fucking shit...

NAZHA: The heart! Aim for the heart!

NEYIF: Ah fuck! Die, you stupid turd, will you shut up and die.

Agonized cries from the sheep.

NAZHA: Watch the carpet!

NEEL: Nelly! Nelly! It's the sheep they're killing for your wedding! Nelly!

NELLY: When are we going to Berdawnay?

Agonized cries from the sheep. Machine gun fire. A violent explosion.

NELLY: When are we going to Berdawnay?

NEYIF: Die, you piece of shit! Die!

Agonized cries from the sheep.

SOUHAYLA: Stop singing lullabies to it and just finish it off, goddammit! Die, you fucker! Die, you dumb bastard! Die!

Machine gun fire.

SOUHAYLA: Do you have anything else to say, you brute?

Agonized cries from the sheep.

SOUHAYLA: Any last words?

The sheep bleats.

SOUHAYLA: What? *(She imitates bleat.)* Behhhh? *(A punch.)* Behhh, you little swine? *(A punch.)* That's the last behhh from you. *(One last hard punch. The sheep dies.)*

NEYIF: The sucker really hung on!

NEEL: That's a surprise in this fucked up country!

NAZHA: Neel, honey, come and help me, we have to shut the windows, it's pouring rain outside. Come, my dear, don't look at that anymore!

NELLY: *(off)* Mama! There are shadows everywhere. Berdawnay has been destroyed! Run mama! They're going to catch you! They're going to kill you! Run! Mama!

NAZHA: I'm coming, Nelly. I'm coming.

Machine guns. Nazha exits. Souhayla goes to help Neel close the window. A hurricane-like wind.

SOUHAYLA: Look down there! There's a bus on fire!

NEEL: Full of children!

SOUHAYLA: There are soldiers there! They're going to try and save them!

NEYIF: Those hyenas aren't going to save anything!

SOUHAYLA: The children are running away. Look, they're shooting at them! Neel! Don't look at it, honey!

NEEL: Where do you WANT me to look?

SOUHAYLA: I'm telling you, we'd be better off downstairs!

NEYIF: We don't have time to go downstairs.

SOUHAYLA: The soldiers are still shooting! There are no more children, the last one just went up in flames!

NEYIF: Now that the sheep is dead, we can really get started!

NEEL: We're going to eat a cadaver!

NEYIF: At least we're going to eat!

Machine gun fire.

ACT 2

Neyif is skinning the sheep, which is hanging from the ceiling. A pail underneath the sheep catches the dripping blood.

NEYIF: Is Nelly getting ready?

NAZHA: When did she ever stop getting ready? Right now she's drying herself off. She's looking at herself in the mirror. She's crowning her head with flowers.

NEYIF: I'm hungry.

NAZHA: Flowers... red ones and blue ones, fragrant ones, wild rose and sprigs of cherry blossoms, daisies around her wrists. Our daughter will be beautiful.

NEYIF: This bugger doesn't want to let go of his skin. Where's Neel? Why isn't he coming to help me?!

NAZHA: It sounds like lots of people are coming to the wedding.

NEYIF: I should hope so! Neel! Neel! Shit! What the hell are you doing?!

NEEL: *(off)* I'm shining my shoes!

NEYIF: Get in here and hold the fucking hooves!

NAZHA: He has to help me set up the table too!

NEYIF: Did you hear me?!

NEEL: *(off)* I'm shining my shoes! I'll come when I'm finished shining my shoes!

NAZHA: He's not in the cheeriest of moods! Leave him alone!

NELLY: *(off)* Are we going to eat kneffay?

NEEL: *(off)* We're gonna eat so much we'll be shitting kneffay for weeks!

NEYIF: Kids! They sure as hell don't make your life easier... They do everything they can to poison it!

NEEL: *(off)* That's a load of crap!

NEYIF: Shut up you little worm!

The siren of an ambulance racing down the street.

NEYIF: *(to the ambulance)* I hope you die!

NAZHA: Maybe they'll be bombing at 4:00! With a little bit of luck, no one will come!

NEYIF: You mean we'd have put ourselves through all this shit for nothing!

NAZHA: Do you remember our wedding?

NEYIF: It was the pits! It was raining, you had "cramps." Three days before we could finally fuck! Now *that* hurt!

NAZHA: What are you talking about? It was sunny! You remember! We looked gorgeous!

NEYIF: Of course! No kids! People look great when they don't have kids. What do you think turned me into such a sour-puss? Your scaly skin? It's no different from mine. Your white hair? It's just a colour like any other. What do you think, huh, my little dumpling? Your plumpness? That, at least, is still exquisite!

NAZHA: I didn't want to talk about all that, Neyif! Let's just drop it!

NEYIF: Ah! I know where you're trying to lead me, my dear! No way, there won't be any tender, tacky, reminiscences. We're not going to sit side by side facing the audience and wax poetic about that special, loving day when we were joined in wedded bliss! You can drop dead! Drop dead! I'll tell you what repulses me about you Nazha, I'll tell you...

Neel enters.

NEEL: Here I am! Are we going to skin this goddamn sheep?

NEYIF: Get the hell out of here! I didn't ring for you! It's not time for you yet!

NEEL: Mama!

NEYIF: I said get the hell out, or else I'll take off my belt! Your bad marks at school last year will seem like nothing next to the bullets of my wrath! Do you hear me! I'm your father, dammit, and I'll use my paternal license to erase every last one of your lines!

NEEL: Good idea. That way there won't be any laughs in this play.

NEYIF: Get the hell out! Scram, you piece of camel snot!

Neel exits.

NEYIF: *(back to Nazha)* It's not over, I still have more to say! Stand the fuck up!

NAZHA: Neyif—

NEYIF: I said stand up! On your feet! Or else I'll hit something. It's not a case of domestic violence here, it's part of my nature. On your feet!

NAZHA: Neyif—Neyif—

NEYIF: Stand up!

NAZHA: Calm down! Relax! There we go.

The thunderstorm and bombing wreak havoc.

NEYIF: Do you smell that odour of freshly cut flesh, Nazha? You might think it's coming from the sheep over there! Do you smell it? It's the smell of your crotch, Nazha! Blood! It's that stench I can't stand anymore!

NAZHA: My God—My God—Neyif!

NEYIF: Shut up, do your hear me! Shut up! It's that faint smell, Nazha, so bitter, almost like mold! That smell that I saw take shape one day, slowly, layer by layer! Then I saw it get bigger and bigger, and then puff up, and turn over again, and again, until it filled up your greedy little belly that continued to swell and swell...

NAZHA: Neyif! Neyif! I can't take this!

NEYIF: It grew bigger than a cannonball! And then one day, without warning, it burst open! Completely exploded—right up to the stars! There was nothing left then, not of you, or of me! Or of our marriage, and even less of the memory of our wedding! There was nothing left but our newborn daughter, a larva! Soft and stagnating, formless, and infested with that incredibly vile stench! I don't remember ever seeing anything so monstrous! And then, you wanted to give it a name, teach it to walk, you wanted me to make "kitchy-koo," and everything that goes along with it, dress it, let it climb on my shoulders, teach it about the world, be a father to it, and today, after 30 years of this daily poisoning, you're determined to make a party for it while bombs are dropping all over the place. Poor Nazha, *you* must be living in some kind of dream world too! You'll see, the war is going to gobble up your Nelly. And later it'll be *our* turn, when people realize there's no fiancé, that there never was a fiancé, maybe then they'll have the guts to kill us. Then it'll all be over...

NAZHA: I think I don't feel very well!!

NEYIF: ...and we'll all be better off!

Nazha staggers.

NAZHA: Dear God!

NEYIF: They'll bleed us dry and that'll be the end of it.

Nazha goes to the window, opens it wide. The shells and the thunder have been wreaking havoc in the neighbourhood for a while.

NAZHA: Dear God! Marry my daughter! Marry my daughter! She's still asleep, lovely as a flower of the sea. Find her a husband! A husband who will make her happy, a sincere and gentle husband, who will stay awake all night to watch over her sleep! Protect her from all the faceless assassins who would cut short her life out of sheer perversity! Protect her, dear God, from the jealous ones, all those whose livers are green with envy! And make sure they all come—men and women—to celebrate her wedding, and have them wear their most beautiful clothes! Nelly's eyes are still shut but they'll see inside her, they'll see through her, they will make of her a continent! They'll want to inhabit her, they'll look everywhere for extraordinary treasures to strew at her feet and the sweetest perfumes to anoint my sleepwalker on her journey!

NELLY: *(off)* Mama! Why are you running away? Stay! I remember the countryside! I remember how you ran towards me among the cedars! The sky was so blue! And your arms around my heart! Why did you die, mama? Why did you leave? When did you leave? When did you stumble? When did you fall? Come back! Don't run so fast! Don't run away! Stay! Stay!

NAZHA: Where will she find the safety to talk like this? Where will she find the salvation that brings peace and rest, the way others find peace and rest in the warm earth? Who will grant her salvation? My Lord! Salvation! Salvation my Lord! That same salvation that, in your grace, you showed me at the very moment of her birth. Do you remember: You appeared to me in all your whiteness, an extravagant form. Then I felt, I felt, I felt this incredibly sweet movement! Something inside me was taking birth! Something inside me was stretching out, unfolding, lifting me, carrying me away. They said to me, "Push ma'am, push," but I was looking at the universe! The universe was between my legs, it slid out of me, it escaped. Do you remember that deliverance, my Lord? What came out of my belly had no body, no flesh, no head, no feet—it was a light I felt slip out of me, a light that has illuminated my whole life! Dear God, that light that spilled out of my depths was your own! Where are you? Where are you? Where is your grace? Your salvation? Your salvation? Ahhh! There is no salvation possible in this carnage! All there is is dust, dust, and more dust!

Machine gun fire.

NEYIF: Nazha! The snipers are shooting at us!

NAZHA: I don't give a shit.

> *Nearby explosion. A storm erupts outside the window. The electricity goes off.*

NAZHA: *(still at the window)* I don't care! Do you hear me, you bunch of animals! I don't care! *(An explosion.)* For all I care you can shove your grenades up each other's asses!

> *An incredibly violent explosion. The shutters fly open, the windows also, the rain and the wind burst in.*

NAZHA: You douchebags!

> *Souhayla enters.*

SOUHAYLA: I'm in a total panic! I'm going to pieces!

> *An explosion.*

NAZHA: You Neanderthals!

> *Neel enters.*

NEEL: Mama, mama, Nelly's crying. She's asleep and she's crying!

> *Machine gun fire.*

NAZHA: You slimebuckets!

NEYIF: Go back and stay with your sister. I'm gonna try to calm your mother down.

SOUHAYLA: I'll come with you.

Neel and Souhayla exit. Nazha grabs a dish and makes to throw it out the window.

NAZHA: We'll throw kibbeh at our brave soldiers! You'll see! We'll make them slosh around in hummous!

NEYIF: No! Not the hummous...

An explosion.

NEYIF: Nazha, not the hummous, no, I'm begging you...

Nazha throws the dish out the window. Machine gun fire.

NAZHA: Troglodytes!

NEYIF: She's out of control!

Machine gun fire.

NAZHA: Fascists!

NEYIF: Nazha! Calm down!

NAZHA: I'm calming down. I am calm. I'm very calm!

Souhayla and Neel enter.

SOUHAYLA: Nazha, Nazha, Nelly is all *(She gestures.)* hunched up—hun—hundled—

NEEL: Huddled up!

SOUHAYLA: That's it! Under the bathroom sink! Could she
be dead?!

NAZHA: That's her spot! Don't wake her up! It could be awful!

NEYIF: Calm down! Calm down, I said, everybody calm down!
(Silence.) All right. The guests are gonna start arriving soon,
so let's have some calm.

NAZHA: The wedding, the wedding! Are we ever going to
show them a wedding!

SOUHAYLA: You're right! Goddamned right. The wedding!
Nothing else matters but the wedding! Neel! Neel come
quick, we're going to set up the table!

NAZHA: Turn the lights on! It's really dark in here.

NEEL: There's no electricity!

SOUHAYLA: I forgot to bring up the warra arrishe and the
baba ghanouj. I'll go get them.

Souhayla exits.

NEYIF: What are we going to do about her?

NAZHA: We could tell her! She couldn't hold it against us!
She's so nice, so dim!

NEEL: You want us to tell her that Nelly isn't getting married after all—that we've told everyone the fiancé was arriving at 4:00, but the whole thing has simply been a joyful little masquerade? For God's sake! She'll die of pleasure! It
could make her so happy she might get pregnant, just like
that, all of a sudden without warning!

NEYIF: Maybe she suspects! Let's pull out now before we really get in over our heads!

NEEL: No, no. She's a lot sneakier than we think. If she had the slightest suspicion, why would that big fat cow have slaved away with her hummous and her fassoulia and her baba ghanouj?!

NAZHA: And her beyleywa!

NEEL: And her beyleywa! Holy shit! We all know how much beyleywa costs! No! No! If she had any doubts about the fiancé, she wouldn't have worked so hard to make believe she was preparing her own wedding!

NEYIF: None of this is getting us anywhere! If we tell her, what's the worst that can happen?

NAZHA: All the women in the neighborhood will find out!

NEEL: And then none of them will come?

NAZHA: None of them will come!

NEYIF: Let's tell her then! In one fell swoop we'll get rid of all the scum around here.

NAZHA: How will we explain to all the nosey neighbours why we've cancelled the wedding?

NEEL: We'll say the fiancé couldn't come because of the situation, and we'll postpone the whole thing until a later date!

NAZHA: It will break Nelly's heart!

NEYIF: She's so sure of it! How will she feel tonight, at 7:00, and at 8:00, and later as the clock ticks on? Will she still be

waiting for her fiancé? Poor Nelly! Eventually she'll understand! Then maybe she'll throw herself out the window! It's
a terrible thing when a fiancé doesn't show up! Especially if
he doesn't exist!

NELLY: *(off)* My fiancé will come!

NAZHA: We can't back out!

NEYIF: Fine! So we won't back out!

NEEL: Goddammit!

NAZHA: Nelly, darling, wouldn't you like to come sit with us
for a few minutes?

NELLY: *(off)* Today, I'll sit at your side dressed in white.

NAZHA: As you wish, darling!

NEYIF: What else can we do but go ahead with it!

NEEL: Goddammit!

NELLY: *(off)* Mama.

NAZHA: Yes, Nelly?

NELLY: Why is the war so beautiful? Why can't I take my eyes
off it? These fireworks! It's so breathtaking mama, I'm kneeling, wide awake, at the wide open window, savouring the
destruction! It's all so beautiful. Down below buildings are
crumbling; the city is falling to its knees, there are fires dancing in the middle of the storm, bombs on the palms; a tree
is exploding!

NAZHA: Nelly! Shut the window and keep getting dressed, darling. Don't look!

NELLY: *(off)* Mama!

NAZHA: Yes Nelly?

NELLY: *(off)* Are the great artists of this country preparing a big celebration? Who else could create something so spellbinding as war. Yesterday, yes, I think it was yesterday, I woke up in the middle of the night mama, and I looked out the window and I saw flames coming from our neighbor's apartment! I saw our neighbor jump off her balcony, holding her baby in her arms. As she fell, she dropped him, she screamed something and then she smashed into the pavement. Her child exploded in mid-air, skewered by a bolt of lightning that came out of the night. Mama, how can something so hideous be so beautiful? Mama, how can something so beautiful?... Mama, how can...

Souhayla enters.

SOUHAYLA: I brought my candelabra and some candles! People will think we turned the lights off on purpose—for ambiance!

NAZHA: Just like in Europe—by candlelight!

NEYIF: Why don't you give me a hand so that we can set up this bitch of a table.

SOUHAYLA: There we go! What else is there left to do!

NAZHA: The battenjen and the coussa to stuff!

SOUHAYLA: Well, let's get stuffing! Let's stuff them my dear!

NAZHA: Anyway, I hope the electricity comes back on for the mutton!

NEYIF: Well, I, for one, am starting to get very hungry.

NEEL: Shit, is this table ever heavy!

NAZHA: A raw mutton joint! That would be a real faux pas!

SOUHAYLA: In wartime people shouldn't complain!

NAZHA: But, you know, some people will complain no matter what!

SOUHAYLA: Now that's true. The Armenian says *our* war isn't so bad. He says lots of countries have been through a lot worse than we have. According to him some people—the Armenians, for example—have lived through far worse atrocities. He says that compared to the Armenians, we're just a bunch of limp dicks.

NAZHA: What does that jerk know about our history?! About our country?! What does that piece of smegma know about it?! That lice-infested baboon's ass! He disgusts me! He enrages me! He makes my blood seethe, that shrivelled foreskin of an Armenian! Dammit! He drives me over the hedge!

NEEL: Edge!

NAZHA: Now what?! I'm warning you, fucking shit, I won't put up with your mental defectiveness much longer! If your brain doesn't stop its high-flying acrobatics, I'll break its fucking trapeze!

NEEL: But I didn't do anything!

NEYIF: All right! Calm down!

NEEL: All I did was say *edge*! I said *edge* because you said *hedge*!

NAZHA: What do you mean I said *hedge*? When did I say *hedge*?

SOUHAYLA: Never mind, it's nothing... She said what you're supposed to say! That's all.

NEYIF: That's right, that's all!

NEEL: She said *hedge*...

NEYIF: Neel! That's enough!

NEEL: I'm sick and tired of this! The minute I open my mouth everyone yells at me! If it was me who said *hedge* everyone would have jumped on me to tell me you're supposed to say *edge*!

SOUHAYLA: What's all this about *hedge* and *edge*?

NAZHA: Let's not talk about it anymore! I'd rather talk about that cockroach of an Armenian! Thank God they're not all like him!

NEYIF: Come on son! Keep screwing those legs in! I'm going to go get the plates.

Neyif exits.

NEEL: "He drives me over the hedge!" Over the *edge*, not over the *hedge*!

SOUHAYLA: So, anyway, according to him it was the *Armenians* who suffered the worst massacre in history! He even claims it's etched into his flesh!

NAZHA: It's etched so deeply he leaves pieces of scab in his lettuces!

NEEL: "Over the hedge!" That's the best one yet!

SOUHAYLA: He said it was the worst massacre ever!

NAZHA: He doesn't know a thing! What about 500 years ago when the Mamelukes massacred the whole area, what was that supposed to be? A manicure session!

SOUHAYLA: You said it!

NEEL: I've got to tell my friends that one. It's hilarious! "Over the hedge!" "Over the hedge!"

The electricity comes back on. All cheer.

ALL: Ahhh!!

NAZHA: Hurry Neyif! We have to put the sheep in the oven! Quick before the power goes off again!

NEYIF: *(off)* Coming!

NAZHA: Good! Now, cut me off that piece there! And then that one! Don't turn the oven up too high, and make sure you baste it well with the arak, all right?

NEYIF: Shit! All this is making me hungry!

The electricity goes off. All groan.

ALL: Ohh!!

NAZHA: Oh no! It's too awful! It's too awful! Everything's going wrong today!

NEEL: We're going to eat the mutton cold, and raw to boot! Don't say I didn't warn you!

NEYIF: We'll just leave the whole thing in the oven. When the electricity comes back on, it'll be all ready!

NAZHA: I'll come and help you! You won't know what to do!

Nazha and Neyif exit.

NEEL: The mutton! We're going to eat it raw! With our hands! We'll fight over the best pieces! We'll club each other with the kidneys!

SOUHAYLA: You're disgraceful! So rude and vulgar! Neel, I'm really disappointed in you! You used to be so sweet...

NEEL: Oh no! Leave the fucking sentimentality to other people! There's no room for that kind of talk around here. Everyone uses it to trick me. No one here knows how to talk in dynamite! Not one single person. Except for Walter! He's amazing! He blasts through everything! He leaves everything sparkling! Spic and span! You know what he says to people who get too close to him?

SOUHAYLA: What does he say?

NEEL: He raises his arm and he yells: "I'm Walter!" A walking neutron bomb. I've come to recite to you, in the bluest depth a poem that will help you rest in peace! And he raises his gun again and he empties his three clips tatatatatatatatata-tatatata and tatatatatatata and tatatatatatataatata. I've seen him do it.

SOUHAYLA: He used to come downstairs to my place and he would sit down with me, and guess what he would do?

NEEL: He would rip off his clothes and run after you yelling, "I'm gonna rape you, Souhayla, I'm gonna rape you!"

SOUHAYLA: He used to come and read me his poems. Poems he'd written himself. Your brother could have been a great poet!

NEEL: He still can be! Tatatatatatatatatatatatatatatatata! That's the title of his latest poem.

SOUHAYLA: Is he coming to the wedding?

NEEL: What wedding?

SOUHAYLA: There aren't fifty-thousand weddings happening around here! There's only one for 200 miles around. There aren't any others, you little brat! There's only one! Only one that everyone's talking about!

NEEL: Everyone?

SOUHAYLA: Yes, everyone! Everyone's talking about it because everyone's wondering. They're wondering all kinds of things about Nelly's famous fiancé! They're wondering— and I'm wondering too—how your sister managed to snare such a rich and handsome European!

NEEL: My sister's gorgeous!

SOUHAYLA: She's attractive, but she's always asleep.

NEEL: So?

SOUHAYLA: So?

NEEL: So?

SOUHAYLA: So, I really don't understand how Nelly could have met such a fiancé when so many *normal* girls, I mean, normal in their heads, in their minds, can still only hope.

NEEL: Don't get so worked up. Because there isn't going to be a wedding! This is all a great big practical joke. That sheep isn't really a sheep, it's just a prop! I swear it! There won't be any wedding because there isn't any fiancé!

SOUHAYLA: You're—euh—euh—disgusting! Yes! That's it! You're disgusting! That's the word! Disgusting! The men in the neighbourhood used to say a lot of nasty things about Walter! But now I see the truth! You're the snake! You're the megalomaniac!

NEEL: I never whistled at women.

SOUHAYLA: Neither did Walter.

NEEL: Yes he did.

SOUHAYLA: You're lying through your teeth! Walter was far too intelligent to sink so low. He was too noble, he was generous, his face was like a clear blue sky... He was handsome and I loved him... I loved him... But he didn't love me! And now he's dead. It's such a tragedy! I'm sick of it, I can't take it any more, I'm cracking up, yes, I'm cracking up! That's it, I'm having a breakdown! I admit it! *(She sobs.)*

NEEL: Souhayla! I tried to make you happy by telling you that Nelly won't be getting married since there's NO HUSBAND. But you don't want to believe me! You're really too stupid!

SOUHAYLA: Well! I didn't come up here to talk to you, or to be insulted, so I'm going back downstairs to my apartment. You can say I'll be back later. And count yourself lucky that I'm not planning to say anything to your mother, you little fool!

NEEL: Tickle my tool!

Souhayla exits.

NEEL: Stupid twit! Twit! Twit! Tweet tweet tweet. Tweedledum and Tweedledee, hee hee hee. Tomorrow I'll be grown up. Meanwhile, everyone knows that children are cruel. And I'm doing my very best. Nelly!... Nelly!

Bombing in the distance. A bomb explodes with distinction.

NEEL: A shining coral! Quick! A wish! Not only do they do unbelieveable damage, but to top things off they have these incredible names! A shining coral! Some people have the luxury of dying in style! Nelly!...

NELLY: *(off)* Softly Neel! I'm right here!

NEEL: Come out! Don't stay there!

NELLY: *(off)* It's nicer to stay in the darkness! Your voice is running around. Now I can see it hiding under the armchair. Like when you were little, do you remember?

NEEL: Little! I used to be little?

NELLY: When mama did the housework, she would stack up all the living room furniture and she would drape the carpet over the pile! It would make a tent and you would crawl inside! You would stay hiding in there! And I used to call you: Neel! Neel! Little brother! Come and see me, come and see me, I'm all alone! Neel! Help! There's no one in my dreams! Come on my little brother, Neel, where are you?

NEEL: No! No, I don't remember!

NELLY: *(off)* And then I would hide, I would slither under the sofa—then you'd start looking for me and you would call me: "Nelly, Nelly, where are you? Look outside, there's a building on fire, quick, hurry, we have to escape, we have to leave in the car, pack our suitcases, close the trunks and go like Aunt Bosra who left with her five daughters! *They're* still beautiful!" And then I would come out of hiding and you would run to me, jump into my arms, kiss me, you loved me so much!

NEEL: You're telling me those stories I've never heard the end of!

NELLY: *(off)* The end is coming! We just have to prepare the wedding, Neel. Have faith. Walter will be here soon. We'll play together, just like he promised you. We're going to play, Neel, we're going to play. Between the three of us, the war won't stand a chance. I'm getting married, Neel, I'm getting married.

NEEL: You really need a fiancé for a wedding!

NELLY: *(off)* Don't you believe in anything anymore? What about fairies, and pumpkins and ice cream and sugar plums?

NEEL: Nelly! My dear sweet sister! Here, Nelly, people only talk about war!

NELLY: *(off)* Do you remember the last poem Walter wrote?

NEEL: Tatatatatatatatatatatatatata.

NELLY: It was a poem about birds, love and light.

NEEL: Walter has disappeared, Nelly. Disappeared. He might even be dead, and all the poetry in the world dead with him.

NELLY: *(off)* You don't have the right to talk about death, Neel.

NEEL: But I sure as hell don't have any right to be where I am! Period! I'm caught in a story way too complicated for my age! The moment I was born they took me away and they tied me up, and ever since then they've been forcing me to watch a bad movie! With a terrible plot! A bad movie in which from beginning to end people get fucked up the ass by one prick after another. So you understand, Nelly, I can't smile at your fairy tales. I just see asses and cocks! Endless slurping of assholes! Big fat cocks rammed up to the hilt in juicy vaginas! Dykes, faggots, dogs with enormous drooling and foaming dicks! Green tongues lapping up the foam that's frothing and overflowing! Do you want some, here you go! Blow job after blow job, a whirl of shafts and knobs, vomiting, ravenous cunts and cadaverous penises, all spinning around, and people suck each other off all over the place, coming and going here and there, and all you can hear are obscene moans, and there's a guy walking around with his tool hanging below his knees, and he stabs another guy and makes him swallow big mouthfuls of his shit, and it goes on and it goes on, over and over, and he pisses on him, and the other asks for more but the first guy is empty so he slits open the other guy's thing, and he sprays himself with the blood that spurts out, and it goes on, and it goes on, he sticks his hand in through the navel to scrape the bottom of the guy's stomach, then he grabs the guy's intestines and his liver and he pulls on them, Nelly, he tugs on them, he pulls on them again, and then he shoots the guy, he shoots the hell out of him, he shoots him, waving his cause like a banner, he shoots him, do you understand? He shoots him, he shoots him, a man, he shoots him and a man falls because he's empty, one less Nelly, one less man, surely the son of a mother! What... What... What will she do now without him? Who will go to get lettuce that smells like fish at the fucking Armenian's! Who? Who? He's dead! He's dead! He's dead!

NELLY: *(off)* Don't fall Neel! Don't fall little brother! Today is my wedding day! Have faith! Listen outside, it's the war digging its own grave with a great blasting of shells! The day is near, believe me, the day when our tired faces will once again be flooded with light.

ACT 3

The table is set up. It is beautiful. Large. White. Plates. Cutlery. Candles. The storm is increasingly ferocious. But is it really the storm? Nazha is in a slip and high heels. Neel is in his underwear and Neyif is in his undershirt and very fancy trousers. They are getting dressed. They are getting ready.

NEYIF: We don't have much time left!

NEEL: You're telling me—the clock just fired three times.

NEYIF: It smells good! Shit, I'm hungry!

NEEL: We're going to eat the mutton cold!

NEYIF: We might get lucky, the electricity could still come back on!

NEEL: It'll go off again right away!

NEYIF: Go get dressed instead of arguing!

NEEL: I already told you it'll start the same way. It always starts the same way, always, always always...

NEYIF: Go get dressed!!

NEEL: I'd love to but I can't find my wedding pants! My dress pants for special occasions!

NEYIF: I don't care! I'm tired of seeing you naked!

NEEL: Mama! I can't find my dress pants!

NEYIF: Let your mother get dressed! A little while ago all she was wearing was her black slip!

NAZHA: *(off)* Hey!

She enters.

NAZHA: I'm still only wearing my black slip!

NEYIF: That doesn't surprise me! You get dressed at a snail's pace!

NAZHA: That may be! But at least *I'm attractive* when I dress up! *I* don't have a pot belly! *I* don't stink of ciga· smoke, and *I* don't have little gray hairs sticking out of my dress! *I* smell nice! You esthetic disaster!

NEEL: All right, I'm getting out of here. Go ahead, it's time for your little duet!

Neel exits.

NEYIF: So, go on. I'm waiting.

NAZHA: I'm not getting sucked into your little game! Insults don't just trip off my tongue! *I'm* not bursting with hatred! But you, poor Neyif, you're another story. Poor Neyif, I pity you! You're skinny! Yes! And ugly! What has your life been aside from me?

NEYIF: Stop! You're making me cry!

NAZHA: Ha! Too late my dear, that's your problem! Cry! You aren't capable of crying! You can't cry you poor old man! All you can do is get angry!

NEYIF: Shut up! You're starting to get on my nerves!

NAZHA: That's what's going to kill you! There's so much anger coursing through your veins that one day your heart's going to confuse your anger with your blood, and instead of pumping the one, it'll pump the other! Then, I'll finally see you blow up for good!

NEYIF: That'll make your day, won't it!

NAZHA: You better believe it. I'll laugh my guts out and I'll spit on your corpse.

NEYIF: Who gives a shit, I'll be dead, I won't feel a thing!

NAZHA: That's just it, you've never *felt anything!* You don't cry anymore, you never get a hard on, you hardly even fart anymore! You're cold and unfeeling.

NEYIF: There we go. Now we're getting somewhere. That's what I was waiting for. Feelings! Feelings!

NAZHA: Yes, feelings! Feelings!

NEYIF: You sound like an aging actress! Feeelings, nothing more than feeelings, how many tons of feeelings do you think there are outside! You can hear their goddamned feeelings falling on our heads! A well-aimed D.C.4, what do you think that is? How am I supposed to love, get a hard on, fart and shit, that's right, SHIT, when all over the place people are venting their feeeelings! Well, *I* don't have any feelings. I don't want to have any, either, and I don't give a fuck about your feelings, Nazha, about their feelings, about anybody's feelings! If those guys out there weren't so busy dealing with their feeelings and their own little selves maybe we wouldn't be in this mess!

NAZHA: You're crying!?

NEYIF: Yes, I'm crying!

NAZHA: Neyif, my love! Anything is possible.

> *A terrible explosion followed by a clap of thunder, followed by several whistles, other explosions, other claps of thunder. Neel enters, still in his underwear.*

NEEL: I've had it! Where are my dress pants? Where are my dress pants so I can put them on!

NAZHA: They're outside! On the clothesline!

NEEL: Oh terrific! That's just terrific! What the hell am I going to do without my dress pants! It's been raining buckets and there are snipers everywhere! How am I going to get my dress pants now!

NEYIF: You're a pain in the ass, Neel! You're pissing us off, do you understand? You're annoying your poor mother and me! Is that getting through to you? The two of us are stirring up the past and you prance back in here yakking on about your dress pants! I don't give a flying fuck about your pants, I want to talk to your mother, do you follow me? So haul your scrawny ass out of here or I'm going to lose my temper!

NEEL: It's not fair! You left Nelly all alone! She's all sad because you're yelling at each other. I don't know how to make her feel better.

> *Neel exits.*

NAZHA: Kiss me!

NEYIF: Nazha!

NAZHA: Kiss me, I said!

> *They kiss. Bombs are still following in the distance, and increasingly closer. The storm continues.*

NEYIF: Let's make love!

NAZHA: On the table!

NEYIF: On the table!!

NAZHA: In the keshk!

NEYIF: I'm gonna do to you what you do to the coussa.

NAZHA: Yes, yes. Fill me up. Stuff your little battenjen.

NEYIF: I'm getting a hard on, holy fuck, I'm getting a hard on.

NAZHA: My darling! Don't worry, I can't have children any more!

NEYIF: Lift up your slip.

NAZHA: Give me your tongue!

NEYIF: I'd forgotten what your ass feels like!

NAZHA: I love you! I love you! You're still so handsome! You're even handsomer! Come inside me!

NEYIF: In wartime, life begins at sixty!

> *Nazha takes off her skirt.*

NAZHA: Oh yes! Oh yes! Oh it's so good. Oh, it's incredible! It goes right to the bottom of my soul! Oops, I'm farting, I couldn't hold it in.

NEYIF: Oh yes, oh yes! Oh that's good.

NAZHA: Do you want me to stick my finger up your ass?

NEYIF: Oh yes, just like in the old days!

NAZHA: Oh yes.

NEYIF: That's good! I'm gonna come!

NAZHA: Yes.

NEYIF: I'm gonna come.

NAZHA: Yes.

NEYIF: I'm gonna come, I'm gonna come.

NAZHA: Oh yes, come.

The electricity comes back on.

NAZHA: Aah! The electricity is back on! Quick! The mutton! The mutton!

NEYIF: Nazha! Who gives a damn about the mutton! We'd just turned into lions again. Where are you going? Where are you going?

NAZHA: The mutton!

She exits.

NEYIF: I've had it! If that's the way it's going to be! Neel! You want your dress pants, you little asswipe? *I'll* go and get them. It's either me or the mutton!

Neyif leaves the apartment.

NELLY: *(off)* When are we going to Berdawnay?

NEEL: Next Friday... *(Shouting down the stairs after Neyif)* Papa! Come back! Come back! Forget about the pants, I'll wear any old pair! It's no problem!

NELLY: *(off)* Next Friday?

NEEL: Next Friday! Mama, mama, papa's gonna get himself killed! He's outside and he's yelling!

Nazha enters and joins Neel on the balcony.

NAZHA: Neyif! Wait! I'll come with you! Wait for me! Don't die without me, don't die without me, I want to get out of here too!

NEEL: Mama stay here!!

Nazha struggles with Neel.

NAZHA: Let go of me! Let go of me! I want to run to the arms of my love!!

Nazha exits.

NEEL: Can she ever be stupid sometimes! Mama! Stay here! Walter! Walter! Damn it Walter, I really need you here!

Neel goes back onto the balcony.

NELLY: *(off)* Next Friday?... Next Friday in Berdawnay ... to eat kneffay.... There's no one anymore! There's no one left! There's only me! It's so sad to be talking to yourself in the middle of the carnage! I'm sleepy, mama! I'm always so sleepy! All naked in the middle of the war! What do they all have to yell about? They must think my fiancé isn't going to come, so they've left. Is it ever sad. *(Yelling)* Hey, my fiancé *is* going to come! They don't hear me, they think I'm still asleep. Maybe I actually *am* asleep at this very moment. "But you're here, Nelly! With your eyes open." I don't know anymore. "You don't know anymore?" I don't know. "You don't know, Nelly?" I don't know, Nelly. "You don't know anymore?" I don't know anymore. "You don't know anymore if you're dreaming or not?" No, Nelly, I don't know anymore. Before, in my dreams, I'd sometimes turn into a big tree; I'd catch on fire in the middle of a wood, I'd run with all my roots and throw myself over a cliff. Then I would wake up. "You would wake up?" Yes, I would wake up and I would know what the words "waking up" meant: finding a peaceful blue sky, a world very different from the one in my dreams, and then yes, I would *know* that I'd been dreaming and that I had just woken up. "And now?" Now? "Yes, now." Now, Nelly? "Yes, Nelly, now?" Now! "No, no, don't cry, Nelly." I can't! Now all I dream about is the toilet, the door and the concrete wall. And when I wake up, I see the same door, Nelly, the same concrete wall, and that's it. Now I no longer know where I am Nelly, I don't know anymore. Can you help me? "I can't do anything, Nelly. Nothing."

NEEL: *(off)* He did it! He did it! He got my pants!

NAZHA: *(off)* It's a miracle! A real miracle!

Neyif arrives flanked by Nazha and Neel. Wet. Trembling.

NEEL: Is my father ever something!

NEYIF: They shot at me!

NEEL: Did you think they were going to toss petunias at you!

NAZHA: Sit down.

NEYIF: Shit!

NELLY: *(off)* Mama!

NAZHA: I'm coming, Nelly, I'm coming!

Nazha exits.

MAN'S VOICE: Wlak ya Neyif?

NEEL: I think someone's calling you!

MAN'S VOICE: Yaaa Neyif!*

Neyif goes to the balcony.

NEYIF: Ahlan abou Lteff!

MAN'S VOICE: Jebtéllak festânn elaarouss!

NEYIF: Tab tcharraff!

MAN'S VOICE: La! La! Lézim rouh lah todroub al mazbout! Ba a stlaa!

---

* MAN'S VOICE: Hey, Neyif!
  NEYIF: Hello Lteff!
  MAN'S VOICE: I've brought the dress!
  NEYIF: Come on up!
  MAN'S VOICE: No! No! They're going to start bombing again. Here, catch!

The man in the street throws him a package.

NEYIF: Take this to your sister!

NEEL: The dressmaker didn't get blown up?

Neel exits.

NEYIF: This fucking cocksucking life! Goddammit! Scumsucking asslicking shit! What a life. It's just a bag of donkey farts. Ahh! Why don't they just put a bullet through my head and get it over with! Shit! I'm hungry!

Neel enters.

NEEL: Thanks for my pants, papa!... But you know, that was a really dumb thing to do! Papa. Papa.

NEYIF: Neel! Calm down! OK? There's a lot of electricity in the air!

NEEL: Give me a break! There's not even enough to cook the mutton! Electricity in the air! You've got to be joking!

NEYIF: No, it's a figure of speech!

NEEL: Yeah! A figure of speech! And when someone says to you "You drive me over the hedge," would you call that a figure of speech too?

NEYIF: Neel! Please, let's talk calmly, do you mind? Quietly and simply without raising your voice, all right?

Neel grunts.

NEYIF: We're going to have a good time, Neel, aren't we?

Later, they're all going to come and they're going to die of
jealousy when they see our wedding table! Their tongues will
be hanging out!

NEEL: You can say that again! The guys are all going to have
their balls in a knot when they see Nelly in her beautiful dress!

NEYIF: We're going to make up incredible stories, you'll see,
we're going to talk about the fiancé's car!

NEEL: And his villa! And about his servants and the old man
who's been his servant since he was small. The servant's
name is Darwish!

NEYIF: No! We need something less suspicious-sounding...
like Alistair.

NEEL: Yes, it's Alistair who's waiting for Nelly and her fiancé
in their villa! We'll tell them the fiancé takes care of an
orphanage, and that the people of his country have nick-
named him Vincent!

NEYIF: Why Vincent?

NEEL: For Saint Vincent de Paul!

NEYIF: The orphanage is a good idea but Vincent is a bit too
obscure. They won't get it!

NEEL: The ignoramuses!

NEYIF: We have to find him a name!

NEEL: Fine! Let's find him a name. Ramón!

NEYIF: Too exotic!... David!

NEEL: No! He's not a David!

NEYIF: Burt, like our plumber?!

NEEL: I don't see him as a plumber!

NEYIF: Fine!

NEEL: How about Giancarlo, like Giancarlo Giannini! That'll make him sound more European. Giancarlo!

NEYIF: Giancarlo?

NEEL: Yes! Giancarlo! Not bad, eh?

NEYIF: Giancarlo! I don't know! We'll ask your mother... Nazha! What do you think of Giancarlo?

NAZHA: *(off)* I don't know any Giancarlo!

NEEL: Yes you do mama... you know very well, Giancarlo, Nelly's fiancé!

NAZHA: *(off)* Oh! You mean François! Oh well, he's a very nice boy!

NEYIF: Well, buddy! She'd already come up with a name!

NEEL: François! He sounds like a shoe salesman.

NEYIF: What have you got against shoe salesmen?

NEEL: Nothing, but they usually don't get to do what they want in life!

NEYIF: What do you know about life?

NEEL: You're right, I don't know much about it!

NEYIF: Lucky shit! I'd trade places with you in a second.

NEEL: Is that why you spend your life yelling at me?

NEYIF: I don't yell at you, I educate you.

NEEL: Don't worry about educating me. The war's doing a good enough job of it, I swear.

NEYIF: This is all such a fucking mess. That's enough. Go get dressed.

NEEL: Thanks for getting my pants, papa!

NEYIF: It was just a stupid pair of pants!

NEEL: It's not the pants, I don't give a hoot about the pants, it's because for a brief moment you turned back into the hero of my childhood!

NEYIF: Oh, shut up. Go and get dressed!

NEEL: Papa!...

NEYIF: I said go and get dressed, dammit! Do you know what time it is? Now go put your clothes on, so at least two of us will be decent when the guests arrive.

NEEL: And it's started all over again! I knew it, right from the start, I even said so: It'll always always start the same way, the same way, always always always...

Neel exits.

NEYIF: Nazha! I'm starving!

A bomb explodes nearby. Another follows.

NEYIF: Nazha! What are you doing?

Another bomb explodes.

NEYIF: Nazha?

NEEL: *(off)* Oh great! Now I can't find my shoes!

> *One bomb, and then another. Incredibly violent thunder. The shutters hold.*

NAZHA: *(off, continues singing under Neyif's lines)*
It's my dear little Nelly
Our smiling Sleeping Beauty
Today's the day of awakening
Today's the day that her heart will sing

NEYIF: Nazha? Maybe we should go downstairs till it quiets down.

> *A bomb explodes. The storm. The electricity goes off. Neyif wants to go see but is pinned to the ground by an explosion.*

NEYIF: Neel! Nazha! We have to go downstairs. They can't hear me.

> *An explosion throws Neyif to the floor.*

NEEL: *(off)* Where the hell have I put my shoes again! Mama, I can't find my shoes!

> *Explosions, the walls shake. The windows break, a submachine gun battle takes place very close to the house.*

NEYIF: They're shooting at me! That's it, I'm going to die! It's now! I can feel it!

NAZHA: *(off, continues singing under Neyif's and Neel's lines)*
    It's our sweet pretty Nelly
    Arising from her bedclothes
    To go join hands with her betrothed.
    Today she'll leave her parents' home.

NEYIF: I don't want to die all alone! Neel! Nazha! Good God, where are you! *(He gets up, another explosion pins him to the ground right away.)*

NEEL: *(off)* Shit! Where the hell are my goddamned shoes!

NEYIF: They're shooting at me, don't leave me all alone! Nazha! Neel!

NAZHA: *(off, singing)*
    The most beautiful birds in sight
    All dance and spin and play

NEYIF: I don't want to die! I don't want to die!

An even worse explosion forces Neyif to remain on the ground.

NAZHA: *(off)*
    On a carpet of rose petals pink and bright
    For Nelly the bride on her wedding day.

Explosions. Sharp whistles. More of them. Explosions. Smoke. Thunder. Rain. The windows break. The shutters open under the impact. The wedding table doesn't move an inch, still there, still beautiful.

NEYIF: Help! Neel! Nazha!

Explosions. Nelly appears. In her white dress. Smiling. She is stunning. Her words are lucid. She has extraordinary dignity and grace. She is beautiful, like women who are free.

NELLY: This is it! I'm marching forward! They won't turn ME into a scowling warrior. They won't turn ME into a terrified, shrinking mouse! Look at me, I'm walking across the killing fields!

NEYIF: We're going to get blown to bits!

NELLY: I'm looking upwards!

NEYIF: The bombs!

NELLY: I refuse to bow down to the missiles to escape their cries of hate! No! No! The missiles will simply go off course when they see the light streaming from my face!

NEYIF: I don't want to die...

NELLY: Corpses will always rot!

NEEL: Yayyy! I found my shoes!

NELLY: And daisies will always grow back on the battlefields!

ACT 4

*The sound and lighting are very important to the sense of
this act.*
*The whole family is dressed. Everyone is seated around Nelly.
The storm is raging outside. The electricity comes and goes,
wavering, flickering, with the surge and ebb of the storm. The
table is there. Appetizing. It is 4 P.M. The clock, if there were
one, would chime as much as it wanted. Everyone is waiting.
A distant thunderclap. A gust of rain. It is very important
for us to feel that all the elements are affecting each other: the
winds whips the rain, and the electricity is in turn affected
by the rain and wind.*
A long pause.

NELLY: My fiancé will come.

NEYIF: Yeah, right.

Long pause.

NEEL: Walter's the one who won't come.

NAZHA: He'll be here soon.

NEEL: He'll be here soon, he'll be here soon. My big brother's
really something. It's 4:00. We won't have any time to play.
And he promised me he'd come and play with me before
the guests arrive.

Long pause. Thunderclap.

NEYIF: What lousy weather.

NEEL: You can say that again.

Long pause.

NEYIF: Shit. I'm hungry.

Pause. He sings to the tune of "I will survive"—ba ba ba ba, etc.—occasionally singing a few words. This goes on or about 45 seconds, becoming louder as he gets carried away.

NAZHA: Stop it!

NEYIF: What do you mean, stop?

NAZHA: I mean you're getting on our nerves. Every time you're hungry you turn into a human juke-box.

NEYIF: I don't care. I'm the head of the household and if I want to sing, I'll sing. *(He sings off and on over the next two pages.)*

A very loud thunderclap.

NEEL: I think God is pissed off at the head of the household.

Very long pause. During which Nelly falls asleep on the table, then wakes up. Then Nelly falls asleep on Neyif's shoulder. Neel adjusts his bow-tie. Very long pause. A bomb explodes.

NEEL: Hmmn, a K72.

Pause.

NEYIF: Maybe we can start eating.

NAZHA: We'll wait for the guests.

NEYIF: The guests, the guests.

NEEL: Don't make me laugh.

Long pause. A bomb explodes.

NEEL: A 448 with a rotating head.

Nelly wakes up. Pause.

NEYIF: Let's eat, for fuck's sake. Let's eat.

NAZHA: No.

NEYIF: But no one's gonna show up!

NEEL: You better believe no one's gonna show up! This is all just an illusion. Even the table! Look at it! There's nothing but appetizers! Where, tell me, is the main dish? Where's the mutton you slaughtered with your own hands, Papa? In the oven? Don't make me laugh! When the guests come, when we tell them the fiancé doesn't exist and that they have to eat the mutton raw, you'll see, they'll hang us up by our feet and they'll poke out our eyes with rusty nails!

NELLY: My fiancé will come.

NAZHA: Yes, darling, he'll come.

Very long pause.

NEYIF: I'm hungry.

NAZHA: Think about something else.

NEYIF: I can't, I'm hungry.

Two bombs explode. A thunderclap. Nelly falls asleep. Very long pause.

NELLY: When are we going to Berdawnay?

NEEL: Next Friday.

NELLY: Next Friday?

NEEL: Yes.

NELLY: To eat kneffay?

NEEL: Yes.

NELLY: When are we going to Berdawnay?

NEEL: Next Friday.

NELLY: Next Friday?

NEYIF: No, I must be dreaming. I'm dreaming! Tell me this is a dream.

Very long pause.

NELLY: *(singing)* The odors spill from the garbage cans
Into the Arabs' coffee cups
All they have left is the sky
To dream their dreams
Of lands far away
Because...

NAZHA: She's having a nice dream! Look how she's smiling like the sun!

NEEL: She's singing one of Walter's poems.

NAZHA: Look at her!

NELLY: *(singing)* A curse on those who forget
    The beauty of the Mediterranean
    The biggest sea
    In all the world!

> *Regular bombing begins. Every five seconds we hear a whistle followed by a rather violent explosion. The whole neighborhood is starting to be bombed. During this, Nelly continues to sing.*

NELLY: I pour out the longings of my heart
    into the Mediterranean.
    She carries them down
    To her deepest waters
    There, among the fish and the reefs,
    My secrets sleep
    In her peaceful embrace.

> *Distant thunder and light bombing. Neyif starts up his song ("I Will Survive") again, quietly. Everyone except Nelly gradually starts to join in. In the middle of Neyif's song, there is a knock at the door. Everyone stops singing. Neyif stops. Everyone looks at each other.*

NEEL: Damnit! The guests!

> *Souhayla enters, dressed for the party.*

ALL: Souhayla!

SOUHAYLA: Is the fiancé here yet?

NEEL: No.

NAZHA: No.

NEYIF: No.

SOUHAYLA: And the guests?

NEYIF: Not yet.

NAZHA: Not yet.

NEEL: Not yet.

> *The family starts singing again. Souhayla slowly joins in. Nelly wakes up. She stands.*

NELLY: Mama!

> *All stop singing except Souhayla.*

NAZHA: She's woken up!

NELLY: Mama, mama, it's now!

NAZHA: What, darling?

NELLY: It's now, it's now, he's coming!

SOUHAYLA: Walter?

> *A huge bomb. Machine gun fire. Another bomb. A very sharp whistle.*

NEEL: A 579 BTX! Everyone take cover!

The bombing starts up again. Explosions. Nelly is still standing.

NEEL: Stay down!

Explosions.

NAZHA: Nelly! Lie down! Lie down!

Ferocious, rhythmic bombing has started. Neel names all the bombs.

NAZHA: Nelly! Get away from the window!

NEEL: Doshka
Doshka
Doshka
Doshka

NAZHA: Nelly! Get away from the window!

NEEL: Doshka
Doshka
45 BTA 4
The thud of a scud.

SOUHAYLA: Dear God protect us!

NEYIF: I think now we really have to go downstairs.

A bomb falls in front of the house.

SOUYHAYLA: *(yelling)* Ahhhh! Ahiiii! Yahaaaa!!

NAZHA: Souhayla!

*An explosion which throws everyone violently to the ground.
Nelly sways with the impact.*

NEYIF: I'll get the bag of food and we'll go down.

He exits. A bomb explodes in front of the house.

NEEL: D.C.A.
Doshka
Doshka
M16
Kalashnikov
M16
Kalashnikov
Doshka

NAZHA: We have to shut the window. Nelly, lie down! Lie down!

NEEL: Stay down, mama.
Doshka
Doshka
A black mass
A black pudding

SOUHAYLA: *(yelling)* AAAAAYI!! I want to get out of here!

NEEL: A black widow alla puttanesca!

SOUHAYLA: Stop! Stop, for heaven's sake!

NEEL: A Louis XIV

SOUHAYLA: AHHHHHH! AHIIII!

NEEL: A Pius XXII

A terrible silence, and then:

NEEL: A blue 101 warhead!

SOUHAYLA: Ahaaaaa! For fuck's sake! This has to end!

Souhayla gets to her feet. Neyif enters and puts down some bags, then exits quickly.

SOUHAYLA: Why are you attacking us! There must be some mistake! Surely this must be a terrible misunderstanding, a monumental diplomatic blunder—go and check with your superiors, this is all just a big joke.

A violent explosion.

NEYIF: *(entering and putting down more bags)* I'll go get the sleeping bags. Everyone get ready to leave.

Two violent explosions force him to lie down.

NEEL: Papa!

NAZHA: Nelly!

A violent explosion.

SOUHAYLA: Stop! *(A violent explosion)* Listen to me! *(A violent explosion)* My name is Souhayla.... *(A violent explosion)* Souhayla... *(A violent explosion)* And I want to get married! *(Two violent explosions)* Does anyone want to be my husband? *(A violent explosion)* I'm 34 but I have nice soft skin! My teeth are bad but I have a very sweet personality *(Three violent explosions)* I do housework, I do dishes, I can sew *(A violent explosion)* and I'm a wonderful cook *(A violent explosion)* I have a sense of humour, I'm cultured *(Two violent explosions)* I like reading and movies *(A violent explosion)* and I have everything it takes to make a man happy *(A violent explosion)* —A beautiful smile, a nice mouth, large tits *(A violent explosion)* a big ass *(A violent explosion)* and I'm still a virgin! *(A violent explosion)* I want to get married.... I want to get married!.... *(A violent explosion)* Is there really no one on this whole fucking godforsaken planet who wants to marry me?!

A violent explosion.

NEYIF: Everything's ready. Let's go.

NAZHA: We've got to do something. They're gonna get themselves killed.

NEYIF: Souhayla! Nelly! Hurry! We've got to go downstairs! *(A violent explosion forces Neyif to lie down.)* Nelly! The bombs!

SOUHAYLA: It's so sad! Nelly, your fiancé won't come, he's probably changed his mind.

A violent explosion.

NELLY: My fiancé will come.

SOUHAYLA: It's raining bombs! How can he come?

A violent explosion.

NELLY: The bombs are nothing. A bit of wind. The bombs don't know anything, but I, I know a poem by my brother.

A violent explosion.

SOUHAYLA: A poem?

NEYIF: I'm gonna count to three, then we'll grab them and force them out with us.

Distant explosions.

NELLY: A poem.

NEYIF: Let's go!

> *Neyif, Nazha and Neel come out of their hiding places and grab Nelly, lifting her off the ground. Just as they lift her, a bomb explodes right outside the window and lights up the whole apartment.*

NELLY: The lilies are still
In the tomblike silence
A reassuring presence
For the night hunter on foot.
In the distance, a face takes flight
And finds its way.
The way is white.
Today I walk,
I walk, and in my head
And in my heart
I remember!
A love is born.
At the detour of a road
I kissed her lips.
The day has risen.
In my hands, your marvelous face!
Three birds take flight!
I smile,
I smile,
I smile with joy.

Nelly falls into Neel's arms. Silence. There are no more bombs. Nothing. There is a knock at the door.

SOUHAYLA: The guests!

NAZHA: My God! The guests!

There is another knock.

NEYIF: It's so quiet.

SOUHAYLA: People must be crazy to leave home when it's like this out!

NEYIF: It's so quiet.

NEEL: You're all pale, Nelly!

NELLY: My heart is beating so fast, so fast!

NEYIF: I'm not hungry anymore. I'm not hungry anymore.

Another knock. Nazha opens the door. A man enters. He is smiling. He is well-dressed. Neatly. He is a foreigner. He is handsome.

NAZHA: Sir?

GENTLEMAN: Bonjour, Madame.

Gentleman offers a bouquet of daisies to Nazha.

SOUHAYLA: The fiancé!

GENTLEMAN: You must be the charming neighbour. Souhayla, isn't it?

SOUHAYLA: The fiancé! It's the fiancé! At last!... Yes... Hurray... Hurray... Why do you look like that! It's the fiancé!

NEYIF: Well!

NEEL: Who is this dude?!

GENTLEMAN: Hello, Neel!

NEEL: Who *is* this dude?!

SOUHAYLA: Ah! You know... don't worry, they're a little bit, in shock, you know... how can I explain... But they've been waiting for you since this morning... You didn't have too much trouble finding the house?

GENTLEMAN: A couple of fishermen showed me the way.

NAZHA: I don't feel very well...

NEYIF: This is incredible!

SOUHAYLA: But what's the matter with you? The fiancé is here, the party can get started!

NEEL: Sonovabitch! It's François.

NEYIF: This is insane!

SOUHAYLA: You managed to avoid the areas that were too heavily bombed? Good for you! Oh, you!!! With this storm on top of everything you must be soaked!

GENTLEMAN: The storm? What storm? There was a clear blue sky! The storm!... I didn't hear a thing! Bombing, you say? No! Why would there be bombing? There was a very slight breeze! You have a delightful country. These trees, this sea, oh, this sea!!

NEEL: Holy shit!

NAZHA: Do you know us?

GENTLEMAN: I recognize you.

NEEL: Papa, Papa, it's François!

NAZHA: Why have you come?

NEYIF: Oh my God, I'm not hungry anymore!

NEEL: It's François!

SOUHAYLA: I don't understand anything anymore. Is this gentleman a guest, or is he the fiancé?

NAZHA: There isn't any fiancé! There never was a fiancé. We made the whole thing up to pass the time, to relieve our boredom a little. There can never be a fiancé.

GENTLEMAN: Oh, yes, I'm the fiancé—if Nelly will have me.

NELLY: Yes, I'll have you, sir.

NEEL: Sonovabitch... it's François. It's really François!

NELLY: Mama! The guests will be here soon! You'll say good-bye to them for us! I'm leaving! Celebrate! Celebrate!

NAZHA: Nelly! Nelly! Don't leave me all alone!

NELLY: I'm awake, Mama! You should be happy! Tomorrow

you'll walk with your head held high! You'll have married off your daughter! Rejoice! I've awakened!

GENTLEMAN: Goodbye, Madam, Sir. See you soon, Neel. Goodbye, Souhayla!

SOUHAYLA: Oh! You!

NEYIF: Take care, Nelly! Be happy!

NAZHA: Be happy? Yes, be happy Nelly!

NELLY: Farewell mama, farewell papa.

NEEL: Are you ever lucky, Nelly! You're going to live in a country where the main concern is the fight against pornography in primary schools! Boy, the people there are happy! Are they ever happy!

NELLY: Don't forget, Neel! A soul old as the cedars, Neel, my little brother, my consolation, my joy, I predict, yes I predict, yes I predict that your bones will grow and burst open your coffin, your bones will slowly grow upwards, turning into an ancient cedar! Later on people will come and make love in the shade of your branches!

GENTLEMAN: Let us go!

NAZHA: Where are you going?

GENTLEMAN: To a villa by the sea. But beforehand we'll drive over to Berdawnay to eat kneffay. It's Friday.

Nelly and the fiancé exit.

NEEL: I'm going to close the window!

More gunshots. One very precise one. The window shatters.
Neel reels and falls on the wedding table. Silence. Nobody moves.

NAZHA: Neel!

NEYIF: Neel! Neel!

NEEL: M.16, new version!

NAZHA: We'll fix it all up! Don't move! It's nothing! It's nothing!

NEEL: It's nothing? An M.16—new version—is nothing?

NAZHA: Neel!

NEEL: I told you it was going to start the same way!

NAZHA: Get up, my baby! Get up! Come, we'll get those potatoes fried, come, my darling! Oh no, no, no, no, I don't want you to... Get up, get up, get up!

NEEL: You know what I'd like?

NAZHA: My little prince!

NEEL: To play "Tickle my..."

NEYIF: I don't know how to play.

NEEL: Souhayla knows.

SOUHAYLA: Once upon a time there was...

NEEL: Tickle my fuzz...

SOUHAYLA: A boy full of fun...

NEEL: Tickle my bun...

SOUHAYLA: He was cute as could be...

NEEL: Tickle my knee...

SOUHAYLA: And he loved a good trick...

NEEL: Tickle my dick...

SOUHAYLA: Till one day in the rain...

NEEL: Tickle my brain...

SOUHAYLA: A bee-sting made him quiver...

NEEL: Tickle my liver...

SOUHAYLA: And by his father's side...

NEEL: Tickle my hide...

A bomb explodes with distinction.

NEEL: A shining coral, quick, a wish...

SOUHAYLA: He breathed his last.

NEEL: Tickle my ASS!

Neel dies.

∾

GLOSSARY

Ya aybeyshoom: Means something akin to "What a disgrace!"
  Pronunciation: rhymes with "but why, fey broom" (ya ay' bey
  shoom). Although both syllables are distinctly heard, the
  "ya" flows quickly into the "ay."

Arak: An anise-flavoured liqueur.
  Pronunciation: rhymes with "a rack" (a rak').

Baba ghanouj: A puréed eggplant dip for pita.

Battenjen: Eggplant.
  Pronunciation: rhymes with buttonmen (bat' ten jen).

Beyleywa: Baklava; a dessert made from phyllo pastry, honey
  and nuts.
  Pronunciation: the first two syllables rhyme with "hey" and
  the last syllable rhymes with "cut." The stress is after the first
  syllable; there is also a glottal stop after the first syllable.

Berdawnay: A beautiful small resort town in Lebanon.
  Pronunciation: rhymes with "Bear down, May" (Ber daw' nay).

Coussa: Zucchini.
  Pronunciation: koo' suh.

Fassoulia: A white bean dish with a tomato-garlic sauce.
  Pronunciation: fuh soo' lya.

Keshk: Tiny dumplings stuffed with ground beef in a spiced
  yogurt sauce.
  Pronunciation: mesh' k.

Kneffay: A traditional lebanese dessert of stuffed shredded wheat in a rosewater and lemon syrup.
Pronunciation: kne' ffay.

Mamelukes: Military class that ruled Egypt from 1254 to 1811.
Pronunciation: Ma' me lukes.

Warra arrishe: Traditional lebanese dish of grape leaves stuffed with beef and rice.
Pronunciation: wa rra a rrishe'. There is a half-stress after the first syllable, and the double r's are trilled.